Harry Potter and the
Cedarville Censors

Harry Potter and the Cedarville Censors

Inside the Precedent-Setting Defeat of an Arkansas Book Ban

BRIAN MEADORS

McFarland & Company, Inc., Publishers
Jefferson, North Carolina

LIBRARY OF CONGRESS CATALOGUING-IN-PUBLICATION DATA

Names: Meadors, Brian, 1969– author.
Title: Harry Potter and the Cedarville censors : inside the precedent-setting defeat of an Arkansas book ban / Brian Meadors.
Description: Jefferson, North Carolina : McFarland & Company, Inc., Publishers, 2019. | Includes bibliographical references and index.
Identifiers: LCCN 2019000152 | ISBN 9781476674971 (paperback : acid free paper) ∞
Subjects: LCSH: Counts, Billy Rae—Trials, litigation, etc. | Cedarville School District (Ark.),—Trials, litigation, etc. | Rowling, J. K. Harry Potter series. | School libraries—Law and legislation—Arkansas. | Libraries—Censorship—Arkansas.
Classification: LCC KF229.C68 M43 2019 | DDC 344.73/092—dc23
LC record available at https://lccn.loc.gov/2019000152

BRITISH LIBRARY CATALOGUING DATA ARE AVAILABLE

ISBN (print) 978-1-4766-7497-1
ISBN (ebook) 978-1-4766-3583-5

© 2019 Brian Meadors. All rights reserved

No part of this book may be reproduced or transmitted in any form or by any means, electronic or mechanical, including photocopying or recording, or by any information storage and retrieval system, without permission in writing from the publisher.

Front cover images © 2019 Shutterstock

Printed in the United States of America

McFarland & Company, Inc., Publishers
  Box 611, Jefferson, North Carolina 28640
  www.mcfarlandpub.com

To Greg Karber

Table of Contents

Acknowledgments — ix
Preface — 1
Introduction — 3

1. An Inspirational Wednesday — 5
2. A Brief History of Harry Potter — 13
3. Legal Backstory: *Gobitis* & *Barnette* (Students Have Constitutional Rights) — 17
4. Estella Fights Back — 21
5. Legal Backstory: *Tinker* (Students Have a Right to Non-Disruptive Speech) — 28
6. School Boards — 31
7. Legal Backstory: *Pico* (Students' Free Speech Rights Apply to School Libraries) — 40
8. Like Magic, a Client Appears — 53
9. Intolerant of Tolerance — 61
10. Adversaries and Allies — 77
11. Legal Backstory: *Sund* (Hiding a Library Book Is the Same as Censoring It) — 91
12. Building the Case — 96
13. "There are schools of magic" — 106
14. Dakota Counts — 119
15. The Expert — 133

Table of Contents

16. Legal Backstory: *Bystrom* (8th Circuit Adopts the *Pico* Plurality)	145
17. Summary Judgment	158
18. Carrot and Stick	164
19. The Fruit of the Litigation Tree	174
*Appendix: Judge Hendren's Opinion (*Counts v. Cedarville School District, *295 F.Supp.2d 996 [2003])*	183
Chapter Notes	195
Bibliography	199
Index	205

Acknowledgments

A decade before the publication of this book, Bob Lescher, a well-established literary agent in New York City, called me. He'd received my query and manuscript, liked my writing, and wanted to represent me.

Anyone trying to break into the writing field is well aware of the "query" system—writer wannabes ask dozens, if not hundreds, of agents if they are interested in representing the author and selling the manuscript to a publisher.

The industry norm is that a "No" is expressed by ignoring the query, or sometimes getting a form letter rejection. Lescher did neither. That an agent of his stature would not only compliment my work but also agree to represent me was a much-needed confidence boost.

Bob Lescher tried, unsuccessfully, to sell the manuscript. Then, advanced in age, he slowed his workload and passed away. He'd been in the literary business for more than fifty years. I'll miss Bob. We lunched a couple of times and spent a day together in the city. He shared personal insights into domestic troubles I was having, and I'll remember him fondly for that.

After Bob's death, years passed with no action on this manuscript. Then, at Gen Con in Indianapolis, Indiana, I stumbled across McFarland and made a pitch. McFarland liked my pitch and had good suggestions for revising the manuscript.

I'd like thank Karl-Heinz Roseman, Charlie Perdue, and Dylan Lightfoot, all of McFarland, for their interest and time in this project. Donna Copeland, Larry Davi, Erika Esterbrook, Amy Hamilton, Robert Makepeace, Carey Meadors, John J. Miller, Speer Morgan, and Meredyth Neilly reviewed earlier manuscripts—thank you for your time and feedback. Chris Finan, now of the National Coalition Against Censorship, has provided

Acknowledgments

guidance and insights, and I'm very appreciative of his help. I know there are others I've inadvertently omitted—thank you, too, for your help.

A special thanks to Simona Gerdts of the U.S. District Court of the Northern District of Texas for making the *Sund* transcripts available electronically and on short notice.

Finally, my wife Mandy has been wonderfully supportive. Projects like this don't happen in a vacuum, and I could not have completed it without her.

Preface

This book tells the behind-the-scenes story of the Harry Potter ban in *Counts v. Cedarville School District*. It is authored by the attorney who successfully fought the ban and is based on his memories, interviews, depositions, and documents produced during case.

In addition to a fun story about a fun topic (Harry Potter), the book also gives insights into the nitty gritty of the legal process: filing complaints and answers; producing discovery; lining up expert witnesses; considering ethics rules; and conducting depositions.

The book also explores how legal principles evolve over time. Interspersed are chapters designated "Legal Backstory." They show the stepping stones leading to the common law as it existed at the time of the *Counts* case. Those "stepping stone" cases start in 1941 and come from West Virginia, Iowa, New York, Texas, Pennsylvania, and Minnesota. The book not only talks about the "stepping stone" cases, but also gives insight into these (sometimes famous) cases by going behind the scenes for them too. For that information, the book relies on the author's interviews with plaintiffs, witnesses, court filings, and scholarly works.

The individual stories that created the "stepping stone" cases ultimately set the stage for the reinstatement of Harry Potter in a rural school district's library in Cedarville, Arkansas. *Counts v. Cedarville School District* is now an important link in the common law chain governing school libraries and has been cited as precedent to thwart censorship elsewhere.

Finally, *Counts* also shows a timeless and optimistic truth: Individuals make a difference. Their stories matter.

Introduction

In the early 2000s, I was a young and obnoxious trial lawyer in my hometown of Fort Smith, Arkansas.

A nearby school district removed Harry Potter books from its libraries because a majority of its school board members thought that Harry Potter was bad for children. I filed suit on behalf of a fourth grade girl named Dakota Counts. A federal court ultimately ordered the return of the books to the school library. The case is called *Counts v. Cedarville School District*, 295 F.Supp.2d 996 (W.D. Ark. 2003).

We take for granted that, of course, a school shouldn't be able to ban Harry Potter books.

But it was not always that way. If the *Counts* case had been brought in 1941, the result would have been different—the school board would have won.

Yet, by 2003, the rules had changed. They changed through a mechanism lawyers call "the common law" or "case law."

In 1941, the general rule was that school boards had carte blanche control of their schools; the concept of Constitutional rights for students had very few applications.

Over time the rule evolved, and it did so case by case, each case being a story in its own right. In deciding those cases, judges relied on what other judges said in earlier, similar cases.

With each new decision, the law evolved. And, like following a long path of stepping stones in a garden, over time the law ended up in a place quite different than where it started and allowed a fourth grade girl to challenge her school board and prevail.

1. An Inspirational Wednesday

> *"The whole problem with the world is that fools and fanatics are always so certain of themselves, but wiser people so full of doubts."*—Bertrand Russell

In the early 2000s, Angie Haney lived in Crawford County, Arkansas. The county, located in the northwest part of the state, is mountainous and rural.

Angie's day job was working as a clerk in the county courthouse. But she anchored her identity and meaning in her role as a 39-year-old mother and being an active member of the Uniontown Assembly of God.

Angie had not always been so committed to church life. As a young adult, she rarely attended any church—Assembly of God or otherwise—despite, as she would later put it, "feeling spiritually empty."

During those Godless days of her mid-twenties, Angie married, but divorced two years later.

She married a second time, but relationship troubles followed her. Even with her second husband, she felt spiritually empty. Like so many people, Angie needed meaning in her life and couldn't find it.

One day, a friend of Angie's invited her to the Uniontown Assembly of God.

Angie went.

She met others like her—others who'd felt lost, others who'd felt lonely, others who wanted to make sense of life and the humbling, hard lessons it deals. She connected with the people she met and, for the first time in a long time, found a group with whom she could feel connected.

As Angie became more and more involved with church, she and her second husband became more distant. The husband blamed the church, and Angie, loath to fail at marriage a second time, acquiesced. She withdrew from the church's embrace.

It didn't help. After a year, the marriage was no better off, and Angie felt as empty as she'd ever had. Angie divorced a second time.

She returned to the Uniontown Assembly of God and built a fulfilling new life with her church family.

* * *

Uniontown is in the Cedarville School District. In the early 2000s, the district was geographically big—it covered a quarter of Crawford County—but it had fewer than a thousand children.

Most folks going to that part of Crawford County start from the interstate in the bottomlands of the Arkansas River valley, go north on a country highway, pass the Walmart, and burrow into oak forests on rolling hills sparsely dotted with trailers.

Incorporating as an Arkansas municipality seems to require nothing more than a post office, gas station, and church. Uniontown qualified and then some—it had three churches: Christian Life Ministries, Uniontown Baptist, and the Uniontown Assembly of God.

On a chilly Wednesday night in November, Angie Haney drove along Uniontown Road, passed the post office—a one-room building at the corner of Uniontown Road and Confederate Lane—and turned right on Church Lane. At the end of the cul-de-sac, she parked in the gravel lot of a 1970s-style red-brick and wood-paneled building. White, nail-up letters on the canopy proclaimed, "Assembly of God." The "y" in Assembly had lost a nail and hung askew.

Wednesday nights are church nights, and members gather for study groups and fellowship.

On this Wednesday night, Angie attended a class being held by Pastor Hodges. The topic? Witchcraft and sorcery in everyday life. Angie, along with about a dozen and a half of her church brothers and sisters, listened and learned.

Pastor Hodges was middle aged and balding; he moved his stocky frame through the sanctuary pews, engaging each soul with a message of certainty and righteousness. Angie Haney took notes and followed along in her Bible. She used the King James version. Her copy was worn and smooth, its passages marked and margins annotated.

1. An Inspirational Wednesday

Pastor Hodges asked the group if they'd heard of Harry Potter. They nodded yes.

Pastor Hodges asked, rhetorically, if the books seemed innocent, and then he explained. These so-called children's books seem innocent enough, but they're not. They make witchcraft and sorcery seem okay. That's how the Devil works. The Devil starts with something small, like the "harmless" spells and incantations in the Potter books, but they're just the first step to something more sinister. Children reading these books are one step closer to darker, serious magic—things like paganism, like the Wiccan religion.

Pastor Hodges continued and linked the Harry Potter books to the larger cultural issue facing evangelicals in the United States. He asked the group to think about the United States today, about its TV shows, movies, and books. Invitations to ungodliness are everywhere, he said. We are being corrupted and led away from the path of God.

After the study group ended, Angie Haney walked to her car and thought about Pastor Hodges' admonitions.

He was right, she concluded. The nation's culture was mounting an ongoing campaign against proper Christian beliefs; the Potter books were a prime example. They were everywhere—even in the schools. Not only were they in the school library, they were, as she knew from her daughter, on the "Accelerated Reader" list, which was part of the schools' reading curriculum. Children got extra credit for reading those books.

She imagined children like her daughter being introduced to witchcraft and sorcery. As she drove home, she knew she had to do something.

❋ ❋ ❋

Mark Hodges grew up in Cedarville. He graduated its high school in 1978 and, like most of his peers, went directly into the workforce, first to a Planters Peanut factory and later a steel mill. Both were in nearby Fort Smith, a manufacturing town.

In 1990, God called Mark Hodges to the ministry. He trained with a Protestant denomination known as the "Assemblies of God," using its "Brean" program, a home study series with thirty-five books and multiple tests.

The Assemblies of God denomination is based in Springfield, Missouri. It has more than twelve thousand churches and more than one and a half million members. If, instead of "member," you count "people who identify with an Assemblies of God church," that number ascends to nearly three million.

According to the Assemblies of God, there are sixteen "fundamental truths." Among these are

- Biblical inerrancy (meaning that the Bible should be read as literal and unerring fact);
- evidence of salvation is shown by speaking in tongues (speaking in tongues happens during fervent religious ceremony—God enables a person to speak in some unknown foreign language);
- the rapture (during the second coming of Christ, dead Christians will "rise from their graves and will meet the Lord in the air" and living Christians will be "raptured" to the Lord); and
- faith healing—which is available to believers only, as God will not divinely heal unbelievers.

These beliefs are not outside the mainstream. Sure, they may be unusual in San Francisco or Boston, but they're common in the Midwest and the South. And these beliefs are not held by just the few million members of the Assemblies of God. These beliefs are common among self-identified "evangelicals"—an identification adopted by about a third of U.S. adults.

After successfully completing his mail-order ministry program, Mark Hodges became Pastor Hodges. By 1998, he was able to quit his manufacturing job and become a full-time pastor—a spiritual and moral leader of his community.

When that community elected him to the school board, he became a leader in government as well.

✳ ✳ ✳

Pastor Hodge's class about the occult in everyday life continued to trouble Angie. The next time she was at church, she approached Pastor Hodges. They started talking at the back of the sanctuary, near the sound booth, and then moved out into the foyer of the church.

She told him that she'd been thinking about what he'd said about the occult. Angie made the observation that Pastor Hodges, as a member of the school board, could do something about the Harry Potter books being in the schools.

1. An Inspirational Wednesday

Pastor Hodges furrowed his brow. He'd not been aware that the books were in the schools.

Angie confirmed that they were—in the libraries and on the reading lists.

Pastor Hodges promised to investigate.

※ ※ ※

In most school districts, school board members do not visit the superintendent and make suggestions about individual books or otherwise micromanage school affairs. But in Cedarville (and, frankly, any small, rural school district), there was precedent for this. School board members would frequently visit, peek into classrooms, and make recommendations to the superintendent. Teachers complained that any time a board member went to the superintendent's office, the visit would result in a new directive. In the past, board members issued commands governing the seating arrangements for bus trips and what material could or could not be published in the yearbook.

None of Cedarville's five school board members had a four-year college degree. One of the board members had only finished ninth grade.

At first blush, this may make Cedarville schools seem like an outlier, but that was not so unusual for rural Arkansas school districts at that time.

For starters, there was a dearth of college-educated adults in the district. In the early 2000s, in the United States as a whole, more than 25 percent of adults have college degrees. But in the Cedarville School District, this number was only 10 percent. Those who were college educated usually had jobs precluding them from having the time to serve on school boards.

Another reason for the lack of formal education on the board is the Cedarville School District's small size. The population from which the board members were elected was only four to five thousand. Combine that with the low percentage of educated adults, and the result is a woefully inadequate pool of talent.

The small size of the district also meant that those who won the largely uncontested school board elections probably had some specific reason for wanting to serve—some agenda to pursue or axe to grind, so it was common for board members to have close relationships with school employees. I heard rumors that one school board member moonlighted as a substitute teacher; another member's wife was a teacher in the junior high school; and others had cousins and siblings employed by the school. In the Cedarville School District, several school employees, by benefit of blood or marriage, had direct lines of communication to board members, who in turn sometimes commanded the superintendent on the conduct of day-to-day affairs.

* * *

A few days after Angie alerted Pastor Hodges to the presence of Harry Potter in the schools, Pastor Hodges, in his capacity as the school board president, appeared in the office of the school superintendent, Dave Smith, and expressed his concerns. Superintendent Smith made a few phone calls to his librarians and learned that all three of Cedarville's schools—elementary, middle, and high school—had the books in their libraries. Pastor Hodges and Superintendent Smith then walked across the parking lot to the high school.

Cedarville High School was a relatively new brick building. Like many schools, it was boxy inside and out. The library was a short walk from the entrance, and its hallway walls were actually windows; passers-by could look in and see the shelves, tables, and chairs.

Estella Roberts was the high school librarian and looked the part—short gray hair, in her early sixties, thin, with a rectangular face and large glasses.

Superintendent Smith walked directly to her and asked if she had the Harry Potter books.

Estella looked down at the top of his head for a moment before focusing on his upturned face and impatient glare. He was a short man. Pastor Hodges stood a few steps behind.

When Estella said yes, Superintendent Smith told her to remove the books.

Estella crossed her arms. Nothing angers a librarian like a whiff of censorship, and she went into a defensive mode.

She knew she couldn't simply disobey the superintendent and the school board president. But she could insist on following policy; nobody could fault her for that. "Gentlemen, we have to follow the policy. I can't just take a book off the shelf. I can't do anything unless somebody first fills out a complaint form."

1. An Inspirational Wednesday

Estella went to her desk, pulled a three-ring binder off the overhead shelf, flipped through the pages, and found a complaint form. She also handed them the form's guidelines, a short document describing how to properly complete a complaint.

Superintendent Smith asked Estella to fill it out for him. She refused.

Superintendent Smith shot her a look of anger and then handed the form to Pastor Hodges, who took the form, sat at a table, and began filling it out. Then Pastor Hodges got to this question: "Have you seen or read this material in its entirety?"

He had not.

Nor could he fully answer the other questions—questions about what specific passages in the book were objectionable or which passages were inappropriate.

Pastor Hodges stopped filling in the form and asked for another blank one. Estella pulled a blank from her binder and handed it to him.

He and the superintendent left.

Estella immediately called the Arkansas Library Association and told them what happened.

It told her to keep following the school procedures and promised to send her helpful materials.

* * *

Pastor Hodges' blank form and guidelines soon found their way to Angie Haney. He asked her to complete it. Angie skimmed the papers and came across the question that had stumped Pastor Hodges: "Have you seen or read this material in its entirety?"

She, too, had not.

Angie told Pastor Hodges that she would need to read at least the first book to complete the complaint form. She looked at him for approval, and he nodded yes.

After church, Angie went to Walmart. When her cart was half-full, she made her way to the book section and located *Harry Potter and the Sorcerer's Stone*.

Angie looked nervously up and down the aisle. Seeing nobody she knew, she took a copy, set it in her cart, and covered it with a bag of chips.

* * *

Harry Potter and the Cedarville Censors

Angie started reading that night. She had a highlighter, a notebook, and a copy of the library guidelines. Rather than make a casual read, she noted each passage that troubled her.

Angie's completed complaint form answered the questions posed by the one taken by Pastor Hodges, but not in the same format. Angie had retyped each of the form's questions, typed in her answers, and attached supplemental pages.

Angie objected to Harry Potter's magic as well as the fact that Harry was rewarded for his defiance of authority: "I don't believe witchcraft or sorcery needs to be available for study, especially in schools.... [The book] depicts bad behavior with little or no consequences for wrongdoing.... They lie to teachers, defy school rules.... It's a starting place to learn witchcraft, sorcery and other satanic ideas. It's a beginning.... If you talk to a child about healing and how good it is, don't they then want to be a doctor? It's the same principle. If you read to a child about witchcraft and sorcery then that's what they want to do."

Angie's anti–Potter essay exceeded a thousand words. She supported her conclusions with dozens of citations to particular passages in the book. Her essay—two full single-spaced pages, Times New Roman font—had no paragraph breaks at all, giving it a rambling, heavy feel.

Estella accepted Angie's written complaint, stamped "Received" at the top, and wrote down the date and time.

"I was ready when Angie Haney brought the complaint form," Estella later told me. "I knew Hodges would find somebody. He found Angie Haney."

Estella sighed. "At least Angie actually read the book."

2. A Brief History of Harry Potter

Estella's first call had been to the Arkansas Library Association, which is a chapter of the national American Library Association. The American Library Association and its chapters are the lead organizations fighting library book bans. The ALA tracks book bans, compiles statistics, and assists in the fights against censors.

The ALA points out—correctly—that throughout history, religious and political authorities have invoked censorship. The motives are always promoted as well-intentioned: youth cannot be subjected to age-inappropriate material; social mores cannot be undermined by obscene or deviant messages; blasphemous or heretical teachings cannot be tolerated.

And America, despite its alleged freedoms, has not been immune. Almost immediately after the ratification of the Constitution, Congress passed the Sedition Act, which forbade "false, scandalous, and malicious writing" against the government. By the late 1800s, the federal government and about half of the states had "Comstock" laws that banned obscene, lewd, and lascivious materials; these laws reached not just the pornography of the day, but also information about contraceptive devices and abortion. In wartime, the federal government censors information it considers to be a threat to national security. And the government has always had the power to censor radio and television broadcasts.

For this country's first one hundred and fifty years, local and state governments frequently enacted censorship laws, and there was little to oppose them. The First Amendment, the courts reasoned, only applied to the federal government, so its protections could not be used against municipalities or states. That was the law of the land until, in 1925, the Supreme

Harry Potter and the Cedarville Censors

Court began issuing a series of decisions that began to apply the First Amendment to state and local governments.

The ALA labels attempted direct censorship efforts as book "challenges." There are hundreds of reported book challenges in the United States each year. The ALA opines that for every reported book challenge, there are four others that go unreported. It is unclear how the ALA determined the number of unreported challenges, but the "hundreds" number of known challenges is alarming enough.

The ALA categorizes book challenges by the type of objections. The most popular categories are "sexually explicit" and "offensive language." Runners up include "racist, "homosexual," and "religious/satanism."

* * *

Enter British author J.K. Rowling's Harry Potter series. At the beginning of the series, Harry Potter is an eleven-year-old orphan who discovers that he is a wizard. He is invited to attend the Hogwarts School of Witchcraft and Wizardry, and his adventures begin. Throughout the books, Harry is faced with a series of problems; he overcomes them by using magic and defying authority.

The Harry Potter series lit up the imaginations of young readers in a way nobody could have predicted. The popularity of the series can hardly be overstated: the series won rave reviews from the *New York Times Book Review*, the *Boston Sunday Globe*, *USA Today*, the *Chicago Tribune*, and the *Seattle Times*. *Publisher's Weekly* declared *Harry Potter and the Sorcerer's Stone* the "Best Book of 1998"; the American Library Association recognized it as "an ALA Notable Book"; and both the New York Public Library and *Parenting* magazine awarded it "Book of the Year" (1998). The money collected by the Harry Potter franchise is measured in the billions, with a "B," and author J.K. Rowling, who wrote the first book while on welfare in Scotland, is now richer than the queen.

In crafting the Harry Potter series, J.K. Rowling used the actual names of alchemists from history and used detailed descriptions of their spells and incantations, complete with Latin words and exotic ingredients.

That kind of detail—that historical "accuracy," as it were—is what really inflamed hardcore evangelicals about the Harry Potter series. Many evangelicals believe in magic, spirits, witchcraft, and the like, and they view them as antithetical to Christianity. The basis for this belief comes

2. A Brief History of Harry Potter

from a passage in the Bible (it's in Deuteronomy) about witchcraft being an abomination.

Thus, evangelicals consider the supernatural (when it is not overtly Christian) forbidden by God. Their reasoning goes like this: the Bible is the inerrant, literal truth; the Bible forbids witchcraft and sorcery; therefore, witchcraft and sorcery exist and are real threats that must be opposed.

Within a year of the publication of *Harry Potter and the Sorcerer's Stone*, religious zealots in the United States had challenged the book twenty-three times in thirteen different states. The Harry Potter challenges grew with the books' popularity, and the ALA later declared the Harry Potter series the most challenged books for the years 2000 to 2005.

Michigan saw at least two of the more publicized challenges. The Bruckner Elementary School in Saginaw achieved the dubious honor of being the first school to remove the books from the classroom. The parent instigating the removal complained, "The books are based on sorcery, which is an abomination to the Lord.... I read a couple of chapters and felt like God didn't want me reading it."

That same year, in Zeeland, Michigan, three parents complained about the books, citing the objectionable themes of magic and witchcraft. In response, the school superintendent restricted access; children could only get the books if they had written permission from their parents.

Florida had multiple Harry Potter challenges. In 2000, the Carrollwood Elementary School forbade the school library from making further purchases of the books. The school took this action absent any complaints; it did so merely on the fear of a possible complaint. Its principal explained, "We just knew that we had some parents who wouldn't want their children to read these books."

The Jacksonville public library faced a lawsuit brought by the paradoxically named Liberty Counsel of Orlando, a right-wing Christian group. The library had been handing out "Hogwarts' Certificate of Accomplishment" to any child who had read the books. The Liberty Counsel objected, saying that the public library was promoting the religion of witchcraft. Liberty Counsel won that battle; the library knuckled under and quit awarding the certificates.

On the West Coast, parents in Bend, Oregon, challenged Harry Potter placements in their school district's twenty schools. That challenge, like the others, was based on religion and witchcraft. The Bend challenge also

Harry Potter and the Cedarville Censors

claimed that the books would lead children to hatred and rebellion. To their credit, school officials resisted and did not ban the books. Interim superintendent Gary Bruner determined that the complaining parents wanted too much. "They want it withdrawn not only for their own child, but for all children," he said. In neighboring California, Simi Valley faced similar challenges, as did the Whittier and Fresno schools.

Indeed, Harry Potter has been challenged not only in Michigan, Florida, Oregon, and California, but also in Illinois, Iowa, New York, Texas, New Hampshire, Alabama, Pennsylvania, and Georgia. Outside the United States, Harry Potter has been challenged in Canada, England, and New Zealand. And it goes without saying that institutions in Islamic countries have always taken a dim (and censoring) view of Harry Potter.

Sometimes censorship efforts succeed; books are successfully removed or prior parental permission is required. But even when these censorship efforts seemingly don't succeed, they actually do. They create a chilling effect. Other school administrators, aware of book challenges and wanting to avoid conflict, spare themselves headache by not stocking the offending books in the first place. It matters not that a complaining parent's challenge would ultimately be rejected; why go through that hassle unnecessarily? The Carrollwood, Florida, incident—when the school removed the books even though no parent had complained—shows that.

3. Legal Backstory: *Gobitis* & *Barnette* (Students Have Constitutional Rights)

In the early 1900s, courts had not yet applied the First Amendment to school boards. They had long given (and, largely, still do give) deference to school boards, recognizing that communities may instill their own values as they see fit. The Supreme Court applied this principle—ruthlessly—in the case of *Minersville School District v. Gobitis*, 310 U.S. 586 (1940).

The *Minersville* case starts with familiar, recurring actors in First Amendment jurisprudence: members of the Jehovah's Witnesses religious sect. Jehovah's Witnesses—known by most for their excessively persistent attempts to convert others—believe that the Bible, as the Word of God, is the supreme authority. Gestures of allegiance to any other symbol would be sacrilege. They rely on passages in Exodus, chapter 20, verses 3 through 5 (no graven images, no gods before me).

Beginning in the early 1900s, states and school boards began passing "flag salute" requirements. Schools required their students, daily, to salute the United States flag and pledge their allegiance, believing that national identity required compulsory respect and allegiance to the flag. These requirements soon spread to all or part of dozens of states.

The Jehovah's Witnesses had long been opposed to compulsory saluting laws.

In Hitler's Germany, the Nazis became so frustrated with the Witnesses that in the early 1930s, Hitler banned the sect and ordered tens of thousands of its members to be shipped to concentration camps.

In the United States, the Jehovah's Witnesses' leader, Joseph F. Rutherford, said at a 1935 convention, "We do not 'Heil Hitler' nor any other creature," and he encouraged all Jehovah's Witnesses not to salute the flag. (The American flag salute was a straight, raised right arm with the palm facing downwards—the same salute used by the Nazis.)

Across the country, Jehovah's Witnesses began disobeying flag salute requirements.

Two of those Witnesses were Lillian and William Gobitis, children in Minersville's middle school at the time. The Minersville superintendent, a Catholic priest named Roudabush, chafed at their refusal to participate in the pledge. After receiving clearance from the state-level education bureaucrats, he convinced the Minersville School Board to pass a regulation compelling students to pledge allegiance.

Roudabush expelled the non-compliant Jehovah's Witnesses almost immediately. Left with no other educational option, the Gobitises' father arranged for his children to go to a makeshift private school at great expense.

Mr. Gobitis brought suit—and won—at the trial level. The judge, a Roosevelt appointee, took a dim view of compulsory patriotism. "Our country's safety surely does not depend upon the totalitarian idea of forcing all citizens into one common mold of thinking.... Such a doctrine seems to me utterly alien to the genius and spirit of our nation...."

The school appealed to the Third Circuit appellate court and lost there too. The Third Circuit (also populated with recent Roosevelt appointees), in a spirited opinion, compared compulsory salute laws to Nazi Germany and framed the dispute, in the first sentence of the opinion, as a sadly absurd and unnecessary David versus Goliath: "Eighteen big states have seen fit to exert their power over a small number of little children."

The school appealed again, this time to the U.S. Supreme Court.

The U.S. Supreme Court rarely takes cases. In general, for every case it takes, there are fifty it does not.

But the Supreme Court is more likely to take a case to settle a "circuit split." That's when federal courts in one part of the country reach different conclusions than federal courts in another part of the country.

Gobitis presented a circuit split. Up until the Third Circuit decision protecting the Jehovah's Witnesses, the federal appellate courts had been upholding compulsory flag salute laws; the Supreme Court took the case to resolve the difference.

It's worth noting that the justices making up the Supreme Court at

3. Legal Backstory: Gobitis & Barnette

that time didn't have legal philosophies favoring the Witnesses' position. And the Witnesses didn't help themselves either when the national leader of the Jehovah's Witnesses fired the lawyers and substituted different lawyers who presented a brief that cited the Bible more than case law.

The American Bar Association and the American Civil Liberties Union each filed their own "amicus" brief, but ultimately did not carry the day. In an 8–1 decision penned by Justice Felix Frankfurter, the Supreme Court reversed the Third Circuit. Compulsory salute laws were deemed to be constitutional.

Justice Frankfurter framed the question differently than the trial and appellate courts. He saw the question of compulsory salute laws as striking a balance between the exercise of religion and cohesiveness of the nation—in other words, he took as a given that compulsory saluting contributed to national cohesiveness. He then morphed his analysis into whether any court should ever second guess any school board. Anyone familiar with Justice Frankfurter will not be surprised to learn that he concluded "No." Justice Frankfurter was a strong advocate of what he called "judicial restraint," but is, in the opinion of many, including me, better described as "having courts abstain from the enforcement of constitutional rights."

With that 8–1 victory, the school had won. School boards across the country had been given, in essence, carte blanche permission to run schools as they saw fit without any regard to protecting religious minorities.

* * *

The *Gobitis* opinion had the effect of egging on a public who already disliked Jehovah's Witnesses. Religious bigots across the country became violent—between June 12, 1940 (nine days after the release of the *Gobitis* opinion) and June 20, 1940, hundreds of attacks on the Witnesses were reported to the Department of Justice, some so violent that the FBI became involved.

Legal scholars panned the *Gobitis* opinion, and three justices later made public remarks that they had second thoughts about *Gobitis* and that it had been "wrongly decided." Shortly thereafter, two new justices, Wiley Rutledge and Robert Jackson, joined the Supreme Court, replacing justices Byrne and Stone.

After the *Gobitis* decision, West Virginia enacted a statute that almost exactly tracked the language of the ordinance in *Gobitis*, presumably to ensure its legality, since the Supreme Court's *Gobitis* case had upheld that same language.

Nevertheless, the Witnesses challenged the West Virginia law.

Their suit was, in effect, the same battle as the one in *Gobitis*, with the only difference being the location, the names of the schools and children, and—most importantly—different judges. The original filing was in a West Virginia federal district court and is styled *Barnette v. West Virginia State Board of Ed.*, 47 F.Supp. 251 (S.D. W. Va., 1942).

The school responded to the suit, predictably, by citing *Gobitis* as binding precedent and asked the district court to dismiss the case.

But the district court did not; instead, it took note of the turmoil following *Gobitis* and the public statements of justices who'd doubted their earlier decision. "Ordinarily," held the district court, it "would feel constrained to follow an unreversed decision of the Supreme Court of the United States ... [but of] the seven justices now members of the Supreme Court who participated in [*Gobitis*], four have given public expression to the view that it is unsound."

The district court found in favor of the Witnesses, and ordered that West Virginia's law could not be enforced against Witnesses' children.

The school appealed directly to the U.S. Supreme Court. This time, good arguments, based on case law and legal principles of religious liberty, were made. And in *West Virginia State Board of Education v. Barnette*, 319 U.S. 624 (1943), the U.S. Supreme Court affirmed the district court. In doing so, it overruled the earlier *Gobitis* decision by eight votes to one, leaving only Justice Frankfurter to write a frustrated and indignant dissent.

Thus, with *Barnette*, came a rule of law that we take for granted today—federal courts may intervene in the operations of public schools to enforce students' Constitutional rights.

4. Estella Fights Back

"Librarians.... That's one terrorist group you don't want to mess with."
—Michael Moore

When Angie Haney gave her complaint to Cedarville's librarian, Estella Roberts, she'd picked a formidable adversary. Estella, no stranger to trouble from school administrators, had been a "troublemaker" from her earliest teaching days.

Decades earlier, Estella Roberts had been the fifth-grade teacher in the neighboring Van Buren School District. She still remembers her first meeting with Van Buren's principal. "He didn't talk much," she later recalled. She described him as odd and thin, with brown hair and unfashionable glasses.

Most teachers had no reason to communicate with the principal, and that suited them fine. They went along and asked no questions—they showed up, taught their lessons, monitored children after school, and went home.

But Estella was different. She was pushy and persistent.

Soon after she arrived, Estella asked a colleague about the library.

She was told there wasn't one.

Estella was incredulous. "None at all."

The colleague elaborated. There was a closet in the hall that had several books. To the extent that the school had a library, that was it.

Estella walked to the hall and tried the door. Locked. She thought back to her first tour of the school, and did not remember there being a library. She walked through the school, taking account of each of the rooms. No library. She went to the principal's office and demanded to know the location of the library. Estella has a blunt and demanding way of speaking that is off-putting to those who do not know her well.

The principal said something to the effect that the school was "working on that," but gave no details. He looked down at his papers, dismissing Estella through his body language.

That week, Estella went to nearby Fort Smith and visited its public library. She spoke with its staff and got special permission to check out fifty books. Estella carted them to her classroom and lined them up on the shelves. Her students would have books.

Estella also innovated with parent-teacher conferences. In her earlier days of teaching, they were not as ubiquitous as they are now. She learned of the concept at a statewide teacher meeting. This meeting was fancier than most, hosted at a downtown Little Rock hotel. The narrow tables had tablecloths, pitchers of water, and mints. Her tablemate extolled the virtues of parent-teacher conferences—something Estella's elementary school did not have.

When Estella returned, she scheduled conferences. To accommodate working parents, Estella went to the principal to get permission to keep the school open after hours.

He stonewalled, promising to get back to her later. When he didn't she followed up and was put off again.

But Estella kept after him. After weeks of nagging, Estella finally cemented the logistics and held her school's first individual parent-teacher conferences. All but two of her students' parents attended personally; the other two attended by phone.

On another occasion, Estella took up the cause of textbooks. She'd gone nine weeks with textbooks for some, but not all, of her students.

After three prior failed attempts to have the principal fix the problem, she tried a fourth time. He dodged her again. Exasperated, Estella went over the principal's head and sent a letter to the superintendent.

By doing so, she placed herself squarely on the administration's list of "troublemakers."

Estella enhanced her troublemaker status further with union activities. She did more than simply enroll in the Arkansas Education Association—she actively participated. When a member from down the hall faced a disciplinary hearing, Estella attended as the union representative. It was one of the few times that the principal could not ignore her.

At the end of her third school year at Van Buren, on a bright and sunny May day, with temperatures climbing into the high 80s, the Van Buren

4. Estella Fights Back

School District distributed teachers' contracts for next year. Estella would be crossing a threshold—her next year would be her fourth at the school district, and she would no longer be on "probationary" status.

With the removal of Estella's "probationary status," she would enjoy a panoply of legal protections preventing the administration from arbitrarily firing her. Those protections had been hard fought. Decades earlier, the teachers' union had achieved those protections by successfully lobbying for the Teacher Fair Dismissal Act. With the passage of the Act, school administrators could no longer fire non-probationary teachers unless they had good reasons backed up by evidence.

Curious of the specifics of her new contract, Estella stood at her mailbox and opened the envelope.

There was no contract.

"Dear Ms. Roberts: This is to inform you that your contract is being recommended for non-renewal."

It also contained her year-end evaluations. Her prior two years' evaluations had top marks in all fields. This evaluation did not. "Needs improvement," it said in about half the categories.

She marched herself to the principal's office and confronted him, demanding an explanation. He refused to comment.

Estella contacted the teachers' union, got a representative, and demanded a hearing. She wanted to see the school's reason for not renewing her contract. The school refused to give one and denied her hearing request. That summer, Estella began looking for another teaching job.

In the meantime, the union's lawyers filed suit against the Van Buren School District. Estella had been fired for, allegedly, no reason whatsoever. That could not happen to teachers covered by the Fair Dismissal Act. But probationary teachers like Estella—those in their first three years at a particular district—remained vulnerable. The Fair Dismissal Act did not protect them.

The union lawyers thought Estella could show that she was really fired in retaliation for union activities and for exercising her First Amendment rights when she demanded better educational materials. They viewed Estella's case as a good test case—winning would chip away at schools' unfettered rights to fire new teachers.

Estella's case wended its way through the courts; it had two hearings, one of them a jury trial, and two appeals. She won, but it was a pyrrhic victory, having prevailed on principle and not much else. By the time the court system finally resolved her case, she was at a new school, with a supportive administration, and the Van Buren School District was long behind her.

* * *

Twenty years later, when Pastor Hodges and Superintendent Smith first entered her library and Angie Haney then submitted a complaint, it would have been far easier for Estella to quietly remove the Harry Potter books. Had she done so, Pastor Hodges and his flock would have been placated, and Estella could have avoided the censure of school administrators who bent themselves to Pastor Hodges' will.

But the intervening years had not eroded Estella's resolve to stand on principle and challenge authority.

And true to form, she did.

* * *

Surprisingly, the Cedarville schools had a formal, written policy on how to handle complaints about library books—a policy that had been created by the American Library Association years before.

For the Harry Potter situation, it was the perfect policy to have. When a book is challenged, it would be reviewed by a specially formed "library committee" of fifteen people total—a teacher, a principal, a student, a parent, and a librarian from each of Cedarville's three schools—elementary, middle, and high.

Estella and the Cedarville schools' other two librarians selected the committee members. Ironically, Angie Haney's complaint resulted in more sales of Harry Potter books. Once the fifteen committee members had been identified, the school district purchased each of the committee members a copy of *Harry Potter and the Sorcerer's Stone*.

Estella provided the committee members with more than just the book. She also prepared folders of pro–Harry Potter materials—essays from pastors and librarians praising the books. She included materials about censorship: a copy of the First Amendment, the American Library Association's Intellectual Freedom Policy, and the Library Bill of Rights. Estella did not even try to present a "balanced" view. Her committee mem-

4. Estella Fights Back

bers got materials that praised Harry Potter on its merits and materials that condemned censorship. The only item in the folders that criticized the books or promoted censorship was Angie Haney's complaint form.

Two months after Angie Haney had submitted her complaint form, Estella personally addressed the library committee. Twelve adults and three children filled the wooden tables and chairs in the high school library. The children had their backpacks, having just come from class, the adults were in their work clothes, having left work early. When all fifteen arrived, Estella got their attention and spoke. "I'm handing out folders that I have created for each of you, along with a memo asking you to evaluate the Harry Potter books. The first book is *Harry Potter and the Sorcerer's Stone*. You should each get a copy of that too. Please read the book as well as the materials that are in your folders. We'll meet back here in three weeks."

Estella answered a few questions from the committee members and then ended the meeting; it had been quite short. As the committee members got up to leave, the youngest, fourth-grader Dakota Counts, went home with her father and fellow committee member Bill Counts.

Three weeks later the fifteen gathered again in the high school library. Superintendent Smith was there too. He had actually read the book by that point, and his view had changed. He admitted that the books were suitable for children. His secretary, also a committee member, was less certain. She wouldn't let her kids read it, but she wasn't going to ban it.

In fact, nobody on the committee thought ill enough of the books to ban them. They kept them on the shelves. One of the librarians prepared a memo to Angie Haney: "The unanimous decision (15 to 0) was to allow the challenged book to remain on the shelves of the Cedarville Public School libraries."

*　*　*

Angie received the memo; she knew the decision was not right.

She prayed.

For Angie, prayer was a still moment—a time to be quiet and listen. In those moments, God would speak.

Angie became still and focused, emptying her mind. Soon, ideas began to form. They were not her ideas; they were God's. And as God spoke to her, she listened.

Harry Potter and the Cedarville Censors

* * *

Ten days after receiving the library committee's memo, Angie Haney appeared at the school board's April 2002 meeting, which was held in the high school library.

Angie's appearance at the board meeting had not been previously announced. The agenda gave no warning about her arrival. But there, in the midst of the books, Angie waited patiently as the board went through its normal routine. It bought a bus and a fence, voted on financial statements, and accepted bids and rejected others. About fifteen people attended the meeting, many of them regulars. Melinda Bigelow, the local newspaper reporter, attended every meeting. Estella was there too.

The agenda allowed a time for visitors, and when that time finally came around, the board recognized Angie. She had come with a few other people from her church. Angie, with the moral support of her sisters in Christ, stood up confidently. She was no stranger to public speaking; she sometimes had to testify in court because of her employment in the clerk's office at the county courthouse. Audiences did not intimidate her.

"I am here about the Harry Potter books," Angie explained. "These books are not harmless. The lead character continually lies and keeps secrets from adults. Instead of being punished, he is rewarded. I don't think that's a proper lesson for children. Children should be taught to tell the truth, not lie."

The board members listened. Pastor Hodges quietly nodded his approval. Angie continued. "There's one scene in which Harry was specifically told that he and other students could not ride their brooms, but he does anyway and gets caught red-handed. The teacher, though, puts him on the school team. This is not what would happen in reality, or least it shouldn't. This simply reinforces the lesson that if you do something you're told not to do, then you will not get into trouble."

Estella rolled her eyes at this, but otherwise sat politely in the audience. She had not been expecting more Harry Potter trouble. The policy didn't say anything about appealing the library committee's decision; Estella had assumed that the library committee vote would have been the last word.

"The book also brings kids to magic. It starts with the basics and builds on them. It takes an imaginary character and lets him dabble in

4. Estella Fights Back

magic. The book is a starting place to learn witchcraft, sorcery, and other satanic ideas."

Angie's voice strengthened and carried an emotional tinge revealing the depth of her conviction. "The Harry Potter book is just a beginning. People just idly purchase some new hot item their kids want and don't give it a second thought. Then they can't understand why, six months down the road, they can't get their kids to behave, to act obediently."

Until Angie had spoken, many of the board members had not realized that she had challenged the books, nor did they know about the library committee.

"Do we have to go along with the library committee?" one of the board members asked. He looked at Superintendent Smith for an answer.

"I think you have the final say-so."

"Do you have a copy of the policy?"

Superintendent Smith did not, but promised to get one.

Another board member spoke up. "I'd like to hear from the librarians about this at our next meeting in May."

* * *

Although Superintendent Smith personally had no issue with the Harry Potter books, he took no leadership role in preventing their ban. Superintendent Smith could have advised the board not to override the library committee or could have said that he had read the book himself, and that it was fine for children. He did none of those things. Instead, he punted. He wrote the board a memo—a memo silent as to his views and without recommendations of any sort. He told the board nothing else except that it had the final word on what to do about the Potter books.

Estella, however, took action.

She called the newspapers. She called the TV stations. She arranged a PowerPoint and video presentation for the next school board meeting in May.

At that next meeting, the Cedarville High School parking lot, normally sparse on board meeting nights, had triple the cars and several TV vans with huge, extended antennae that looked like portable telephone poles.

Estella had her audience. If Harry Potter were going to be banned, it wasn't going to happen quietly.

5. Legal Backstory: *Tinker* (Students Have a Right to Non-Disruptive Speech)

In the days leading up to December 16, 1965, the Des Moines, Iowa, school board held an emergency meeting. School administrators had learned students were planning to wear two inches of black fabric on their arms to mourn Vietnam war casualties and support a proposed Christmas truce.

Not wanting to condone such un–American ideas, the board banned armbands.

Nevertheless, Mary Beth Tinker, age thirteen, wore her black armband the next day.

Her morning passed uneventfully, but after algebra in the afternoon, the principal called her to his office. Her counselor was there too.

They ordered her to remove the armband. She did. And then the school suspended her anyway.

Several other students across the school system also wore armbands, including Mary's older brother John. The school system suspended them, too, although it chose not to suspend Mary's youngest siblings, who were still in elementary school.

The armband-ban escalated quickly and unexpectedly. The Iowa chapter of the American Civil Liberties Union got involved and its attorney appeared at the next school board meeting.

That meeting was raucous and crowded, with speakers on both sides of the issue. As is typical in these kinds of cases, the issue was framed as "disruption" versus "free speech."

Ultimately, the board voted 4–3 to keep the ban. The ACLU filed suit, and the case began its journey through the courts.

5. *Legal Backstory:* Tinker

The district court judge ruled against the Tinkers. He reasoned that the Vietnam War was a controversial issue. Wearing armbands would be disruptive, if for no other reason than others may be angered by the speech. "While the armbands themselves may not be disruptive, the reactions and comments from other students as a result of the armbands would be likely to disturb the disciplined atmosphere required for any classroom." In other words, the district court in *Tinker* chose to allow a theoretical "heckler's veto," i.e., preventing speech because of the mere possibility that some people would react poorly.

The Tinkers appealed. But a divided Eighth Circuit ruled against them too.

This created a circuit split. Another circuit—the Fifth—had ruled that schools in Mississippi could not prevent students from wearing "freedom buttons" in support of civil rights. So when the Eighth Circuit ruled that schools could stop black armbands, yet the Fifth Circuit already had precedent that students' "freedom buttons" were okay, *Tinker* became a prime candidate for Supreme Court review.

In his (excellent) book, *The Courage of Their Convictions*, scholar Peter Irons opines on the factors affecting the U.S. Supreme Court when it heard the *Tinker* case years later, in 1968, and reversed the Eighth Circuit and found for the Tinkers. Irons points out that from the time of filing of the Tinkers' case until the Supreme Court heard oral arguments, the cultural landscape had changed. More than 20,000 Americans had died in Vietnam, Martin Luther King and Bobby Kennedy had been assassinated, and continuing the war had become even more of a major, national issue.

The Supreme Court's *Tinker* opinion opens with a citation of *Barnette*—the West Virginia case allowing Jehovah's Witnesses not to salute the flag—for the proposition that "symbolic acts" are protected by the First Amendment, including within a school environment.

"Our problem," said the Supreme Court, "lies in the area where students in the exercise of First Amendment rights collide with the rules of the school authorities."

And here's where *Tinker*'s good facts—two of them—come in.

First, the school system had singled out black armbands. Prior to the anti-war armbands, students had been allowed to wear buttons from political campaigns and other symbols, such as a German Cross. This selective punishment strengthened the idea that the armband students were being singled out for their viewpoint and not some other reason.

Second, the record in the case was clear that the *Tinker* plaintiffs "caused ... no interference with work and no disorder."

The combination of actions that were purely political speech and lacking any disruption of school business made *Tinker* a win for students and established a framework for future analyses of student free speech: (1) is it speech? and (2) is it causing disruption?

6. School Boards

*"In the first place God made idiots. This was for practice.
Then he made School Boards."*—Mark Twain

At that May 2002 meeting, the Cedarville School Board moved quickly and perfunctorily through the non–Harry Potter portion of the agenda. When her turn came, Estella stood and started her presentation.

Her large glasses hung from decorative and heavy eyeglass chains around her neck; Estella put them on. Straight, gray hair and a black sweater gave her an austere presence.

"Lights, please," she said, waving at the switch on the wall. She began playing a video called *The World of Harry Potter*. It was a good start, given that so few of her audience knew what was actually in the books. Once the video finished, Estella walked through the materials that the library committee had reviewed—the Library Bill of Rights, articles on censorship, book reviews on Harry Potter, and discussions concerning Christianity's relationship to Harry Potter.

Those materials had persuaded the library committee—even those members who had been initially opposed. Could Estella persuade the school board too?

The school board members sat and listened. Four of them wore crisp, ironed, striped button-up shirts with blue jeans. The fifth, Pastor Mark Hodges, had his own kind of formal wear—a silky, collarless t-shirt with a gray suit jacket. He wore tinted lenses—the kind that never fully clear up inside. They obscured his eyes.

Estella finished. "Any questions?"

A board member said, "We need to go into executive session."

Arkansas' freedom of information laws are some of the most powerful in the country. They are much more comprehensive and revealing than the federal freedom of information laws. Under the state's version, no government agency may deliberate in secret. The only exception to this rule is "executive session," which is reserved solely for discussion about employment matters.

On the one hand, "executive session" is an understandable exception—employment decisions sometimes require frank discussions that really ought not be in the press. On the other hand, "executive session" can be abused—for example, when non-employment matters are discussed in secret. And, since it's in secret, there's no way for outsiders to tell if those in "executive session" are cheating.

The timing of the Cedarville School Board's "executive session" was, at best, suspicious. Estella Roberts remembers the board going into executive session immediately after her presentation. The school board minutes show that the board went into executive session a little bit later. Cynical observers are convinced that the Harry Potter matter was discussed in executive session.

Regardless, that night, the board decided not to decide. Board member Gary Koonce looked at the room crammed with people and reporters. "I move we table this. We can look at it again in June." The motion carried 5–0.

The press, anxious for a story, went away disappointed.

Estella went away harassed. As she walked to her car that night, two men yelled at her in the parking lot. "That's the devil's work. You shouldn't be giving that stuff to children." The men made Estella nervous. After she got home, she called the police and asked to file a report.

※ ※ ※

Estella Roberts was convinced that the media attention and high turnout at the May meeting dissuaded the board from banning the Harry Potter books—at that time. The visitor sign-in sheet from that the May meeting listed more than thirty-five people in attendance, many with the press.

June was different. Only eleven visitors attended. There were very few reporters and no TV vans with their antennae sticking up like giant soda straws.

At the June meeting the board members decided to discuss Harry Potter—and with fireworks not usually seen at school board meetings.

6. School Boards

Board member Jerry Shelly moved to sequester the Harry Potter books. They would be pulled from the shelf, placed on the librarians' desks, and available only with written parental permission. The motion also would remove the Harry Potter books from the Accelerated Reader list, which was part of the schools' reading curriculum.

"Second," said Pastor Hodges.

Audie Murphy, one of the younger school board members, spoke up. And that was unusual for Audie Murphy. A high school graduate and four-year veteran of the school board, Audie Murphy is normally the kind of person more comfortable listening than speaking. He turned toward Pastor Hodges and Jerry Shelly. "You don't have the right to tell me what my daughter can and cannot read. This is a public school. You don't have the right to tell her what she can or can't read here. If I don't want my daughter to read it, I'll tell her not to read it, and I'll deal with it."

Jerry Shelly was unswayed. "Well, are you going to tell your daughter not to read it?"

Audie Murphy raised his voice and tightened his face. "It's my business and nobody else's!" He glared at Jerry Shelly. "This Board doesn't have to take any action on this, because that is not the way the policy is set up. I could understand if the recommendation from the library committee came back 10 to 5 or something like that, but it didn't. It came back 15 to nothing. These people went to college and are trained."

"Are they trained in the occult?" Pastor Hodges shot back. "Are they trained enough to tell me that this book doesn't deal with the occult?"

At this point, the best response would have been that whatever the books dealt with, be it the occult or not, did not matter; a public school has no business censoring books based purely on the prevailing religious sensibilities. Sharon Partain, a well-known community activist who happened to be in the audience, came the closest to making this argument. "I don't think our school board needs to step over into the area of censoring books on our shelves," she said. "The Harry Potter books are no different than *The Wizard of Oz*. They're only fairy tales."

The debate ended; minds were made up; the vote was called.

"On the matter of removing the Harry Potter books, how do you vote?"

Ayes from three—Mark Hodges, Jerry Shelly, and Gary Koonce.

Audie Murphy and board president Mike Shumard voted nay.

Harry Potter and the Cedarville Censors

"Three to two, ayes have it."

The board minutes memorialized the event, and Superintendent Dave Smith made a note to himself to have his principals issue a memorandum effecting the new Harry Potter ban.

* * *

Estella received the memorandum just before the start of the new school year:

To: Estella Roberts, Librarian
From: Glennis Cook, Principal
Reference: Harry Potter books

Please make sure that the following items are attended to before the students arrive back to school on August 19, 2002. These items have been voted on and are part of board policy at this time.

1. Remove all Harry Potter books from the shelves.
2. Place these books where they are highly visible, yet not accessible to the students unless they are checking them out.
3. In order for these books to be checked out, the student must have a signed permission statement from their parent/legal guardian.
4. Make sure that all Harry Potter books are blocked from Accelerated Reader points.

If you have any further questions on this matter, don't hesitate to contact me.

/s/ Glennis Cook, Principal

And, as much as she disagreed with it, Estella complied. To do otherwise would be insubordination and cost her job. Estella gathered the papers she had presented to the library committee and school board and waited. There were other ways to fight this. And when her sister Dorothy called with the name of an interested attorney, Estella knew how that fight would take place.

* * *

I first heard about Cedarville's banning of Harry Potter books from my then-mother-in-law.

Not banning, really. More like a mild restriction. Students could still read the books if they were willing to jump through the procedural hoops imposed by the school board. I would later learn that this was typical in censorship cases. The censor can truthfully claim that it had only partially, not completely, banned the books.

At this time, I had just moved back to my home state of Arkansas

6. School Boards

from Washington, D.C. My D.C. days had been spent in law school and, later, at a posh, genteel corporate firm wherein I got paid entirely too much money to generate esoteric memoranda opining about nuclear energy regulations. And while the money was good, the glamour was not there. That kind of work would confine me to an office for my whole career.

Wanting the thrill of trial work, I moved my then-wife and infant son to my not-so-bustling hometown of Fort Smith, Arkansas, population 80,000, the largest town in a six-county area.

You know the saying—be careful what you wish for... When I arrived, my new partners had several files on my desk; my make-shift inbox, a cardboard juice container, held the assigning memos. My first Arkansas cases included child custody fights, a quarrel between a building contractor and his concrete man, a will for a woman who, literally, signed it on her deathbed, and a fight with the local prosecutor about the legality of some video games that allowed poker options.

So when I heard about a book banning—a good, old-fashioned book banning—how could I help but become excited? Isn't that what everyone went to law school for?

At the time, my mother-in-law, Ana, lived with us, and she made me breakfast each morning while my wife and infant son got much-needed sleep. Ana was particularly fond of olive oil, convinced it has near-magical powers of health. She added it to most everything, including scrambled eggs.

Ana told me about the Cedarville case one morning as I ate my olive-y eggs.

"Do you want more coffee?"

"Please."

"Did you see in the paper about the books at that school? Seekerton? Seedville? See-something."

Completely confused, I looked up from the eggs.

Ana poured more coffee. "It's near Van Buren."

"Cedarville?"

"Yes. That sounds right. Is that near Van Buren?" she asked.

"Yes."

"Oh. Well, the school board there—would that place have its own school board?"

"Maybe. There's more than a hundred little bitty school districts in this state. That's why there's all that fuss about consolidating them." The Cedarville School District, like so many Arkansas school districts at that time, had fewer than a thousand students for all grade levels, kindergarten through twelfth grade. At that time, some Arkansas school districts had only a couple hundred students for all grade levels.

"What happened at Cedarville?" I asked.

Ana told me about the school board's restrictions on Harry Potter.

I rushed through breakfast and left for the computer. Research. Must do research. Surely this was unconstitutional.

※ ※ ※

Some readers may be chuckling to themselves right now about these backward Arkansas rubes with their strange and fervent religious beliefs. And they're right to do so. The notions that fueled the Potter ban are the very definition of narrow-minded.

The Potter censorship wasn't without precedent in Arkansas. Various groups in Arkansas had protested other movies and book in the past, such as the allegedly heretical movie *The Last Temptation of Christ*, which no theater in Arkansas showed, save one, and that one theater was vandalized for it.

But if we are going to cast stones at my fellow Arkansans, then we must cast stones at other, equally deserving folks. Neither Arkansans, nor right-wing evangelicals have a monopoly on censorship. This is because the axiom of the Potter censors is the same as any censor: certain beliefs are dangerous, and their cure is not vigorous debate, but suppression.

I first learned this lesson fifteen years prior to taking on the Harry Potter case. At that time, back in 1987, I had graduated from Southside High School in Fort Smith, Arkansas, and matriculated at the University of Michigan, Ann Arbor.

A more different locale can hardly be imagined. Not only is Ann Arbor's weather opposite—Arkansas gets snow about every other winter, while Ann Arbor has snow on the ground continually from November to February—but its culture is opposite. Ann Arbor is a Berkeley-wannabe, and the university's most vocal political groups have a Stalinistic left-wing fervor. That vocal left has a great deal of support among students, faculty, and university administration.

My sophomore year at UM–Ann Arbor greeted me with the "Code."

6. School Boards

The Code, an official UM–Ann Arbor policy blessed by the university and its lawyers, forbade students from uttering things that the university administration deemed offensive. At that time, things on the "offensive" list included remarks perceived as racist, sexist, or anti-homosexual.

One of the things in the Code that caught my eye was in its list of examples of forbidden speech. Among the examples: "You display a Confederate flag on the door of your room in the residence hall."

That caught my eye because my alma mater, Southside High School, had as its mascot Johnny Reb. In fact, a big wooden mascot of a Confederate soldier greeted students as they entered the front door of my high school. At pep rallies we were led in chants of "The South [meaning the Southside High School football team] shall rise tonight." Really spirited students would wave Confederate flags at the rallies; the cheerleaders were known as the Dixie Belles. My high school yearbooks, honoring the school mascot, have pictures of Confederate flags on their covers.

I have since learned, thanks to higher education and a smidgen of worldliness, that my high school mascot was outrageous and offensive. Once I went north to school, people hearing my tales of a Southside High School pep rally reacted, uniformly, with shock. Having a Johnny Reb mascot and encouraging youth to wave Confederate flags are not the most appropriate activities for a public school.

Nevertheless, Southside was where I came from, and I had brought my yearbooks—with their pictures of the Confederate flag—with me. And now, I learned, UM–Ann Arbor had declared my high school yearbooks verboten.

UM–Ann Arbor enforced the Code with glee. It punished a dental student who thought that minorities had a difficult time in the course and had the temerity to say as much. It punished a student for telling a sexist joke: "Q. How many men does it take to mop a floor? A. None, it's a woman's job." The university also disciplined a student for opining that homosexuality was a disorder that could be treated.

Thus, in a university environment—an environment that allegedly promotes free inquiry—UM–Ann Arbor punished people for parroting viewpoints once held by the country's leading psychiatrists or that were, rightly or wrongly, widely held cultural beliefs.

The Code at Michigan had offended me, and so I joined one of the only groups on campus fighting the UM's censors—a small libertarian and conservative campus newspaper called *The Michigan Review*. We railed against the Code every chance we got and, with the exception of a few supportive faculty members, were the lone voice against it. The editors of the main student newspaper—*The Michigan Daily*—supported the Code. After all, it was being used to enforce their own sensibilities.

One brave soul, a teaching assistant named Wesley Wynne, also disagreed with the Code. He contacted the American Civil Liberties Union and brought suit. A federal judge promptly found the Code unconstitutional and threw it out.

Wesley Wynne initially brought his lawsuit as a "John Doe" action. He sued anonymously because he, justifiably, feared retaliation from the university.

After winning the court case, he contacted the *Review* and wanted to go public. Another *Review* staffer and I were to meet him at a tea and sandwich shop called Drakes.

Drakes bordered the campus, and following an afternoon class, my staffer friend and I ducked away from Ann Arbor's perpetually cloudy-gray sky into the dark and aromatic Drakes. We walked by the cash register, with its menacing display of bounced checks and a "cash only" sign, and peered into the various booths. It was hard to meet someone at Drakes. The seating was mostly booths, and the benches had tall, five-foot-high, painted wooden backs. Their pale green paint and black trim conspired with the poor lighting to keep customers and conversations isolated and well hidden.

Finally we spotted a pudgy, searching face that we later learned was Wesley Wynne. My staffer friend and I sat down, pulled out a tape recorder, and got started.

"Just imagine sitting, for example, in class." Wesley Wynne, after some initial reticence, had begun talking with us in earnest. He'd refused my offer to buy him tea, so he spoke without distraction; I dunked the corner of my grilled cheese sandwich into a hot cup of the (for this occasion) aptly-named Constant Comment tea and listened. "Imagine," he says, "you're in class, and class hasn't begun yet. You lean over to your buddy and say—and this is something that you happen to believe—'You know, I don't think women are as good as men are.' Well, say somebody in back of you, maybe some radical feminist women's studies major, gets all ticked off and goes to the Affirmative Action Office. Well, it says right here, by

6. School Boards

God, you're guilty of discriminatory harassment." Wynne thumped a copy of the UM's Code for emphasis.

"Every student at the university," said Wynne, "received this pamphlet. And there's a good chance that many people, on the basis of this policy, will refuse to make certain comments for fear of being punished."

Wesley Wynne was exactly right. UM–Ann Arbor's Code gave me proper perspective. In Arkansas, the censors were right-wing "Christians"; in Ann Arbor, the censors were left-wing "Progressives."

Both were equally dogmatic and morally smug, and the solution used by both—censorship—was wrong. In one locale, condemning homosexuality or the Confederate flag or traditional roles for women was a must; in the other, a mustn't. This convinced me that the power to censor is a bad power indeed—it will be used to enforce the prevailing notions, whatever they may be, of the people who happen to hold that censoring power.

Wesley Wynne's story was one of my favorites at *The Michigan Review*. We wrote it in the spring of 1990. "John Doe Tells All," said the headline. We included a rather unfortunate photograph of Mr. Wynne that rivaled most DMV photos. I can still recognize Drakes' retro wall paneling in the background. When the article first came out, Wynne complained about the photo, but there was nothing we could do. Several thousand copies of the *Review* had been printed and dispersed.

Nevertheless, it was one of the better issues of *The Michigan Review*, and I remembered the story fondly.

And even though a decade had passed, I wanted an encore. I wanted to give the Cedarville School District the same licking that the University of Michigan got, but this time, I'd be doing it, not just reporting it.

7. Legal Backstory: *Pico* (Students' Free Speech Rights Apply to School Libraries)

The watershed case for students' First Amendment rights in a school library began in the 1970s in Levittown, Long Island, New York.

After World War II, anticipating a tremendous demand for housing, a New York company, Levitt & Sons, began developing the onion and potato fields of unincorporated Nassau County. They named the development as originally as their near-identical houses: Levittown. It was the nation's first mass-produced, cookie-cutter suburb.

Levittown properties had "restrictive covenants"—a clause in property deeds forbidding buyers to sell or rent to non–Caucasians. William Levitt justified the clauses by saying, "As a Jew, I have no room in my heart for racial prejudice. But the plain fact is that most whites prefer not to live in mixed communities. This attitude may be wrong morally, and someday it may change. I hope it will."

The United States Supreme Court declared those kinds of restrictive covenants unenforceable in a 1948 ruling, but Levittown's covenants still had their desired effect. By 1975, the time of the *Pico* case, Levittown was a virtually all-white, middle- and working-class neighborhood whose residents were socially conservative and suspicious of people not like them.

In late 1975, several members of the Island Trees school board (the district covering Levittown) attended a conference in upstate New York organized by "People of New York United" which was, behind the scenes, sponsored by the ultra-conservative John Birch Society.

At the conference, the school board members received a list of books

7. Legal Backstory: Pico

deemed unsuitable for children. A federal court would later describe the list as "two sets of crudely typed and reproduced sheets."

The sheets listed books and excerpts (offending passages) from each with no context whatsoever. For example:

The novel *A Hero Ain't Nothing but a Sandwich* by Alice Childress featured an adolescent black teen who was struggling with issues related to drugs, poverty, and relationships with family. *Hero* was critically acclaimed and won multiple awards. It gave insights into the challenges faced by some poor, black, urban children, which were a world apart from the comfortable, homogeneous existence of the middle class white kids of Levittown.

Yet, according to the "crudely typed ... sheets," *Hero* should be kept out of the school library because of these excerpts.

- 10: "Hell, no! Fuck the society."
- 64–65: "The hell with the junkie, the wino, the capitalist, the welfare checks, the world ... yeah, and fuck you too!"
- 75–76: "They can have back the spread and curtains, I'm too old for them fuckin' bunnies anyway."

The sheets gave no other information about *Hero*; those excerpts, standing alone, put *Hero* on the ban list.

Kurt Vonnegut, Jr.'s *Slaughterhouse Five* was also on the list. The conference's sheets identified a few passages with profanities and a passage unflattering to Jesus. For those sins, Kurt Vonnegut, Jr., a well-known and celebrated author, had his novel banned.

An anthology containing a short story by Jonathan Swift (of Gulliver fame) was on the ban list because of Swift's satirical short story "A Modest Proposal for Preventing the Children of Poor People in Ireland from Being a Burden to their Parents or Country." Swift's short story suggested—again, satirically—that overpopulation could be solved by selling children for food. Literary critics have long recognized "A Modest Proposal" as an early example of satirical hyperbole; Swift's goal in producing the essay was to mock the prevailing heartless attitude towards the poor.

The Fixer, by Bernard Malamud, told the story of a Jew unjustly imprisoned in Tsarist Russia. The book won a Pulitzer Prize and the U.S. National Book award for fiction, and had, for several years prior, been a part of the school's literature program (at the same time the board members removed the book from the library, the school system had sixty copies

Harry Potter and the Cedarville Censors

of *The Fixer* for its curriculum, which had been previously approved by an earlier board). As noted by *Newsday*, in a March 19, 1976, article, "A school employee, who did not want to be identified, said the passage considered offensive in *The Fixer* concerned an anti-semitic remark made by a Russian boatman.... 'It's not anti-semitic [the employee said]; it's about how the Russians persecute Jews.'"

There were thirty-two offending books on the conference list, most of them banned for using profanity, discussing sexuality, or—with disturbing frequency—banned for no other reason than giving voice to the concerns of feminists, Black Panthers, the irreligious, and the other usual suspects from the political left.

The three school board members returned from the conference, sheets in hand, and a month later, in the dark of night—literally, at night—they asked the custodian to unlock the school. They descended on the high school library, found nearly a dozen books also on the conference list, and removed them.

Somehow, the faculty learned of the board members' actions. Court records and newspaper articles aren't clear how that happened. Perhaps the custodian told someone, or maybe the principal who'd accidentally come across the members as they were removing books (but did not stop them) told somebody.

Regardless, the faculty found out, and several were angry. Among the angry was an English teacher, Mrs. Othalie Pepper.

Othalie Pepper was an attractive woman, in her forties, with an average build. She stood 5'3". She took pains to dress nicely and sported a Julie Andrews haircut with blond highlights.

She loved language and loved teaching. She'd earned a master's degree from the City University of New York. She also had children and a husband, which made her even more unusual for that era, since prevailing sensibilities were that a woman should not work if she had children and a husband.

Mrs. Pepper understood the realpolitik of her school district, and while, as a teacher, she had some protections from the union, she knew that being personally vocal against the administration would accomplish little except make her a target.

So, one morning, not long after the dark-of-night removal, Mrs. Pepper sat behind student Russ Rieger at a school assembly. She leaned forward and whispered to him about the banning.

7. Legal Backstory: Pico

Russ was the perfect person for Mrs. Pepper to have selected. His older sister was politically active, and Russ admired his sister. Like his sister, he was civil rights minded and questioned authority.

And most importantly, for Mrs. Pepper's purposes, Russ wrote for the school newspaper.

In researching this book, I spoke with Russ Rieger to get his memories of the events leading up to the *Pico* case. "Mrs. Pepper was cool," he told me. "She was very much about the arts, very ethical.... She was someone I looked up to, [and] my peer group ... enjoyed being with her."

Russ believes—and I have no reason to dispute this—that the furor started when Mrs. Pepper discreetly brought the book ban to the attention of those who could publicly protest. "That took courage," Russ told me. "It's not an easy thing to do as a teacher ... she could have easily been named [and retaliated against].... She risked her job doing that."

At Mrs. Pepper's suggestion, Russ wrote an article for the school newspaper, exposing the book ban to all the students. "It was the first time ... everybody was outed for their actions." When I asked Russ how he could report on such a thing when the school administration would take a dim view of that kind of story, he explained.

"This was Island Trees. It was about football. There was no money. There was no journalism [class]. There was a teacher who oversaw the paper.... I'm sure [the teacher] got in trouble for that [allowing the article to be published]" but by having the students do it, there was plausible deniability.

Predictably, the school administrators later banned the student newspaper. They cited what were obviously pretextual reasons. The school claimed that a later-published article had not been supportive of the school's football team and therefore the paper would be discontinued. That incident would spur its own separate controversy (but, of course, not going to the Supreme Court), with Russ and his fellow students appearing at school board meetings wearing black armbands in protest.

After Russ' article exposing the book banning, the teachers' union filed a grievance. It claimed the removal impacted its members' academic freedom.

Then the school superintendent got involved. He wrote a surprisingly candid and prescient memo to the board. "We already have a policy ... designed to expressly handle such problems.... It is a good policy—and it is a Board policy—and that it should be followed in this instance ... [following the policy would] perhaps avoid the public furor which always attended such issues in the past."

The policy that the superintendent was referring to was, for all intents and purposes, the same that Cedarville ended up using: an American Library Association process of creating committees of faculty, students, and parents, reviewing the books, and making recommendations.

The superintendent's memo went on to predict that "unilateral banning by the Board ... would surely create a furious uproar.... I don't believe you want such an uproar, and I certainly don't."

Nevertheless, the school board members continued their efforts, targeting the junior high school library in February 1976.

Not long afterwards, the local newspaper, *Newsday*, picked up the story, running its first of many articles on March 19, 1976, "School Board Purging 11 Books."

Board president Richard Ahrens adamantly defended the banning. "[The Board has the right to remove] any books we want. The taxpayers don't have to subsidize garbage. If the teachers union doesn't think we have the power, let them take us to court."

The next day, *Newsday* ran "Board Removal of Books Makes Critics of Students." The article quoted several students who were confused by or objected to the ban. It also quoted a statement released by the school board: "With the elections of school board candidates just two months away, the teachers union is once again attempting to discredit the board and win seats for two union-backed lackeys ... these books contain obscenities, blasphemies, brutality, and perversion beyond description.... When most of the parents review these books, we are confident they will back us to the hilt, grateful that we have done our job and remained as they elected us ... their faithful Watchdogs."

Thus, the lines were clearly drawn. The school board saw itself as gatekeepers for acceptable ideas to be presented to children, and those opposed believed that academic freedom was more important.

The controversy continued to escalate. The local chapter of the American Civil Liberties Union threatened a lawsuit.

But the board refused to budge. It defied the ACLU and chastised the teachers' union for complaining about the book ban. "[The teachers' union] is fighting to keep books in our schools which are offensive to Christians,

7. Legal Backstory: Pico

Jews, Blacks, and all Americans in general. One such book [referring to *Slaughterhouse Five*] refers to Jesus Christ as a 'man with no connections.' One must ask oneself what motivates [the union]? Why ... does [the union] insist that these books remain in the hands of our children?"

And as for the ACLU, the board president said, "no amount of pressure from any group is going to make this board back off. All they do is make us get more adamant in our position."

At the next school board meeting, according to *Newsday*, "some 500 parents and students crowded into the auditorium" of one of the schools.

The superintendent—the same gentleman who'd warned the board earlier to not to create a furor—made a lengthy statement to the board opposing the book ban. "It is wrong for a board ... to act to remove books without prolonged consideration of the views of both the parents ... and the teachers. It is wrong to judge any book on the basis of brief excerpts from it."

Allow me to make an aside here. In my ten years as a trial lawyer in Arkansas, I had the opportunity to be frequently involved in legal matters concerning schools. Sometimes I represented students, often I represented teachers, and towards the end of my time in Arkansas, I represented a school district.

For a school superintendent to criticize his or her board, and to do so publicly, is unheard of. A superintendent, like any normal person, has a strong motivation to not be fired. School boards hire and fire their superintendents. I've simply never seen a situation where a superintendent would cross the board, and certainly not in a public forum. So for the Island Trees superintendent to have done that—well, that's remarkable. Wow.

The superintendent recommended the board restore the books pending review by a proper committee. The board did appoint a committee, but it refused to restore the books.

The local ACLU chapter held off on suing until the committee review.

Two months passed, and in May there was a school board election. The voters in the Island Tree district re-elected the book banners 53 percent to 47 percent.

Then came the summer. By the end of July 1976, the committee was ready. It had read ten of the eleven books; not all the books had not been available to all the committee members, but ten were.

Harry Potter and the Cedarville Censors

The board scheduled a meeting to discuss the committee recommendations. More than a hundred people attended.

The committee recommended that two of the books—Piri Thomas' *Down These Mean Streets* and Desmond Morris' *The Naked Ape*—continue to be banned.

The former, *Down These Mean Streets*, was, as a federal judge would later describe, "an autobiographical account ... of a Puerto Rican youth growing up in the East Side Barrio (Spanish Harlem) in New York City. Predictably the scene is depressing, ugly and violent. [The book is] replete with four letter and twelve letter obscenities.... Acts of criminal violence, sex, normal and perverse, as well as episodes of drug shooting are graphically described."

It seems that the sense of the committee was that if white, middle class high school students were to learn about the troubled lives of the urban poor their own age and living only thirty miles away, then it should at least be a sanitized, PG version.

The latter, *The Naked Ape*, had no swear words or illicit drug use at all. Its author posited that human nature is largely the result of evolution, rather than culture. For the 1970s, this was a decidedly unorthodox view (a view that would, by the way, become more accepted by academics over the next several decades). The "crudely typed sheets" objected to *The Naked Ape* because of three passages discussing how certain specifics of human sexual activity may be explained by evolution. The school district had a policy against teaching "sex education," which apparently was applied broadly, so *The Naked Ape* was out.

Those are the two books that even the committee thought should remain banned. Which, I must say, shows that not even book committees can get the censorship question right.

The committee also recommended

- *Laughing Boy, Black Boy, Go Ask Alice,* and *Best Short Stories by Negro Writers* be retained.
- *The Fixer* be "returned to the Modern Literature curriculum, subject to parental approval."
- *Slaughterhouse Five* be "put on the restricted shelf."

The committee was split, 4 to 4, on *Soul on Ice* and *A Hero Ain't Nothing but a Sandwich*.

7. Legal Backstory: Pico

But the committee was merely "advisory"; the board had the final say-so.

The board largely ignored the committee; it voted to ban every book it had originally purged except *Laughing Boy* and *Black Boy*.

Nobody on the board had read all the books. Nobody on the board gave specific reasons for overriding the recommendations of the committee.

※ ※ ※

Russ isn't entirely sure how his parents and the ACLU got in touch with each other, but he surmises that the ACLU "did research, made some phone calls, and found out who'd be receptive." Russ' parents would definitely have been receptive, as they were some of the few liberals in town.

Russ remembers more than one meeting with the ACLU lawyers, and one of those took place in his basement. "It was a rather large basement, fully finished. Our house was on the edge of Levittown," Russ told me, "so it wasn't a standard Levittown house." The basement was L shaped with a couch, television, and coffee table. It had linoleum floors.

The meeting was at night. Four other students in the district—Pico, Gold, Yarris, and Sochinski—joined Russ. Their parents were with them, too, because they had to sign the lawyers' paperwork allowing the ACLU to sue on the teens' behalf.

Russ recalls the ACLU lawyers discussing the case and going through what their strategy would be. The lawyers ensured that everyone participating understood what would happen and what being in the lawsuit would entail. The lawyers said it would be a landmark case and they were prepared to take it as far as it could go.

On that point, the ACLU lawyers were right, and it was one of the few points on which they would agree with the school board. In a point/counterpoint sort of editorial presentation in *Newsday*, the board said, "Make no mistake about it, this action in Island Trees has national significance. Every board of education, and every parent, has a stake in the outcome of this lawsuit."

Why were the predictions of "landmark case" correct? The answer is because this debate had been brewing for some time, across many courts and with varying outcomes. Thus, there was "circuit split," and the Supreme

Harry Potter and the Cedarville Censors

Court was much more likely to take a case if it would resolve a circuit split.

And that was the situation here. A federal appellate court, in a case called *Presidents Council, District 25 v. Community School Board # 25*, 457 F.2d 289 (2nd Cir.) *cert. denied*, 409 U.S. 998 (1972), had held that a school district could legally ban *Down These Mean Streets* from a junior high school. That case was binding law in federal courts in New York, and its existence explains the confidence that the Island Trees School Board had about its own actions.

On the other hand, courts in other federal circuits had reached different results in cases about school boards censoring books.

* * *

The ACLU filed on January 4, 1977, and held a press conference. Russ was there. "I remember being on a dais with Kurt Vonnegut, who was really friendly and polite to me. And chain smoking. That's what I remember, him being very friendly and smoking the entire time."

Newsday covered the press conference and published an article and a picture of Russ along with Steven Pico (the "lead" plaintiff, meaning that his name was listed first on the court papers) and Jacqueline Gold. There was further coverage, too, of course. For example, Steven Pico appeared on Phil Donahue's television show, and I'm fairly certain the case got picked up by the UPI/AP.

The *Pico* case did not actually go to trial. The school and the students suing the school (read: the ACLU) actually came to an agreement about the facts of the case. Together they created a document with those facts: the process (or lack thereof) of the book ban, the impetus behind the ban, and how the ban was implemented. With that in place, both sides wrote briefs to the court and awaited a decision.

The judge sided with the school, citing the binding precedent, *Presidents Council*. The ACLU had argued that the judge should look at (and follow) the decisions from other circuits, but the judge declined that invitation.

Technically, that judge had no choice but to rule the way he did. He was a "district" judge, which is a low rung on the federal judicial ladder. The next level was the appellate "circuit" courts, and above them the

7. Legal Backstory: Pico

Supreme Court. A district judge is bound to follow appellate decisions from the circuit she or he is in.

The ACLU dutifully appealed to the Second Circuit. By this time most of the student-plaintiffs had graduated from Island Trees, although Shochinski was still around, since he was the youngest.

The Second Circuit empaneled three judges to review the district court decision. They reversed the district court in a 2–1 vote. In reaching that decision, they noted that *Pico*—as with all school library banning cases—pitted two important values against one another.

The first, of course, was the First Amendment, the right of students to freely read and receive material.

The second, though, was the right of school boards to set their own curriculum, molded in the community's values and mores.

Federal courts are loath to be called upon to rule on what they see as small and minor matters (like a book in a school district library), especially when a governing body, like a school board, already exists to make such a determination.

It was this point that the dissenting judge glommed onto. "[There is no] effort by school authorities to suppress speech or ideas.... The ideas expressed in the removed books may also be freely discussed, in or out of the classroom, without using the profanities, vulgarities, and indecencies objected to by the Board.... There are few, if any, thoughts that cannot be expressed by the use of less offensive language."

The dissenting judge also complained that his colleagues on the bench weren't following the precedent set in the Second Circuit's *President's Council* case, which had allowed removal of a book from a school library. And, in my opinion, he had a point there. Not that I agree with *President's Council*, but it was binding precedent in the Second Circuit.

The two judges whose views prevailed in the Second Circuit decision sidestepped *President's Council* by saying it was different enough to invoke a different rule. In legal parlance, this is known as "distinguishing" a case, which means finding a difference in that case's facts so that a judge can apply a different rule to the facts before her. That sort of thing happens with some frequency, not only with judges, but with people in general. Psychologists call it "motivated reasoning."

With *President's Council* out of the way, the Second Circuit's opinion made clear that it did not want to set precedent allowing folks "bring to court every decision by a school official involving the shelving or unshelving of a book in a school library [or else] the federal courts will become 'the school board for the country.'"

Nevertheless, the two judge majority felt that the First Amendment considerations outweighed the interest in letting school boards control their schools. The judges explained their decision this way: "The books were removed from school library shelves before any concerned school official had read them, solely on the basis of mimeographed quotations collected by anonymous readers whose editorial comments revealed political concerns reaching far beyond the education and well-being of the children of the Island Trees Union Free School District."

The Second Circuit ordered that the case be sent back down to the district court for a trial so that the district court could gather more facts and evidence and rule with the recognition that the law allowed the district court to second guess the school board.

The story could have ended there, but it did not. The school board appealed to the United States Supreme Court.

Having the Supreme Court take your case is a long shot. As one lawyer friend of mine put it, "There is no greater legal certainty than the certainty that the U.S. Supreme Court will not take your case." And that's pretty true, since the odds of the Supreme Court taking a case (called "granting certiorari" or "granting cert") is about one in a hundred. Certainly, there are some factors that may favor a case getting cert, but the overall odds of requests to acceptances are about a hundred to one.

The Supreme Court granted cert to *Pico v. Island Trees*.

In researching this case, I listened to the recording of the *Pico* oral arguments before the Supreme Court.

The first thing that struck me was how reasonable and measured the school board's attorney seemed. Prior to hearing the recording, I'd demonized that gentleman as a smug conservative seeking to limit children's free inquiry. On the tape, he was unfailingly polite. And he hammered away at the specter of federal courts forever being bothered to intrude upon each and every book selection and curriculum choice made by the thousands and thousands of school districts across the country.

Pico's lawyer, on the other hand, argued with indignation and raised his own specter—that of narrow-minded local officials improperly imposing their views on children under the guise of "education" or "protecting morals."

7. Legal Backstory: Pico

For the Supreme Court, it was a tough case. It was so tough, it didn't even get a 5–4 decision; it got a 3–1–1–4 decision and was (is) a real mess to understand.

Here's what I mean by that.

Normally, when the U.S. Supreme Court decides a case, the decision is made by a majority of the justices. When that happens, the majority's pronouncement is law.

But sometimes, and this is what happened in *Pico*, there is not a clear majority. In *Pico*, three justices gave one reason for siding with the students; one justice agreed with some, but not all of the three justices' opinion; another justice voted for the students for totally different reasons; and four justices sided with the school board. The students won on what is called a "plurality"—there's a win, but not a clear win.

A review of that final decision, officially known as *Board of Education, Island Trees Union Free School District No. 26 v. Pico*, 457 U.S. 853 (1982), shows the following.

For the students: three justices, Brennan, Marshall, and Stevens, were the "plurality." They held that a school board has broad discretion in determining its curriculum, but libraries are different. Unlike classrooms, libraries are places of "voluntary inquiry" by students, and so First Amendment protections, such as the right to receive information, can be enforced.

For the students: Justice Blackmun pretty much agreed with the plurality, but in a narrower way. He said yes, school officials can and should be able to set their curriculum and run their schools as they see fit, but they cannot restrict access to political ideas or social perspectives. He said that the *Pico* case put these two principles in tension, "[b]ut that tension demonstrates only that the problem here is a difficult one, not that the problem should be resolved by choosing one principle over another."

For the students: Justice White thought there needed to be more facts developed than the ones that were agreed upon by the parties at the district court level. He thought the case should be sent back to the district court for a trial and didn't think anyone needed to opine on the First Amendment issues until after all the facts had developed at trial.

Against the students: Chief Justice Burger and justices Powell, Rehnquist, and O'Connor dissented. They thought that there were plenty of other avenues for children to receive information; it would be improper

Harry Potter and the Cedarville Censors

to insert federal courts into the middle of decisions that are best left to school boards and the parents who elect them. Further, they pointed out, there are 15,000 different school boards in the country, and having federal courts become avenues for anyone objecting to boards' decisions about their libraries is unwieldy.

The dissent also picked at problems with the plurality's holding. For example, why is a school board being forced to continue to host books it finds objectionable? Why, under the plurality's decision, can school boards can still select books, but once selected, they can't easily be removed?

* * *

The *Pico* students won their case, but could that victory really be translated to other cases? If I were to cite *Pico* as precedent, the other side could say, "That's not really the law. Fewer than five justices supported Mr. Meadors' position."

After reading *Pico*, I made a note to do further research to see if I could find other, later cases that cited *Pico* and relied on the plurality opinion. Frankly, I just assumed, without checking first, that I would find some. I just couldn't imagine a judge allowing a ban of Harry Potter books.

So, even with incomplete (but promising) research, I pressed ahead with figuring out how to bring a lawsuit against Cedarville.

8. Like Magic, a Client Appears

> *"Never stir up litigation. A worse man can scarcely be found than one who does this."*
> —Abraham Lincoln

The initial legal research on *Pico* I did after breakfast had given me hope. I was ready to take the Cedarville schools to court, ready to vindicate poor Harry. The Cedarville case had good facts. Even the banned material was pleasant. It is not as though I would be defending some borderline pornographic book or some other edgy work—it was Harry Potter. I didn't have to worry about all the f-bombs and sex talk at issue in *Pico*.

But I had a problem—I had no client.

There's a concept in Anglo-American law called "standing." Colloquially, gotta have a dog in the fight.

An example: I hire a painter and, foolishly, I pay the painter $400 up front because she promises to show up tomorrow and do the job. Tomorrow comes around, no painter. When I call her, she's drunk and refuses to live up to her end of the bargain. I could sue the painter for the $400. She plainly owes it. But I decide, for whatever reason, not to sue her. Maybe I just don't want to mess with it, maybe I know suing her is fruitless because she couldn't pay the money even if the court told her to, or some other reason.

A week later, over coffee, I tell my friend about the painter. My friend is indignant. "How dare she!" says my friend. "She shouldn't be able to get away with that." And the friend then files a lawsuit against the painter to get her to pay me the $400.

No.

That's a non-starter. The friend's case will fail—the friend has no standing. It's not the friend's $400 that was lost. The friend never had a contract with the painter. Standing requires that only a person who is actually hurt can bring a lawsuit.

Applying this to the Cedarville case meant that I had to have a client. It wasn't enough that I, a lawyer living in an adjacent county, was indignant about censorship. My only realistic option was finding a student at the Cedarville schools to challenge the removal of the Harry Potter books.

I decided to overcome that obstacle later, and I went ahead and drafted a complaint. A "complaint" is the name of the legal document that initiates a lawsuit. In the caption, I put "xx" for plaintiff—where the client's name would ultimately be. "Plaintiff" is the legal term for the person who is bringing the lawsuit.

I determined that I would file the lawsuit, should I ever be able to find a client, in federal court. I considered Arkansas state court, but the case would have gone to an elected, local judge—a judge elected by the same people who had elected the school board members who had banned the book. So, federal court it would be. Its judges are more insulated from political pressure—they're not elected; they're appointed for life. While those lifetime appointments bring about their own set of problems, in a case like this, the federal court seemed to me to be the lesser of two evils.

After the caption, I started the meat of the complaint. Federal rules require that the complaint say why you are suing, who you are suing, and what you want. The complaint cannot be one long narrative; it must have separately numbered paragraphs.

My first few paragraphs recited information about jurisdiction, venue, and the residency of the parties. Federal rules require complaints do that, and typically that information is put at the beginning.

I then moved on to the "facts," and told the story of what happened, cribbing from the newspaper articles that I had found—articles headlined "School Board Makes Harry Potter Disappear" and "Rule Riles Librarian." The articles were quite detailed.

Starting from my initial draft of the complaint, and throughout the case, I only attacked the school board's decision to remove Harry Potter from the library. The board had also removed the books from the Accelerated Reader list, which is a list of books that children may read for extra credit. The Accelerated Reader list was really a question of curriculum—and my research had taught me that school boards have much more leeway in matters of curriculum than they do in removing items from libraries.

8. Like Magic, a Client Appears

So I never directly addressed the Accelerated Reader list issue; I focused only on the library issue, hoping that the Accelerated Reader issue would resolve favorably on the library's coattails.

The complaint also included rousing (at least, rousing to me) First Amendment arguments. I pointed out that the board was motivated by its members' personal religious views, and that by restricting access to the books, the board was stigmatizing the books and its readers.

The complaint also pointed out that the school board's restriction had the effect of preventing children from "discovering" the book as they browsed the library shelves. Children, unaware of the books' existence, would not be able to ask for permission to access the books, as they would not know that the books even existed. And if children were to learn of the books' existence, parents unfamiliar with the books would be reluctant to grant access to books that have been stigmatized and separated from the rest of the library's collection.

Finally, I argued that the First Amendment violation was two-fold. Not only was the board preventing the dissemination of the books—it was also infringing on the students' right "to receive information." People usually think of the First Amendment as the right to give information—a speech on the street corner, passing out handbills, publishing a newspaper, and so forth. But the First Amendment covers more than that; our courts have ruled that it also protects the right to receive information. Which makes sense. If the First Amendment protected only the speaker, then in the Cedarville case, the only person who would be allowed to sue would be author J.K. Rowling.

In the complaint I also put in the exact law I was suing under. "The restriction abrogates Plaintiffs' rights under the First Amendment as applied to the states under the Fourteenth Amendment to the U.S. Constitution.... Cause of Action, 42 U.S.C. § 1983."

I worded it that way because of an interesting legal nuance. We're all taught that the First Amendment protects our free speech rights. And it does—against the federal government. But the First Amendment—indeed the whole Bill of Rights—does not apply to the states, meaning that state and local governments can violate the Bill of Rights.

So why don't they? The answer is the Fourteenth Amendment. This is one of the "Reconstruction Amendments" passed shortly after the Civil War. "No State shall ... deprive any person of life, liberty, or property, without due process of law." Over the years, the courts have, a little bit at a time, interpreted "life, liberty, or property ... due process of law" to include the protections of the Bill of Rights. So the First Amendment's free speech protections now apply to state and local governments—via the Fourteenth Amendment.

I closed the complaint with what is known as the "prayer." "This Court should ... order the Harry Potter books to be returned to the libraries' shelves without any restriction other than those administrative restrictions that apply to all works of fiction located in the libraries and were applied to the Harry Potter books prior to the School Board's action.... WHEREFORE, Plaintiff prays for the relief requested above and for attorney's fees and costs."

I chose not to ask for monetary damages. Was my client, whomever that would ultimately be, really going to be monetarily hurt by the board's actions? I did not even want to go down that road. So I only asked for the books to be put back on the shelf.

And for attorney's fees. Of course.

* * *

I returned to my client problem. How to get one? Ethics rules limit lawyers soliciting business. That may come as a surprise, given all the TV and phone book advertising, but they do. A lawyer cannot phone a stranger and ask her to bring a lawsuit. The only way that a lawyer is allowed to "cold call" a client is by sending a letter. At that time, in Arkansas, the letter had to say "Advertisement" in big red letters on the envelope and had to open with the sentence "If you already have a lawyer, please disregard this." The rules also required the solicitation letter to give the name and address of the ethics committee in case the recipient wants to complain. There are other requirements, too, and missing any of them puts a lawyer into hot water with the ethics committee.

After reading Estella's comments in the newspaper articles, I seriously considered sending her a solicitation letter. But my law partners asked me not to do that. They thought it "unseemly." "If anybody wants to do something about the book ban, they'll find us," my partner Greg Karber told me.

It was true that Karber was known for doing civil rights and First Amendment cases. But we weren't the only game in town. Other firms

8. Like Magic, a Client Appears

could have been easily contacted about the matter, and I doubted that they would refer away a case as fun as a Harry Potter ban.

I wasn't content to wait. I needed to put the word out that I was available for Harry Potter business. And if my partners didn't want me to do it directly, then I'd do it indirectly—in a "seemly" way.

* * *

My then-mother-in-law Ana worked at my city's public library—the Fort Smith Public Library. I had learned from her that all the local librarians knew each other and had a well-developed gossip network. I tried to tap into it. "Ana," I said, "I've got to find a client. I need a parent with a child at Cedarville. How can we find one?"

"My boss' wife's sister works at Cedarville."

I paused and tried to process the relationship chain. After further questioning, I understood. Ana's boss, Larry, had a wife. The wife had a sister. That sister was none other than Estella Roberts, the librarian at Cedarville High School. And Estella would know sympathetic parents.

"Listen," I said to Ana, "you've got to get the message out. Here's my card. Please give this to your boss, Larry, and ask him to have somebody call me. Please."

"Sure, Brian. I'll give it to him today at work."

My business card made its way to Ana's boss, to his wife, who then called her sister Estella. After Estella got my contact information, she picked up the phone and called the elementary school librarian, Betty Franklin. "Betty, it's Estella. I need the names of your parent and student—the ones you put on the library committee." Betty gave Estella the phone number for Bill Counts and his fourth grade daughter, Dakota.

* * *

Bill Counts was a fireman for the neighboring city of Fort Smith. His 24 hours on, 48 hours off schedule has allowed him to be the primary caregiver to his two children. His wife Mary had a traditional eight-to-five job as the chief financial officer for a non-profit.

Bill Counts would have told you that he "never succumbed to any particular religion." He and his family attended no church, and that was unusual for Cedarville residents. Wife Mary shared his same (lack of) religious views. Growing up, Mary's parents had been hardcore evangelicals, and she rejected that.

The Countses were an over-scheduled, over-achieving family succeeding in the meritocracy. Their daughter, Dakota, was in fourth grade. Her elementary school teachers remember her fondly; at time of the Harry Potter hubbub, Dakota was one of just a half-dozen fourth graders in the Cedarville schools' gifted program. Years later, when Dakota was in high school, she would have an academic ranking of second place among 413 students. She would achieve that despite her other commitments—softball on a traveling team and the school's volleyball team.

The Countses were readers and regular bookstore customers—the kind of family that is loved by the marketing departments of the New York publishing houses. Their love of reading fits nicely with Bill and Mary's counsel to their children: do not rush to judgment; only form opinions after considered research. Dakota has taken this advice. In the years after the Harry Potter ban, when that fourth grade girl had reached high school, Dakota was well read on various religions, committed to none, and intrigued by Buddhism.

Bill and Mary Counts tell me that Bill's involvement in the lawsuit was Bill's decision, and that Mary really had no say-so. I don't believe that. Mary Counts is too serious a person to let her family get involved in a federal lawsuit without her blessing. But Mary gave it. Her idealism overcame whatever pragmatic concerns she may have had.

※ ※ ※

"I hear you want to get mixed up in this—this Harry Potter thing." The husky voice came from my law office speakerphone. The receptionist had announced a call from a Bill Counts—I had never heard of him before.

"I do want to get mixed up in this Harry Potter thing," I said. "I surely do."

"Estella Roberts gave me your name. My daughter goes to Cedarville, and I was on the book committee. We want to fight this."

I checked my calendar. Wide open. "When can you come in?"

"This afternoon."

I gave him directions.

A few hours later, Bill Counts and his daughter, Dakota, arrived at my law firm's single-story, gray brick building, located a few blocks from

8. Like Magic, a Client Appears

downtown. Within the building, a dozen lawyers' offices ring the outside—we lawyers kept the windows for ourselves. The staff's offices and our conference room were on the inside. Bill and Dakota were led from the light and airy reception area to my office with its deep green carpet and wood trim.

Bill Counts entered my office and extended his hand. Dakota, ten years old, both her body and hair wispy thin, extended her hand too. I rose from behind my desk, reached across its green marble top, shook both Countses' hands, and motioned for them to sit in the two client chairs.

"Tell me why you're here."

"I hate censorship," Bill said. Those were his first words to me when we met in my office. Talk about a motivated client.

"We all hate censorship," I said, smiling. "Hopefully we can do something about it. Dakota, I assume you're a student at Cedarville?"

Dakota, who had been watching her father and me attentively, nodded yes.

Good, I thought. Dakota had standing.

I spoke with Bill and Dakota some more and learned that both had been part of the elementary school's library committee. Their votes were among those overturned by the school board's decision.

"Here's the deal," I said. "I'd love to have you as clients, and I need you as clients in order to challenge the Harry Potter ban. And I'll do it free, or at least free to you. Under the civil rights laws, if we win, the school district will have to pay my fees. If we lose, then I won't charge you anything."

Bill agreed, and I signed them up on the spot. No win, no fee. I had a special form for that and handed it to Bill. He signed for himself and Dakota. Dakota, being a fourth grader, was a minor and could not sue on her own.

Normally, under the American Rule (as opposed to the English Rule), each side in a lawsuit has to pay their own attorney's fees—win or lose. But civil rights actions are different. If, in a civil rights case, a plaintiff successfully sues the government—and that includes local governments like school districts—then the government has to pay the winner's attorney's fees. That's what I was banking on—I anticipated a win and therefore a fee. Fighting for justice is all well and good, but I wasn't in a position to be doing major cases for free.

Harry Potter and the Cedarville Censors

That rule—that government defendants must pay the attorney's fees of successful civil rights plaintiffs—is the main reason First Amendment cases are brought at all. Otherwise they would not be economical. Unlike car wreck cases with their big money medical bills and attorneys taking a third of the verdict, there's no money in esoteric values. How does a lawyer take one-third of a court order against censorship? First Amendment cases are about the principle, not the principal.

As Bill and Dakota left my air-conditioned office for the heat of July, I opened the complaint on my computer, deleted the "xx" in the caption, typed "Bill Counts, individually and as parent and next friend of Dakota Counts," and saved the final version to the firm's network.

"You're going to love this case," I wrote to my secretary, Donna, as I emailed her the complaint's document number. "Let's get it filed today."

9. Intolerant of Tolerance

"Thank goodness I was never sent to school; it would have rubbed off some of the originality."—Beatrix Potter

At that time, Greg Karber was one of my law partners and the closest thing to a mentor I've had in the law.

Karber was a classic left wing, ACLU trial lawyer. In his twenty-five years of litigating, he, at one time or another, had sued, and gotten a judgment against, every county and school district in the northwest quarter of the state. You could tell Karber three sentences about a new case, client, or opposing counsel, and he'd have a pithy one-liner summing it all up, and with the added benefit of being dead-on correct.

Here's an example, just one of many: I had a case in which an unknown, out-of-town lawyer on the other side missed some deadlines to produce papers to me. Now, that's typical, but this lawyer, when challenged, would get apologetic, beg for an extension (which I granted), and then all would be okay. This happened about three times, and on the third time I went to Karber in frustration to ask for advice.

"How do I handle this? I'd file a motion to compel, but he comes through at the last minute. I don't understand; I've not seen this before."

"Ah," Karber said, nodding. "A lawyer with a drug problem. There's nothing you can do. You just have to wait for him to flame out. Make sure you document everything."

"How can you possibly conclude that on what limited information I just gave you?"

"I know," he said. "I've seen it all. That's what this is."

And, as usual, Karber was right. Four months later, the lawyer was removed from the case and, I later learned, from all his cases due to a substance abuse issue.

Karber's instinct for discerning people's true motivations was uncanny.

When Karber first started practicing law, few Arkansas lawyers brought civil rights cases. The federal civil rights law was (and is) complex, strange, and nuanced. And the clients are often problematic—they are often prisoners or others in trouble with the authorities and, it follows, have little money.

Immediately after law school, Karber clerked for a federal judge. "I hardly ever saw the judge, though," Karber explained. "He sent me to work for the magistrate."

A federal magistrate is a "helper judge." Unlike the federal judge, the magistrate does not have a lifetime appointment, nor is a Senate vote required for a magistrate to be appointed. Federal judges send the more pedestrian work—administering plea bargains, resolving scheduling disputes among lawyers—to the magistrate for resolution. Often the federal judge will ask the magistrate to review a case or a motion and make a recommendation, which the federal judge may or may not accept. If the federal judge is Batman, then the magistrate is Robin.

As the helper to the helper to the judge, Karber was assigned the unending stream of judicial paperwork flowing from the prisons. It should come as no surprise that prisoners, who have a great deal of time on their hands, use that time to become learned in the law, particularly in the area of the law that is keeping them in prison. The prison population is forever filing petitions, writs, and complaints about the unfairness of their trials, the sneakiness of the prosecutors, the meanness of the guards and warden, incompetence of their defense counsel, and whatever other gripes they can imagine.

The judicial system must review them all.

As a clerk, Karber was on the court's front line in dealing with the prisoner litigation, summarizing the prisoners' filings for the magistrate. Many of the petitions were brought under the part of the civil rights act dealing with the Bill of Rights—things like free speech, taking of property, due process, and search warrants. This is the same law that is used by non-prisoners challenging improper police conduct and free speech violations.

After his clerkship, Karber returned to Fort Smith, armed with unusually detailed knowledge of civil rights litigation. With his love of the under-

9. Intolerant of Tolerance

dog as well as the propensity of local, small-town officials to engage in constitutionally questionable behavior, his civil rights practice grew.

"When I first started, the civil rights area was great. I could represent the little guy against the government and immediately level the playing field. We could bring these officials to court, make them answer for what they did, and get paid for it." Karber was referring to section 1988 of the civil rights laws. Under that section, if the government lost, then the government had to pay Karber's attorney's fees. "I got some good fees too; it was good money. And," Karber told me, "nobody else did it. I was the only one that would take those cases, and other lawyers referred them all to me."

But nature abhors a vacuum, and as time went on, Karber's niche became less of a gravy train. He attributed it to several things. "Over the years, the defendants became more savvy. Nowadays, government officials know better than to say, 'I'm firing this person because he's a Democrat' or 'I searched the house without a warrant because I didn't feel like going to get one.' Officials know better than to say things like that or, heaven forbid, actually put it in writing. That's made it tougher to bring these cases. Also, there's more competition. If there's a really good civil rights case, other lawyers will now keep it rather than refer it out. Another reason is the Reagan appointees. The appellate courts have taken the teeth out of these laws. Eight years of Reagan packing the appellate court with his judges has made it tough to bring these cases."

Karber is not being partisan on that last observation; it is a statement of fact. Over time, appellate decisions have chipped away at the civil rights laws. More and more government actions are considered "immune" from civil rights cases, and recovering attorney's fees has become more difficult.

The Harry Potter case, though, was as strong a civil rights case as I could imagine, and I wanted Karber's input right away. I walked into Karber's office and sat, uninvited, in one of his client chairs.

Like most of the firm's lawyers (and secretaries too), Karber had a television in his office. The firm paid for the cable—a perk we'd not had in my D.C. firm. One of the cable channels always ran Cardinals baseball games and Karber, a lifelong baseball and Cardinals fan, watched as many as he could.

The whole television-in-the-office thing scandalized me when I first moved from D.C. back to Arkansas. D.C. offices are terribly stuffy and professional. Nobody would dream of having a television in his office, much less having it on. But the work environment in Arkansas was kinder and gentler than on the East Coast. I was also, when I first moved back, scandalized by the fact that our firm had no voicemail, just an answering machine activated after hours. But I soon became accustomed to the low-tech phones, and I did not miss voicemail at all.

I feigned interest in the ball game for a minute or two and then got down to business.

"I've got a slam dunk," I said. "I cannot lose the Harry Potter case."

That caught Karber's attention. "A slam dunk? Can't lose?"

"That's right. No federal judge is going to let himself be known as the judge that banned Harry Potter."

Had we been in a kung-fu movie, this scene would have been set in a Tibetan temple at night, with Karber and me in orange robes and illuminated by candles. Karber would have begun his next sentence with "Ah, grasshopper, you have much to learn."

But we were in a law firm in Fort Smith, Arkansas, and no candles were to be found among the mishmash of knickknacks that populated Karber's office. "Brian," he said, peering at me over his glasses, which is something he had started doing once he turned fifty, "Brian, there is no such thing as a 'slam dunk' or a 'no-lose case.' No such thing. I promise you."

Karber paused to let that sink in. He continued. "You'll draw Hendren, right?"

"Fifty-fifty," I said. There were two federal judges in our local district—Hendren and Dawson. Each new case is assigned at random. There were even odds that I would draw Judge Jimm Larry Hendren for the Cedarville case. That is not a typo; there are two "m"s in Jimm, and thus he was called, by some, "Double-m Jimm."

* * *

A person meeting Double-m Jimm would like him. His face is ruddy and round, and he speaks to folks in a friendly, conversational way that is atypical of long-serving judges. He has such a nice personality that it's hard not to be angry at his adverse rulings until they are long past and you're out of his presence. It's been said that a person does not have to be

9. Intolerant of Tolerance

a politician to become a federal judge, but it certainly doesn't hurt. Judge Hendren shows the truth of that statement. He may not be a politician, but he could have been had he wanted to.

After serving in the Navy JAG Corps during Vietnam, Jimm Hendren returned to Arkansas and practiced law for a few years before becoming a state court judge. Shortly thereafter, in 1992, George H.W. Bush appointed him to the federal bench.

A person doesn't have to go back far into Judge Hendren's prior generations to find a time when the Hendren family lived in log cabins in the Ozark Mountains. Judge Hendren restored those cabins, and he and his family occasionally gathered there and played music. The judge himself played the banjo, guitar, piano, and, I'm sure, many other instruments. His children shared his love of music. His brother, Kim, was a state legislator and owned car dealerships.

The conventional wisdom among employment and civil rights lawyers at that time was, that in Judge Hendren's court, corporations and the government get the benefit of the doubt at the expense of the individual or the underdog. That conventional wisdom has led many lawyers to file their cases in state court and to plead them in a manner to keep them there. Studies done by the trial lawyers' association confirmed that this is a good strategy, not just for Arkansas' federal courts, but all federal courts. Statistically, the average plaintiff was more likely to lose in federal court than in state court, and my anecdotal evidence was that Judge Hendren's court was no exception.

* * *

Karber considered the Harry Potter situation and thought about Judge Hendren. He leaned back in his chair and folded his hands. "A sure thing, you say? Well, let me tell you. It damn sure isn't a sure thing if it's a civil rights case in front of Hendren."

And then Karber told me the story of Jeff Thomas (not his real name—see notes).

* * *

Jeff Thomas, with the assistance of the American Civil Liberties Union, made a federal case out of a $10 newspaper ad.

Jeff grew up and graduated in Mountainburg, Arkansas, a teeny tiny town in the Ozark Mountains. As the crow flies, it is close to Cedarville; as the car drives, it is farther. It's close culturally. Rural and religious.

Every community seems to produce a few citizens that, for whatever reason, are different from the rest. For Mountainburg, Arkansas, Jeff Thomas was such a citizen. New Age ideas—druids, pagans, witchcraft, palmistry, psychics, and so forth—fascinated Jeff from elementary school on. After graduating high school, he worked in various restaurants until, at the age of twenty-two, Jeff opened The Talisman, a small boutique in Fort Smith, Arkansas, specializing in New Age books and accessories. The Talisman also hosted lectures and workshops—Herbal Healing, How to Meet Your Guardian Angels, Astrology, Wicca, Palmistry, Healing Energies of Stones, and Past Life Regressions.

Jeff, like all good Wiccans, believed in tolerance and acceptance of all. He lived by the Wiccan creed, "And Ye Harm None, Do What Thou Wilt." Running The Talisman may not have made him rich, but it made him happy.

Given its out-of-the-way location, not to mention the offbeat and unusual items for sale, The Talisman needed to advertise. Jeff ran radio and newspaper ads. One day, he decided it would be a good idea to run ads in the Fort Smith high school newspapers.

Fort Smith has two high schools, Northside and Southside. Jeff called Northside and asked if The Talisman could advertise in the *Northside Grizzly*, a school-sponsored, twice-per-month student newspaper with a circulation of 1,400.

The school said yes. It dispatched journalism student and high school senior Rebecca Bock to follow up.

People mistakenly think that Rebecca Bock is Italian; she is not. Her straight, raven hair, strong, black eyebrows, and brown eyes are the product of an indeterminate mix of Eastern European stock. She has a small frame and jealously claims every bit of height she can.

"How tall are you?" I asked, when interviewing her about The Talisman case, many years after the fact.

"Five three and three quarters." She paused and then added the extra quarter-inch. "Go ahead and put five-four," she said, pointing at my notes. Her nose is pointy and face freckly. She is pretty in a youthful way.

Northside High School expected its journalism students to sell ads. The ads did not make any significant contribution to the paper's finances,

9. Intolerant of Tolerance

but ads, being a part of the real-world newspaper business, were part of the course. Rebecca had, on her own, sold two other ads—one to her grandmother's video game company, another to a next-door neighbor with a photography business. The ads cost $10 per issue.

After receiving the message that The Talisman wanted to buy an ad, Rebecca made the five minute drive to the store.

Rebecca had to be looking for The Talisman to find it. On Grand Avenue—a not-so-grand street of dilapidated houses, paycheck advance stores, and gas stations—was a four-bay strip mall hidden behind an E-Z Mart convenience store. The Talisman occupied the fourth bay on the end. A wise choice, financially. The location could not have commanded premium rent.

An odiferous mix of incense and patchouli addressed Rebecca as she entered The Talisman. The small and uncluttered shop had few bookshelves, but those few—glass and bamboo—invited the curious to explore the topics of Wicca, Homosexuality, Spirit, and New Age. A papasan chair in the corner beckoned her, and the glass and rectangular cash register counter offered tarot cards, magic crystals, and beads.

"Hi, can I help you?" Jeff greeted Rebecca.

Rebecca told him that she was from Northside. She had come about the ad.

Jeff and Rebecca spoke at some length; he showed her the store and identified the items for sale. The conversation strayed into those ethereal topics that define The Talisman. Rebecca liked Jeff and found him to be soft spoken, almost effeminate.

The next day, in her journalism class, Rebecca created The Talisman ad. She presented it to her journalism teacher.

> TALISMAN
> Books, Tarot, New Age, Crystals, Body Oils
> 4119 Grand Avenue (Behind E-Z Mart) 782-7522

"Hmmm." Her teacher studied the ad. "I don't know about this 'body oils.' Change that." The teacher thought that "body oils" sounded too much like sex.

The journalism teacher didn't have any written guidelines when she gave that order. As she later testified, she relied on her "gut feeling," and "body oils" didn't pass muster with her gut feeling. It wasn't the first time that the teacher censored ads. In the past, she barred ads from a pregnancy crisis center. The crisis center considered abortion a possible solution to unwanted pregnancies, and the teacher felt that such options should not be presented to high school students. Permissible options were more along the lines of attending local Baptist churches—the teacher allowed advertising from them. Several flavors of Baptist churches—First, Eastside, Grand Avenue—ran ads in *The Grizzly*.

After receiving the "body oil" edit, Rebecca changed the ad, replacing "body" with "new":

> TALISMAN
> Books, Tarot, New Age, Crystals, New Oils
> 4119 Grand Avenue (Behind E-Z Mart) 782-7522

There was no picture with the ad—just text. Her teacher approved the change.

Rebecca took the ad proof to The Talisman and showed it to Jeff. He liked it and signed up for four issues.

The Talisman ad only ran twice before it caught the eye of one Kevin Plame (not his real name; I've changed the name to avoid embarrassment), whose daughter attended Northside. Kevin and his family worshiped at Fort Smith's First Baptist Church, a sprawling downtown mega-church. The Plame family blessed First Baptist Church with their presence at least twice per week, being regular Wednesday and Sunday attendees.

The Plames' piety carried through all aspects of their lives. They were known to the neighborhood children as the strictest parents on the block. Mrs. Plame would take it upon herself to tattle on the other neighborhood children. One time, she called a parent about a neighborhood snowball fight that had, in her view, gotten a little too rough.

Mr. Plame called Northside's principal and complained about The Talisman ad. Mr. Plame objected to tarot cards. He also objected to homosexuality. Mr. Plame had been to The Talisman and had seen its books on homosexuality. He did not think that high school students should be exposed to such things. It apparently never dawned on Mr. Plame that many of those same "homosexual" books were also available in mainstream bookstores in Central Mall, like Waldenbooks.

Besides Mr. Plame, other parents complained too. At least according to the school they did. Northside's principal said that he received fifteen to twenty complaints from parents. But Rebecca Bock doubts that the school received "fifteen to twenty complaints." "I find that very hard to

9. Intolerant of Tolerance

believe," she told me. And indeed, in the federal court case that followed, when asked for the names of those complaining, the principal could only identify two or three.

Nevertheless, unbridled by any sense of specificity or notions of protecting the minority from an alleged majority, Northside High School pulled The Talisman ads. The journalism teacher obeyed her orders without complaint and sent a letter to The Talisman:

> To Whom it may Concern: Due to the overwhelming complaints about your ad that has appeared in the past issues of the GRIZZLY, we will no longer be able to carry your ads in the future. Our balance shows that Talisman still has not paid $10.00. Please mail your check to the address below.
> Journalism Department, Northside High School

The school, for good measure, also yanked the ad for Mystic Domain, a store that sold Dungeons & Dragons games.

Kevin Plame's daughter smiled at the news. She bragged to her friends. That Talisman store, she said, was evil. Satanic. Her daddy, a representative of First Baptist Church, had gone to the principal's office, demanded the ad be pulled, and succeeded.

Rebecca went to The Talisman and told this to Jeff. "Sorry." She shrugged. There was nothing she could do.

"This is really unfair," Jeff said.

Rebecca shrugged sympathetically. "I'm really sorry."

Jeff pushed through the hanging colored beads dividing the store from its back stock room, located a day planner, and looked through the addresses. Here, he thought, I'll call her. And he dialed his friend Gypsy's number. Gypsy, a Massachusetts Wiccan, was part of the Witches Anti-Defamation League, a group of Wiccans devoted to protecting themselves from negative publicity. As you can imagine, the Witches Anti-Defamation League had its work cut out for itself.

"Call the American Civil Liberties Union," Gypsy said.

While Jeff called the ACLU, a Mystic Domain supporter wrote the local newspaper. The paper assigned the story to a reporter, and he called Northside's principal.

"I had 15 to 20 calls complaining that young people were exposed to things in the stores that were inappropriate," the principal said to the newspaper reporter. "We've got a strong religious group in the community. When you advertise tarot cards, they were opposed to that."

Harry Potter and the Cedarville Censors

The school superintendent was more savvy. He knew better than to identify religious motivations as the reason for pulling the ads. "Basically, you've got two people who ran ads at the paper and both were in arrears in their accounts," said the superintendent to the reporter. "Regardless of what the issue was, the fact was they owed money, and that was the reason the ads were canceled."

The superintendent was, however, lying. Payment had nothing at all to do with pulling the ads. After the ACLU initiated suit and was able to inspect the school records, it showed that "The-Talisman-didn't-pay-its-bill" excuse was a sham. Multiple *Grizzly* advertisers waited to pay until all ads had run, not just the Mystic Domain and The Talisman. None of those other advertisers had been targeted. When the ACLU pointed this out, the school and its lawyers abandoned that position and shifted gears. They instead cited the "disruptive" effect The Talisman ads were having. They also claimed that the *Grizzly* was not some open forum like a library—it was part of the curriculum. And a school, they argued, has complete control of its curriculum.

※ ※ ※

"Is that when you got involved?" I asked Karber.

"It is, it is." He nodded. His phone had buzzed half a dozen times while he told me the story, and he'd asked the receptionist to take messages on all the calls. I could see Karber's email inbox on the monitor behind him, and the receptionist's messages stacked up in bold lettering. Karber's law practice had reached that level where all he did was talk on the phone to clients. I don't think I ever saw him with a law book in his hand. A person could not sit in Karber's office for more than five minutes without being interrupted by the receptionist announcing calls.

※ ※ ※

The Arkansas ACLU sent Jeff Thomas to Karber. The two met, Karber took the case on contingency (in other words, his fees would be paid under the civil rights laws if, and only if, he won), and filed suit. Karber never had much love for the Fort Smith School District, and his complaint showed it. After reciting the standard jurisdictional language, he wrote: "The refusal of the school to permit The Talisman to advertise in the *Grizzly*

9. Intolerant of Tolerance

was based upon the belief of the school that the advertisement was of a religious nature and, being so, was contrary to the religious preferences of residents of the City of Fort Smith."

Now, for the purposes of filing a complaint, that was enough. Karber didn't have to be very particular about the details. Only a rough outline was required. But Karber wasn't content with that and heaped additional, well-deserved abuse into the complaint. For example: "This pattern of establishment of religious preferences is exemplified by numerous other practices and policies of the Fort Smith School District. For example, the District's formal policy is that prayers shall be permitted at extracurricular events, even if contrary to established constitutional law. As a further example of the absurd reaches of these policies, the District prohibits the wearing of apparel at Southside High School that is considered too 'otherworldly' and 'humanist.' As a result, the motto 'Just Do It' of the world's largest athletic apparel manufacturer, the Nike Corporation, cannot be worn on school grounds."

After filing the complaint, Karber marshaled his evidence. In addition to speaking with Jeff about what happened, he interviewed Rebecca Bock and the newspaper reporter who had spoken with the superintendent and principal.

In the legal world, formal interviews, called depositions, are taken under oath and transcribed by a court reporter. Karber took the depositions of several school personnel, including one of the school board members.

When the board member read the article in the paper about the ad cancellation, he visited The Talisman to see what all the fuss was about. Tall, with militaristically short blond hair, light blond eyebrows, and clean-cut clothes, the board member must have looked odd entering The Talisman. He walked in, hands behind his back, and scanned the bookshelves, touching none. He, literally, judged the books by their covers. Three books, or at least their titles, particularly offended him—*Gay Spirit*; *The Complete Book of Spells, Ceremonies, and Magic*; and *Lesbian Sex*. He also noticed, with disapproval, that The Talisman sold crystals typically used by Wiccans. Without saying a word, the board member left The Talisman and wrote down the book titles so he would remember.

The Talisman visit convinced the board member that the school had done the right thing in pulling the ads. Schools, he later explained at a speech to students, faced many problems. "As a school board member, I have to deal with a wide range of issues, issues including weapons on campuses, witches in student newspapers, and complaints regarding how much the schools charge for ice in the cafeteria." The board member did not explain where, exactly, "witches in student newspapers" fell in the gamut between weapons and cafeteria pricing. Nevertheless, he identified witches as a problem.

Karber tried the case in Fort Smith's federal courthouse. Like many federal courthouses, it used to be a post office. Federal security screening set its perimeter near the old post office boxes where, nowadays, cell phones and other everyday contraband can be stored. Two elevators around the corner ploddingly took visitors to the second floor courtroom.

The trial lasted more than a day. On the first day, a Wednesday, Karber called his witnesses and showed Judge Hendren his evidence. He proved that the "complaints," such as they were, came from religiously-motivated people. He showed that the decision to pull the ads was religiously motivated. He introduced copies of the *Grizzly* in which the Baptist churches were allowed to advertise, but The Talisman was not. Rebecca Bock, who was a freshman in college by the time the case went to trial, flew down to testify. Karber paid for her plane ticket.

The school had an "expert witness" lined up for the next morning. He opined that running The Talisman ad "disrupted" the school. But Judge Hendren questioned him on the specifics.

"The school had a disruption," the witness said.

Judge Hendren turned and looked at the witness. The witness sat to the Judge's left, and about three feet lower. Judge Hendren sat the highest beneath the courtroom's twenty-foot ceiling. His black robes (judicial, not magical) were mostly hidden by the elevated judge's bench. Elderly furniture and somber carpet darkened the courtroom.

"Who is the 'school'?" Judge Hendren asked.

"The school is made up of 1,300 students—"

"No, no, no," interrupted the judge. "You know what I'm talking about. Who is 'the school' that was disrupted that you're talking about? Who is 'the school' that was upset?"

"The heart of the school, of course, is the student body."

"The what?" Judge Hendren peered down at the witness.

"The heart of the school is the student body. It is the school."

9. Intolerant of Tolerance

"So you understand the student body was upset?"

The witness squirmed. "I'm having a real struggle with answering—"

Judge Hendren cut him off again. "You think you're having troubles. I'm really having troubles. I don't think those are tough questions. When you sit on the witness stand as an expert and tell me under oath that you were made to understand that 'the school' was upset, it looks to me you ought to be telling me what you mean by that. What school is upset? Who?"

Karber, spectating from his counsel table in the well of the courtroom, relaxed and shifted in his unpadded, federal wooden chair. Judge Hendren was doing his work for him.

"The school is the student body, obviously, with a faculty, with a staff." The expert was still struggling.

"Is that what you mean?" asked Judge Hendren.

"Yes."

"The school, the student body and the faculty was upset?"

"Yes."

"All right." Judge Hendren looked forward, paused for a moment, and then turned back towards the witness. "Did you make any further inquiry to see what was the basis for that notion that the student body was upset?"

"No."

"So you didn't talk to any students?"

The witness said that he had not.

"And nobody's indicated to you that any student was upset at all?"

"No student has been named."

Further questioning by Judge Hendren revealed that the witness had no basis for claiming "disruption" except that the school officials—primarily the principal and journalism teacher—had told him so.

"You're released," said Judge Hendren, dismissing the witness. He looked at the lawyers. "All right, gentlemen, do you desire to make closing arguments?"

At first, Karber thought that he didn't need to. He thought his case was air tight. The school's only defense was that hokey "disruption" defense, and the judge himself had taken care of that.

But, just to be safe, Karber reiterated his case. "Your Honor, just want to make two points that may not have been readily apparent through the pleadings and trial today." Karber had moved to the podium, but stood beside it in a casual manner. "Number one is the original pretext for the termination of the ads was that The Talisman was in arrears. The school completely abandoned that."

He then moved on to his second point. "The real reason for terminating the ads was the religious complaints made by the religious community as a result of what they perceived to be a sacrilegious store."

Karber paused for effect. He put one hand in his pocket, gestured with the other, and continued. "The school's speech policy is this: If the school gets so many complaints about a particular speech, then it's going to terminate that speech. That's their policy, your honor, and it's patently unconstitutional."

Karber sat down. The judge looked at the school's lawyer, Mitch Llewellyn. This wasn't Mitch Llewellyn's first rodeo. A substantial portion of his practice was representing schools, just as a substantial portion of Karber's practice was suing them. They regularly faced off in court.

Llewellyn stood and went to the podium. Like Karber, he used no notes. "I don't think I can be as brief as Mr. Karber, but I'll be quick."

Llewellyn had a gentle voice and Soft southern accent. His tufty white hair, obvious ears, and wide, buggy eyes made him appear harmless. He was not. He smiled pleasantly as he inserted his legal daggers into opponents. "Your honor, the plaintiff, not the school, has injected religion into the case. It was not an issue at the time the ads were terminated. There was no reference to religion by any of the complainers, by the principal or the journalism teacher at the time they made their decision."

It was all Karber could do not to leap to his feet in protest. The principal did talk about religion! He said it to the newspaper reporter, and that reporter quoted the principal in the newspaper article. Karber figured that Judge Hendren would remember that and realize Llewellyn was playing fast and loose with the facts.

Llewellyn continued. "Only when the plaintiff himself went out and brought the witches leagues, the anti-defamation leagues, in the correspondence with the district did the issue of religion ever enter into it. That was not a part of the decision and it was not a part of any infringement of the plaintiff's right to establish or practice a religion."

Llewellyn then made his "disruption" argument, but with a twist. Fifteen complaints, he said, triggered the whole issue. "It's the number of complaints combined with either the disruption or the potential for dis-

9. Intolerant of Tolerance

ruption in the curriculum in the delivery of education in the building that forms the foundation for these complaints."

And there it was. "Curriculum." The school paper wasn't an open forum where all ideas could be heard. It was more like a textbook, subject to the control of the school. "Fort Smith Schools," argued Llewellyn, "have always dealt with the *Grizzly* as a non-public forum. This whole issue is a rather simple one—its effect on the curriculum, the disruption in the school—and for that reason, we think the court should rule in favor of the school."

Judge Hendren bought it, hook, line, and sinker, although Karber did not know it at the time. Judge Hendren did not make his ruling then. "I will take the case under advisement," he said after Llewellyn had finished his closing argument, "and I'll do my best to issue a written opinion within approximately ten days."

A week or two later, Karber received the judge's written opinion in the mail. It came in a large 9" × 12" white envelope with the federal court's black lettering on the return address. His secretary had opened the envelope for him, but had not read the opinion herself.

He stood at her desk, near the inbox, and began reading. Some judges' opinions helpfully tell the ruling on the first page, and then give the reasoning on the subsequent pages. Lawyers reading those opinions know, right away, if they've won or lost. Judge Hendren's opinions were not like that—he typically waited until the last page to disclose his ruling. This opinion was no different. It began with a recitation of the testimony and what happened in the case. Karber flipped through the pages quickly.

But then he paused. He noticed a sentence that concerned him. "The principal testified, without contradiction, that the placement of advertisements in 'The Grizzly' is an optional part of the curriculum." The judge had underlined "optional." The judge had forgotten the fact that, at the time, Northside journalism students were required to find advertisers. Later parts of the opinion also bode ill. When discussing the testimony, Judge Hendren gave full credit to the school's witnesses, and disregarded the others. For example, the newspaper reporter had testified that the principal said the ads were pulled for religious reasons; the principal had denied that. Judge Hendren sided with the principal.

Thirty-three pages into the opinion, Judge Hendren delivered the final blow. Even if the school were motivated by religious beliefs, wrote

Judge Hendren, the school has "absolute discretion in matters of curriculum.... The solicitation and publication of the advertisements in 'The Grizzly' clearly constituted part of the curriculum, since it was taught as part of the journalism [class]."

Karber threw the papers back into his inbox and walked out.

※ ※ ※

"I hope you appealed that," I said. "That's messed up. Can schools, under the guise of 'curriculum,' promote the Baptist churches to the exclusion of other religions? Schools can use the 'curriculum' excuse to promote one religion over another?"

"Yes, that's exactly the law. At least it is in Judge Hendren's court and in the Eighth Circuit."

"You lost the appeal?"

Karber nodded yes.

"How?"

"I don't know. I know I wasn't treated well. During the oral argument, one of the three judges looked at me and said, 'So, Mr. Karber, what's the A-C-L-U have to say about this,' and the judge tick-tocked his head back and forth as he said each letter. I knew then that the Eighth Circuit was going to rule against me. It was really uncalled for."

"What reason did they give?"

"They didn't give a reason. The Eighth Circuit didn't even issue an opinion. It just wrote, 'affirmed.'"

Several seconds of silence slipped by. I watched Karber's computer screen stack up more phone messages.

"So there's your lesson," Karber said. "There's no such thing as a slam dunk in front of Hendren. Or the Eighth Circuit, for that matter. If I can lose The Talisman case, you can lose the Harry Potter case."

10. Adversaries and Allies

"To accept good advice is but to increase one's own ability."
—Johann Wolfgang von Goethe

When I was in law school, I never really understood "filing." What did it mean to "file" something at the courthouse? As I sat in my civil procedure class, there was lots of talk of starting a lawsuit with a "complaint," and then "answers," "motions," and the "filing" of each. It wasn't until later that I actually figured out the mechanics.

The mechanics were pretty straightforward. Everything in a lawsuit is either done on paper or said in court. If somebody wants the court to do something—for example, make a ruling on who's right, or order one party to pay money or to disclose certain information—then that person must "move" the court. You don't "motion" the court; you "move" the court by filing a written memo.

At that time, before filings became electronic, the physical act of filing happened at the courthouse. Once Donna put the finishing touches on the complaint, she had me sign it, made several copies, and gave them to one of our couriers. The courier walked to the federal courthouse, only three blocks away from my office, and handed the original and copies to the woman at the desk, the clerk. The clerk stamped them (called a "file-mark"), assigned a case number, kept one for the official court file, and returned the rest.

When the courier came back, I looked at the case number. 02-2155-JLH. The last three letters grabbed my attention. JLH. The case had been assigned to Judge Jimm Larry Hendren.

* * *

It was now my job to "serve" the complaint, meaning that I had to get a copy of the complaint to the person being sued. You cannot successfully

Harry Potter and the Cedarville Censors

sue people unless they know they're being sued. That sounds like a rather obvious proposition, but you'd be surprised how often that comes up.

I didn't need the drama of somebody personally finding the superintendent of the Cedarville schools, handing him papers, and saying, "Sir, you are being sued." That really serves no other purpose than to make people mad. It's also more expensive. I took a more practical route. I sent, by certified mail, return receipt requested, a copy of the complaint to the Cedarville School District's superintendent. That's also proper "service" under the court rules.

At this point, I did not know which lawyer Cedarville would hire. I assumed it would be attorney Mitch Llewellyn. Mitch represented every school district in a 75-mile radius. Since Karber regularly sued every school district in a 75-mile radius, he was quite familiar with attorney Llewellyn and had established a cordial, professional relationship with him. Lawyers opposing each other often establish that type of relationship and should. As aptly stated by a lawyer friend of mine, "We can disagree without being disagreeable." So I sent a courtesy copy of the complaint to Mitch on the assumption that he would be handling Cedarville's defense.

Late in the day, I faxed a copy of the complaint, along with a soundbite, to the main newspaper in our area, the *Southwest Times Record*. That is, of course, not at all required by the court rules. But it is good PR. Typically, in the newsworthy cases I had in my pocket of Arkansas, here is how that strategy played out: the reporter would receive the complaint, see the file-stamp, and know it was a real lawsuit. The reporter's attempts to get comments from the defendants would fail because either the defendants would have already left work (which is why I sent it late in the day) or, at a minimum, not yet seen the complaint. As a result, my version—and only my version—was the one reported first.

The *Times Record* loved the story and ran it the next morning on the very appropriate day of July 4, 2002. It was the first of many news articles about the case. Subsequent stories about the case would use clip art showing books, quills, and Harry Potter. Who knew that there was Harry Potter clip art?

The initial July 4 story—above the fold, on the front page of the local paper—was headlined "Parents Sue Over Books. Children have right to read Harry Potter, Lawsuit says." The article included my hamfisted soundbite: "As we celebrate Independence Day, we should also remember that

10. Adversaries and Allies

the price of liberty is eternal vigilance. Heavy-handed bureaucrats in the Cedarville School Board are trying to use government as a tool for censorship and to impose their own peculiar religious views. Luckily, our Constitution protects citizens from this abuse of power." When I had sent a copy of the complaint to the newspaper the day before, I had figured that the school superintendent would be out on the afternoon of July 3 and unable to respond. I wanted to have the last and only word before the story ran—and I got it. The newspaper noted that Superintendent Smith "was out of the office late Wednesday and could not be reached for comment."

The newspaper reporter did manage to get a quote from Staff Attorney Kristen Gould of the Arkansas School Boards Association, a lobbying and support group for school districts. "My recommendation would be not remove it from the school library, which would raise constitutional issues," she said, "but to restrict access to that material based on whatever criteria they deem appropriate." Her quote irritated me when I read it; I expected a more cogent analysis from a lawyer, especially one whose job it was to advise school boards. Ms. Gould believed that school boards—and I can only assume that when asked for her legal advice, she so advised them—had every right to restrict library books "on whatever criteria they deem appropriate." That appropriate criteria included, apparently, fear of sorcery and witchcraft.

* * *

Sorcery and witchcraft concerned far more people than just Cedarville's school board members. The media attention accompanying the case drew letters from pro– and anti–Potter forces. Throughout the case, both the Crawford County local paper, the *Press Argus-Courier*, and the multi-county regional paper, the *Southwest Times Record*, ran letters from readers.

Every anti–Potter/pro-censorship letter cited particular notions of the Bible and Christianity as their underlying authority. From this premise, all other arguments followed. Witchcraft is evil; children should not be taught spells and sorcery; if we can ban *Playboy* from schools, why not satanic books like Rowling's books; what's wrong with letting parents control what their children read. All these arguments were best summarized by a woman's letter to the *Press Argus*: "I would rather see a child spend a lifetime in ignorance than an eternity separated from God."

Harry Potter and the Cedarville Censors

Indeed.

That was certainly the paradigm of the anti–Potter/pro-censorship crowd. "Make no mistake about it," read one letter, "there is war raging against Christianity."

And the suggested way to fight that war, they believed, was to limit access to allegedly anti–Christian information.

* * *

At that time, my town of Fort Smith had the region's central mail processing facility, a fact that I found to be quite convenient. Prior to the rise of the Internet, lawyers lived and died by the mail. Virtually everything we did was on paper, and almost all that paper was mailed. My firm sent out and received boxes of letters and packages each day. Our official mailing address was not a "P.O. Box"—it was a "P.O. Drawer" because it was so big. It had to be—we got so much mail.

Having the local processing facility, combined with having a P.O. drawer at the post office, resulted in us getting our mail first thing in the morning. At that time, we got our mail by 9. (In later years, the post office relocated the central processing facility to a town seventy miles north. This slowed down our mail service, much to my annoyance.)

I was a late riser and did not get to my firm until 9:30. Each day began with me getting the day's mail. It sat in my secretary's office in a cheap, black, plastic inbox atop an equally inelegant gray metal filing cabinet. About two weeks after filing the complaint and mailing a copy to Superintendent Smith, I saw a green postcard in that inbox. "Domestic Return Receipt," it said in pre-printed black letters. Separately stamped big red letters read, "Restricted Delivery." There, in the "Received by" block, was the name "Dave Smith," and his signature appeared in the block above.

The Cedarville School District had been served. It now had twenty days to respond.

* * *

After being served, Superintendent Smith showed the lawsuit papers to Pastor Hodges. The superintendent's first inclination was to forward the papers to Mitch Llewellyn, the school district's regular attorney. "No," Pastor Hodges said, "not him. I know who to call."

10. Adversaries and Allies

✳ ✳ ✳

The Cedarville School District hired attorney David Hogue to defend the Harry Potter case.

David Hogue, a good Louisiana boy, grew up with God. He and his parents attended Monroe's First Baptist Church; David went to the town's private high school.

Unlike Angie Haney, who will tell you that she is not proud of her youthful behavior, young David Hogue both "talked the talk and walked the walk." The high school-aged Hogue took as axiomatic that smoking, drinking, swearing, and sexual activity were immoral, and he avoided these activities. After high school, his parents sent him to nearby Louisiana College, a small Baptist school populated by other students whose parents wanted to keep them sheltered. Louisiana College offered a semester abroad program, though it had few takers. But David Hogue accepted the opportunity and traveled to England.

The young Christian returned with broadened views. Granted, his faith and morals remained resolute, but his tendency to be judgmental had subsided. There is a certain "condemning" and "judging" aspect to evangelical Christianity; England taught David Hogue differently.

After college, David matriculated at Mississippi College's law school, graduated, and began practicing in Gulfport, Mississippi.

He hated it.

A hundred files faced him, all of them from some person's terrible, stressful problem: an injured father who could no longer work and support his family; a mother who wanted to get custody of her children back; a small business owner facing a ruinous lawsuit. He fretted. What if he handled the cases wrongly? What if the father's family went hungry, the mother could not see her children, or the business went bankrupt? What would happen then? Sometimes the stress brought him to tears.

The stress reached critical mass while David was mountain biking one weekend. With tears in his eyes, David prayed, and sent his message to God. David waited. He listened. He waited more.

And a thought crossed David's mind. Jesus handled all the sins of the world—all of them. And Jesus was crucified too. If Jesus could handle that, then surely David Hogue could handle some stress at work.

"That's not very helpful," David thought.

Harry Potter and the Cedarville Censors

Another idea popped into his head. Establish a Christian Legal Service: represent the poor for free, take conservative Christian causes, and serve as a Christian mediator.

David didn't know how he would be able to do this, and he wasn't sure how this would change the stress of legal work. But David knew that God would provide.

At about this same time, in 1997, David's father, who lived in Arkansas, died from a heart attack. David moved to Arkansas, learned the ropes of Arkansas law from a Conway lawyer, and then put his plan into action. He opened Christian Legal Service.

David sent letters to the local women's and homeless shelters. The shelters' clientele are the very definition of "poor people needing legal help," and they readily responded to his offer. David took their cases for free; his caseload swelled.

David had been right, God did provide. The women and homeless whose cases he'd taken referred friends with personal injury claims, and David handled enough of those to keep the electric bill paid. As David's Christian practice progressed, he came to the attention of various right-wing religious groups like the Alliance Defense Fund; they flew him to various seminars and provided him training on handling constitutional issues for conservative Christians.

Five years after he'd moved to Conway, David Hogue was on the short list of specialized, evangelical Christian lawyers.

∗ ∗ ∗

David Hogue made the two-hour trip from Conway to Cedarville and met with Superintendent Smith and the school board. Angie Haney was there too.

As is often true in lawsuits, one aspect of the case is emphasized more than others, and decisions are made at the outset that will affect the trajectory of the litigation. For the Cedarville School Board, the religious objections to the books mattered most. The board felt that it should have the right to control the books in its library, especially un–Christian books like Harry Potter.

Angie heard this tactic and seethed. She thought it was a mistake to pursue the religious angle in court, because it probably wouldn't win. She believed that there were plenty of other, and very good, reasons for remov-

10. Adversaries and Allies

ing Harry Potter, such as its celebration of rule breaking and disrespect for authority figures. David Hogue, who, ironically, looked like Harry Potter—youthful, thin, glasses, and with a full head of straight black hair—was not, in Angie's eyes, what the board needed. They needed an older, more experienced lawyer like Mitch Llewellyn. Angie had seen enough of the courtroom to know that.

But it wasn't up to Angie. It was the board's decision, and the board liked David Hogue. David contacted the State Board of Education, received the necessary bureaucratic permissions, and signed on as the school district's attorney.

* * *

My first legal job was not in my hometown of Fort Smith; it was in Washington, D.C., at one of the big, corporate law firms. At a D.C. firm, lunch out was a rare and special event; few wanted to spend that time away from the office when they could be billing more lawyers.

Typical corporate firm lawyers ate at their desks, usually grabbing a sandwich at the firm's cafeteria. That, by the way, should give a sense of how large the D.C. firms are—they have their own cafeterias, complete with daily specials and dedicated food-preparation employees.

Fort Smith was a different story. Even though my firm had only a dozen lawyers, it was the second largest in the city. And in Fort Smith, frankly, lawyers just don't work as hard as those on the East Coast.

This resulted in a rather pleasant, albeit substantially less remunerative, nine-to-five lifestyle with an hour for lunch. On one of those hours, I told my lunchmates and law partners about the new Harry Potter case.

"You got your fee up front, I hope," said Tom Robertson. Tom was my father's age and, appropriately, kept tabs on my legal work during my first several months in practice in Arkansas.

"No. It's a contingency case."

"Brian, you need to get your money up front, at least for costs."

"The client is not paying costs. I didn't even ask. I can't charge somebody thousands of dollars for getting a book un-banned. Nobody is going to do that. It's full contingency."

Tom began asking pointed questions. "Why should the courts tell schools what books they can and can't have? If the courts can make a school keep a book, can the court make the school buy a book? Can the courts control the curriculum, too? If a school board can keep a *Hustler* magazine out of its library, why can't it make that decision with other books?"

I had glib and easy answers to these questions and was so convinced of the invincibility of my legal position that I became frustrated with Tom.

At this point, some background on Tom would be worthwhile. Tom almost always represented "the man." Tom's clients were typically banks, medium-sized corporations, and other businesses. If you were trying to "stick it to the man," then "the man" hired Tom Robertson. Thirty years of doing that made Tom unsympathetic to those challenging authority. He would deny this observation, but I'm right.

Tom was also not sympathetic to plaintiff's civil rights cases, by which I mean this: when my partners and I took a client on contingency and sued some business or government entity for violating employment or constitutional rights, Tom Robertson was always pessimistic about the case. And saying "pessimistic" is a kind description. "Hostile" would be better.

In fact, I can remember only one time that Tom sided with the plaintiff and against the government in a civil rights case. I was sitting in Karber's office.

Karber was in the middle of dispensing his usual pithy wisdom to me one morning when Tom Robertson came in.

"Let me ask you a civil rights question, since y'all are the ones that do this stuff all the time."

Karber and I looked up at Tom.

"Is this legal?" Tom asked. "The bank loans some ol' boy the money to buy a car. Takes a security interest in the car, gets the first lien on it, holds the title until the money is repaid. Bank files the lien, does all those things it's supposed to do to keep its security interest.

"The owner is down in Texas, some county in the middle of nowhere down there, and gets pulled over by the cops. They arrest him—they've got a warrant for him or something. Cops take the owner to jail, and there he sits.

"Now, all that's fine. I don't care about the owner, and he's probably a drug dealer or something anyway. That owner quits making his car payments, no doubt because he's stuck in jail, defaults on the car note, and the bank wants the car back. The bank gets a call from the sheriff of that Texas county. Says he has the car, bank has a lien, and if the bank wants it, come get it. But first, the sheriff says, the bank has to pay the storage

10. Adversaries and Allies

fees, which are like $2,000. The bank pays it and sends a rep down there to get the car.

"Listen to this part. The cops never told the bank, but they had searched the car. And they don't just search it, they ripped the damn thing apart, tearing off the door panels, knifing open the seats, pulling out the stuffing. Thing's totally ruined. Totally. The bank rep shows up there, having already paid that bogus storage fee, and the damn thing's not even worth the $2,000. It's totaled.

"That has got to be a civil rights violation, right? They can't do that, can they, just ruin the bank's security interest that way?"

After a half second pause, Karber and I burst out laughing. "Tom, why is it, of all the civil rights cases we've ever had and you've ever heard of, why is it that the only one that has ever gotten you personally angry is when a bank's civil rights were violated?"

※ ※ ※

Tom Robertson's civil rights cynicism was, nevertheless, a good thing. He acted as a good reality check against what is known as "litigator's myopia."

"Litigator's myopia" is a common affliction among trial lawyers and arises from the nature of our jobs. Our job is to be an advocate—an advocate for our client. Good advocates, like all good salesmen, actors, or other people in the persuasive arts, truly believe in their product and role. Thus, good trial lawyers truly believe in their client's position, and when that True Belief shines through, the trial lawyer is all the more persuasive.

The problem with True Belief is that it hampers lawyers' abilities to see the weaknesses in their cases. And that can be very dangerous. Not recognizing weaknesses can lead to disaster.

For example, once I defended a termite company. The termite company had been hired to inspect a house for termites; the mortgage company would only loan the buyers the money if the house were termite-free. The termite company came in, inspected, and declared the house termite-free. The buyers, relying on the termite-free declaration, got the loan and bought the house. After they moved in, though, they discovered that the house was totally infested with termites. But the infestations were not obvious. The termites lived behind the paneling and underneath the house.

Thus, the buyers of the house had really bought a house worth basically nothing, as it was all eaten up by termites. Yet the buyers were stuck with a house payment for the full amount. The buyers' only sin? They made the mistake of trusting the termite company. That mistake cost the buyers at least $60,000.

So they sued. The termite company had insurance, and the insurance company hired me to handle the defense.

To me, the termite company had a great defense. Before the termite company did its inspection, it had the buyers sign all these forms saying, "We are not responsible for hidden termite damage," and in this case, all the damage had been hidden. And there were other disclaimers too. At trial, I showed these forms to the jury. On cross-examination, I beat up the buyers by repeatedly asking them about the disclaimers they had signed.

The jury would have none of it. The jury found that my clients tricked the buyers and committed fraud. In fact, the jury was so mad at my clients that they wrote at the bottom of the verdict form, "We think the buyers should get their attorney's fees too."

Ouch.

Lesson learned: Look at your case from the other side, even if you think the other side is totally wrong. Do the mental gymnastics necessary to get you there. If you don't, it could be ugly.

And Tom Robertson, bless his heart, was one of the few who would actually argue with me about the banning of Harry Potter books.

* * *

July's days passed, burned away, and melted into August. The Cedarville response, due soon, had not yet come.

My morning routine had me still in bed at eight, grabbing a mocha at nine, and in the office shortly thereafter. Each morning my secretary, Donna, opened my mail, unfolded it, stamped its receipt date, and put it in my inbox. Donna also gave editorial comments on the mail, but always in pencil or on yellow stickies so that her incriminating comments could later be destroyed. "About time she paid," Donna wrote about a late-paying client for whom I worked wonders in a child custody case. "Uh-oh," was her comment on a motion by an opposing attorney who, from the looks of the motion, was going to win.

August 5 started like most days, my dusty, beat-up—yet paid for—blue Honda Accord motoring the twelve miles from home to work. The August

10. Adversaries and Allies

sun had long since beat away the morning dew, and I broke a sweat just walking from the parking lot into the office. I went directly to Donna's desk, stood by the metal file cabinet, and grabbed the stack of mail.

"What's the mail today?" I asked. "Anything going to make me mad?" The day's mail often set the tone for the rest of the day, bad news spoiling it, good news the opposite. I liked Donna to brace me for any bad news.

"Nothing bad." She brightened. "But something interesting. I saved the envelope. You'll see it."

"What?"

"You'll see. Go to your desk."

Walking down the hall, I sifted through the stack, skimming various court orders, nasty letters, and motions. Then I saw it. Cedarville's answer.

* * *

An "answer," like all documents generated by lawyers, is best analogized to the arguments of children.

In a child's argument, one child makes an accusation: "Your mother wears combat boots." The other child has various responses: "Does not" or "So what if she does?" or "Oh, yeah? Well you're ugly and your mother dresses you funny."

Lawyers use these same types of arguments with such frequency that they have names.

"Your mother wears combat boots." This is the "complaint." It is the initial shot in the battle to come. In the grown-up world it is, nine times out of ten, a demand for money and usually arises from things like contract disputes, dog bites, car wrecks, credit card collection, employment squabbles, and the like.

"Does not." This would be called an "answer." It is a "general denial." Here, mom's boot status is simply denied. Were the complaint something different, for example, a demand for money, then the answer would deny that any money is owed.

Another possible response is "So what if she does?" This is called a "motion to dismiss." This can be filed instead of an answer. Rather than denying the complaint, a motion to dismiss takes a different approach: "So what?" the argument goes. "Even if everything you say is true, you still don't win." Here's a good example of the use of a motion to dismiss. Suppose people owe me money, and it's clear that they owe me money. I still have a letter from them, written ten years ago, and in the letter they say, "Yes, we owe you money." But they never pay.

Finally, exasperated, I sue, and in the complaint I say, "For the last ten years, these people have owed me money, they have admitted it, and I've attached their letter as proof." In response, the people file a motion to dismiss. "So what?" they say. "Even if that complaint is true, it is still a loser. That happened ten years ago. The statute of limitations ran out five years ago. If he wanted his money, he had to sue us much earlier. He didn't. Therefore, judge, please throw this case out of court."

And that's a good motion to dismiss. It would win. The "So what?" defense is often a good defense.

Or, operating under the theory that the best defense is a good offense, there's a third possible response. "Oh, yeah? Well you're ugly and your mother dresses you funny." This is called a "counterclaim." If someone sues you, sue him back. That'll teach him.

* * *

The fact that Cedarville filed an answer, and not a "So what?" response (a motion to dismiss), surprised me. I fully expected to get a motion to dismiss claiming that schools had every right to control library material, that Miss Counts was not a proper plaintiff, or that my complaint was somehow deficient. Dismissal motions are the tactic typically taken by large corporations and governmental defendants, if for no other reason than it makes the plaintiff's lawyer have to work harder. Merely getting an answer was a pleasant surprise.

The answer had another surprise for me. It didn't come from Mitch Llewellyn, the school district's regular lawyer. It was from someone who I had never heard of: David Hogue of the Christian Legal Service.

Both the envelope and letterhead of Christian Legal Service displayed a "Jesus fish," which is my moniker for the Ichthys, an early Greek symbol for Jesus.

Some people put a Jesus fish on their cars. Others have the fish, but with feet attached and the word "Darwin" written in the middle. I had never seen a Jesus fish on legal letterhead before.

Like most answers, Cedarville's admitted a few allegations, denied most, and said that it reserved the right to raise additional defenses—standard stuff of answers.

10. Adversaries and Allies

The preliminaries were out of the way. Each side had now appeared by filing documents in court. Further legal maneuvers now required nothing more than sending the documents to the court with a regular mailing to the other side's lawyer.

I prepared a letter to the Countses forwarding Cedarville's answer, recorded the time spent doing so, and then turned to the rest of the mail.

* * *

The Harry Potter case was, of course, not my only case. In a small-town practice like mine, I typically had about fifty open cases at any one time. Contrast that to my days in the big corporate firm. There, I never had more than ten things on my plate. Those things paid very well and kept me occupied—there were just fewer of them. A small-town practice has a great number of small, lower-paying matters as compared to the big town practice of fewer, higher-paying matters.

I'm not minimizing the importance of the "lower-paying matters." On the contrary, they are critically important to the clients, and I do not forget that. I am simply observing the economic realities of a small-town practice. There's only so much a lawyer can make in fees from a client who's not financially well off; to make a living, I had to have many clients.

A few days after receiving Cedarville's answer, I had an all-morning child custody hearing in one of those lower-paying matters. The hearing had been in Greenwood, a town about half an hour away. I had finished with the hearing, was driving back, and used the time to return phone calls. One of them was from a Daniel Mach, and he had a 202 area code—Washington, D.C.

It turns out that Dan Mach was a lawyer at a big corporate firm called Jenner & Block. Dan had all the credentials necessary to be esteemed in the big-firm lawyer social circles of D.C.—politically left wing, well read, geeky in a good way, and an impassioned First Amendment aficionado. I liked him immediately.

"We'd like to give you some help," he said. "I read about your case in the news, and my client, the American Library Association, wants to do what it can to assist."

"I'll be happy to take whatever help you can give me."

"Take a look at *Sund v. Wichita Falls*. It's out of north Texas. We got a good result in that case, and the facts there apply to you."

Harry Potter and the Cedarville Censors

As he talked, I held the cell phone with one hand, scribbled notes on an old ATM receipt with the other, steered with my knees, and tried not to wreck the car.

"In *Sund*, the library didn't actually ban the book. It removed certain children's books from the juvenile section and put them in the adult section so that children would have difficulty finding them. The judge found that violated the First Amendment, because certain children's books were being singled out based on their content, and the library was 'burdening' access to the books."

Dan was right. That seemed to be my situation exactly. Cedarville hadn't made an outright ban on the Harry Potter books. Children could still access them—if they had parental permission. I could see how Cedarville's lawyer might argue that's not really censorship.

11. Legal Backstory: *Sund* (Hiding a Library Book Is the Same as Censoring It)

Wichita Falls is a city of a hundred thousand people in north Texas, close to the Oklahoma border and far enough away from Dallas and Oklahoma City to be considered its own metropolitan statistical area.

In 1997, the city's library purchased two children's books, *Heather Has Two Mommies* and *Daddy's Roommate*. These books were, according to the library administrator, "a wonderful way to explain to children that you may live a different lifestyle, but the important thing is people love you."

The books had received critical acclaim. Professional reviewing publications recommended the books for children of homosexual parents. *Publishers Weekly* described *Daddy's Roommate* as having "text [that] is suitably straightforward, and the format is easily accessible to the intended audience. The colorful characters ... lend the tale a stabilizing air of warmth and familiarity."

One day, a parishioner of the largest Wichita Falls church, the First Baptist Church, discovered *Heather Has Two Mommies*. According to the head librarian, Linda Hughes, the parishioner "was appalled" and wanted the book out of the library.

Linda presented the parishioner a five-page form for challenging books in the library—"A Request for Reevaluation of Material." Linda explained the length of the form by citing one of her professors: "The longer you make it, and the more detailed the questions, the less likely they are to fill it out."

Nevertheless, the parishioner completed the form. "She didn't want anything about homosexuals in the library," Linda explained.

Harry Potter and the Cedarville Censors

The library reevaluated the book and considered the challenger's request to ban all materials related to homosexuality. Relying on recommendations from the National Education Association and an association of child psychologists praising the book, the library rejected the challenger's request.

Unhappy with the decision, the parishioner alerted her minister, the Rev. Robert Jeffress, a charismatic, telegenic man, that the library's children's section had books about homosexuality—not just *Heather Has Two Mommies*, but also *Daddy's Roommate*.

The Reverend Jeffress read *Daddy's Roommate* and sermonized about it on his television show. "Here is a library book—purchased with your tax dollars—promoting sodomy, which is illegal in the state of Texas, is largely responsible for one of the deadliest epidemics in history (AIDS), and is an abomination to God.... It is time for God's people to say, 'Enough!'" The Reverend Jeffress then asked his church to petition the city council to remove the books.

Jeffress' statements set off a firestorm with the left. As he explained in his book *Outrageous Truth ... Seven Absolutes You Can Still Believe*: "Media outlets including the *New York Times*, Associated Press, NBC television, ABC radio, and Rush Limbaugh carried the story. PBS sent a crew to Wichita Falls and filmed a documentary on the furor that divided our city. I was fervently denounced by the American Civil Liberties Union (ACLU), People for the American Way (PFAW), the American Library Association (ALA), and Americans United for Separation of Church and State (which later threatened our church's tax-exempt status). The editor of the local newspaper wrote an editorial condemning me for promoting censorship and suggesting that I should be jailed for my act of civil disobedience."

In addition to sermonizing against the books, Jeffress had also kept the library's copies. He refused to return them, opting instead to send a check for the cost.

If Jeffress' goal was to keep the book out of the library, he failed. The media attention prompted people from around the country to send the Wichita Falls library replacement copies of the offending book. Linda Hughes received far more books than the library needed; she sent the extra copies to nearby libraries so they would have copies too.

But I don't really think censorship that was Jeffress' true goal. I think

11. Legal Backstory: Sund

his real goal—as it is often in situations like this—was to grandstand for himself and his cause. And that he certainly did, and successfully too. The name he made for himself in Wichita Falls would lead to him becoming the pastor of a mega-church in Dallas, Texas, and then a prominent evangelical affiliated with the Trump administration.

Jeffress had, in his congregation, both the city attorney and a council member named Altman. The city council, under pressure from Jeffress and his congregation, passed the "Altman Resolution." The resolution allowed the relocation of any children's book if any three hundred library members signed a petition. The library had more than ten thousand members.

In legal parlance, this is a classic "heckler's veto."

Unsurprisingly, the library soon received petitions to remove both the books.

Using freedom of information laws, the local paper obtained the petitions. When it published the names, Linda Hughes received a frantic call from one of the petitioners, a woman, who wanted her name off the petition. That petitioner's boss had a gay son, and the petitioner worried it would jeopardize her employment. Linda explained that the petitions were a public record and couldn't be changed.

At the next city council meeting, a lawyer, Thomas Allensworth, warned the council it was making a mistake. He said he'd seen this sort of thing before when he practiced elsewhere. "You will lose. It will cost you over $20,000."

Councilman Altman treated the warning dismissively; the council stood its ground.

It didn't take long for several library users to band together with a local ACLU lawyer, John Horany, and file suit.

Because Linda Hughes, in her official capacity as librarian, had been the public official to remove the books (as she was compelled to do by the ordinance), the suit had to name her as a defendant. Attorney Horany visited her prior to filing, though, and assured her that she was being sued in name only, and that he recognized she was, in actuality, a friendly witness.

And Linda was. At the trial, she told the judge about the importance of books like *Heather* and *Daddy's*, because children in similar situations could identify with the books and feel normal and included. She also gave testimony explaining why it's necessary for children to find books by browsing on their own and not asking for them.

Attorney Horany didn't just use Linda's testimony. He called the president of PFLAG—Parents, Family and Friends of Lesbians and Gays; an elementary school teacher who opined that the books were age appropriate; a member of a lesbian couple who had a seven-year-old son; and some expert witnesses.

He also called city council members, the Reverend Jeffress, and local lay religious figure Janie Hill. Ms. Hill was a leading protestor in Wichita Falls against books "supportive of the homosexual agenda." During the trial, Ms. Hill distributed religious tracts to those in attendance, including the judge. At the conclusion of her testimony, after the judge excused her, she turned to him and said, "I hope you will consider the little children."

The judge ruled in favor of the books, ordered them back into the children's section, and assessed attorney's fees against the city in an amount more than $20,000.

Thomas Allensworth, the lawyer who'd warned the council prior to the litigation, attended the meeting following the judgment. He stood up, said, "I wanted to tell Councilman Altman 'I told you so,'" turned around, and walked out.

* * *

The formal *Sund* opinion written by the judge walked through all the witnesses—the librarian, the local censors, and various experts. Those experts cited the American Library Association's Library Bill of Rights and some other materials regarding how to select library books for children.

I also noted how the *Sund* opinion treated the "restriction." In other words, what reasoning did the *Sund* opinion use to find that moving the books from one place to another was the same thing as "banning."

Sund found that the books were originally placed in the children's section—as they were children's books—but were moved to the adult section in order to limit children's access to the books. That fact—the limiting of the children's access—was critical to the *Sund* decision. I needed to establish that same fact in my case. I wrote in the margin, "Deposition on this."

I also took heart with *Sund*'s legal analysis. *Sund* explained why

11. Legal Backstory: **Sund**

merely moving the books was just as bad as an outright banning: although the books are not banned entirely by the library, the burdens on the First Amendment are still constitutionally objectionable. Censorship is not okay just because the censor could have imposed even more draconian censorship than what it did.

For me, *Sund* had only one down side—it was a low-level court case decided in a different jurisdiction. That meant that Judge Hendren did not have to follow *Sund* if he didn't want to. Had *Sund* been an Eighth Circuit or Supreme Court decision, Judge Hendren would be required to follow it. But it was neither; I could only cite *Sund* as "persuasive" authority, not "binding" authority.

Nevertheless, persuasive authority is better than none, and *Sund* had some good, persuasive language.

12. Building the Case

"There is no substitute for face-to-face reporting and research."—Thomas Friedman

This may sound obvious, but it is not, at least not to many lawyers. Evidence, not the law, wins cases. No amount of legal research can undo a bad fact. If there are three eyewitnesses who will testify that your client shot the victim in cold blood, then you're going to lose that case, regardless of how much legal research is done. On the other hand, if you discover that those three eyewitnesses are convicted perjurers with a vendetta against your client, then maybe you have something to work with. But it takes investigation to get to that point. And good investigation requires a lawyer to leave the office and see things firsthand.

Normally, under the legal ethics rules, I'd not be allowed to communicate with people on the other side unless their lawyer were also present.

Yet, I wanted to interview the librarians and learn what they had to say without having their bosses or the district's lawyer present. I wanted their thoughts without them being intimidated. Brief research into the ethics rules provided an answer. For organizations represented by counsel, the rule only applied to decision makers in the organization—for example, school board members, the superintendent, or principals. The librarians had no authority to speak for the school district, and I concluded they were fair game.

I left my air-conditioned office and headed to the Cedarville schools. I drove for half an hour uphill from the Arkansas River valley into the Ozark Mountains.

The Cedarville schools—elementary, middle, and high—are all on the same plot of land, all next to each other, right off of a country highway.

12. Building the Case

"The school is in Cedarville," Estella had told me when I'd called her on the phone.

"Where in Cedarville?" I asked. But I'd asked a dumb question. Cedarville is small; everything there is on the same road.

"Just off the highway," Estella said impatiently. "You'll see it. The elementary school—we'll meet Betty Franklin there—is around the back, so drive to that building."

I followed Estella's directions, such as they were, to the schools, and after some searching among the buildings, I found the elementary school and went in.

The elementary school's library is close to the front office and is an open, inviting space with rows of books, tables, and chairs. Estella had wanted to meet there, instead of the high school library where she normally worked.

"You're here," Estella said abruptly. "Let me tell you what happened." Estella got straight to business. Betty Franklin, the elementary school librarian, was there too, but Estella took the lead in talking. I didn't know this at the time, but Betty Franklin was related to one of the school board members, and that may also explain her deferring to Estella. Perhaps Betty, while personally opposed to the ban and wanting to discreetly assist, also wanted to maintain familial peace.

We sat at one of the tables. The chairs, built for children, were too low, and my knees uncomfortably high. Estella recounted for me her visit from Superintendent Smith and Pastor Hodges. I took notes on my yellow pad.

"You know," Betty Franklin said, "he called me that same day."

"Who?"

"The superintendent. Dave Smith."

"What did he say?" I asked.

"He asked me if we had the Harry Potter books at the elementary school. I told him that we did. Then he asked me what I thought about them."

"What did you tell him?"

"I said, 'Oh, they're delightful.' And they are delightful. The children love them. Then he told me that he wanted them off of the shelf."

Betty explained how she, Estella, and the third school librarian, Debbie Griffin, had met later that week to discuss the situation. By that time

Harry Potter and the Cedarville Censors

Estella had already called the Arkansas Library Association and gotten a copy of the Intellectual Freedom Committee's pamphlet. Thus, when Angie Haney's form arrived, the librarians were prepared.

Estella handed me the documents that she had distributed to the committee members that had reviewed the Harry Potter books. "This is what we gave the parents," she said.

I nodded appreciatively and then asked Betty, "Where are the Harry Potter books now? May I see them?" I stood and stretched my legs.

"They're here." She pointed to a cluttered shelf several feet above her desk. The Harry Potter books were buried in stacks of paper near a three-ring binder, some magazines, and a box of computer disks. A child would not even be able to see the books, much less reach or discover them. I took a picture.

"Before you removed them, where were they?"

Betty walked across the room to the shelves along the wall. The shelves started at the floor, but only went up by three feet, which made sense, considering the target audience was typically four feet tall.

I found the spot where the books used to be—between children's authors Jean Rogers and Ron Roy. For dramatic effect, I pushed them apart and made a space before snapping a photo.

Estella then took me to the high school. Her desk was in an office adjacent to, but separated from, the library. The Harry Potter books had been moved to Estella's office. My camera captured two more scenes—the sequestered books and the library shelf where they used to be.

I envisioned presenting these pictures in court. "Here is where they were.... This is where they are now."

※ ※ ※

Have you ever watched *Perry Mason*? I love *Perry Mason*. That show is before my time, but it's great. For starters, it is classic 1950s—the cars, the suits, the bulky telephones. Secondly, as we all know, Perry Mason is the greatest lawyer ever because he invariably gets his (always innocent) client an acquittal by shaming the real murderer into confessing on the stand.

The third thing that strikes me about Perry Mason is surprise evidence. There is always some sort of surprise evidence that Perry introduces. And the prosecutor, the hapless Hamilton Burger, can do nothing more

12. Building the Case

than make the objection "This is highly unusual, Your Honor," which is really not an objection at all, but is more of the show's writers' way of telling us that Perry is much more clever than Hamilton, a fact that the audience needs no reminding of.

Federal courts, though, are not set up to make great television. In civil cases—meaning noncriminal—surprise evidence is not allowed. The "discovery" rules, Rule 26 to be exact, have "mandatory disclosures." Each side must tell the other their witnesses and exhibits; in other words, you must show your evidentiary hand.

That's not to say that all your evidence has to be ready and known from the beginning of the lawsuit—not at all. But as each side learns of witnesses or gathers more documents, that information must be made known. You can't "Perry Mason" the other side. At least, you're not allowed to.

* * *

As I've mentioned, in federal court, if you're going to use a document in evidence, you have to disclose it in advance. It was my regular practice to disclose all documents; I didn't want to be in the situation of having a good document but not being able to use it because I never gave a copy to the other side. So I printed my photos, added Estella's papers, and organized them all into a single stack.

After organizing the photos and documents, I "bates-labeled" them, meaning that I numbered each as though they were pages in a book. Each sheet of paper had its own unique number in its lower right hand corner. I started at 00001 and ended at 00090. Lawyers are well advised to bates-label. If each document in the case has its own unique number, there's never any doubt if it has been produced. This avoids disputes like the following example:

> "I'd like to introduce Exhibit One."
> "Your honor, I object. I've never seen this document before. It's unfair for opposing counsel to spring this surprise evidence on me."
> "Judge, I don't know what he's talking about. This document was in a big stack of paper I gave him last month."
> "Was not!"
> "Was too!"

And so forth.

But if the document has been bates-labeled, there is no dispute—the lawyers' records will show which range of pages had actually been delivered—"Your Honor, my records show that I delivered pages bates-labeled 1 to 90, and this document is number 57, so he must have gotten it."

After stamping my ninety pages, I sent them, along with a letter listing my potential witnesses, to David Hogue.

* * *

In addition to exchanging documents and witness lists, lawyers have another weapon in their arsenal of trial preparation—the deposition. A deposition is an under-oath interview. In a deposition, the lawyer can question witnesses before the case goes to trial, and the lawyer can do so even if the witness doesn't want to cooperate.

There are as many different theories about how to conduct depositions as there are lawyers. The lawyers I encounter have their own notions about depositions, their own theories, and their own methods. Here's mine.

Depositions should serve several functions. First, they lock somebody into a story. After I deposed witnesses, I knew what they were going to say at trial because I asked them, in their deposition, what they were going to say. Oftentimes I asked the question exactly that way: "When this case goes in front of a jury, what are you going to tell the jury about…?" At trial the witness would either match the deposition testimony or the witness would say something different and look like a liar.

Now, most lawyers stop there. For most, the overarching strategy is to lock in the story.

But good depositions, in my opinion, require more.

They are good opportunities to test the witness. How does the witness react to harsh questioning? How does the witness react to pleasant questioning? Does the witness ramble, or does the witness give short answers? Depositions reveal this, too, and that information is useful in preparing for trial.

Finally, I think that depositions are good for developing particular answers. Sometimes, witnesses can be persuaded to put their answer in the lawyer's terms.

And that is a valuable deposition.

It takes preparation, though.

I prepared to take the depositions of the school board members. My

12. Building the Case

preparation started with a study of five permissible categories of "banable" material in schools: obscene, libelous, vulgar, illegal, or disruptive. My deposition outline included questions on each of these categories—Is there anything in the Harry Potter books that are "obscene"? If so, show me. Anything else? And then I'd move on to the next category.

I also knew from case law that material cannot be censored if a "decisive factor" in their censorship is the material's "message or viewpoint." The board members would be asked questions using that exact phrase.

Besides the three board members who'd voted for the ban, I also wanted to take Angie Haney's deposition. Part of me could not believe that Pastor Hodges would actually admit that he banned the Harry Potter book for religious reasons. Saying such a thing would be very hurtful to Cedarville's case. The cynic in me assumed that Pastor Hodges would, after consulting with legal counsel, back away from that. Therefore, I wanted to take Angie Haney's deposition first and lock in her testimony about what Pastor Hodges told her—prior to the lawsuit—about the Harry Potter books.

After calling Cedarville's lawyer's secretary and getting his available dates for depositions, I asked my secretary, Donna, to prepare a subpoena for Angie Haney. Donna did so and wrote a check for the witness fee; at that time, court rules required a witness fee of $30 plus mileage. I signed both and gave them to our runner. "Serve this on Angie Haney at the Crawford County courthouse. Ms. Haney just so happens to work there."

An hour later, the courier returned.

"Did you serve it?"

"Oh yes."

"And?"

"She was very excited. After she read it, she said, 'Oh, I'll be there. I'll definitely be there.'"

"Really?" I paused. "I've never had that reaction before."

"That's what she said."

* * *

I had scheduled Angie Haney's deposition for 8:30 in the morning on a Thursday in January 2003. I took advantage of the cold weather to wear my long black dress coat. I liked that coat quite a bit, but the mild Arkansas winters afforded me few opportunities to wear it. This morning provided an opportunity, as the night's biting cold persisted.

Normally I would not have scheduled a deposition for 8:30 a.m.; that was just too early for me. But we had a full day of depositions scheduled. Cedarville's lawyer had driven up from Conway—a two-hour drive—and to minimize the number of trips he'd have to make, we wanted to get as many depositions done as we could in a single day. We'd scheduled the board members' depositions after Angie's.

A word about depositions.

A deposition requires four people.

The first is the lawyer asking the questions. In this case, this would be me.

The second is the deponent. That's the person being questioned. In this case, it was Ms. Haney.

Ms. Haney arrived at the office promptly at 8:30. She wore a dressy orange blouse. She was smiling and excited and remained so throughout the deposition, which pleased me, because often when I subpoenaed people for depositions they showed up defensive and angry, and that makes the whole day no fun at all. But Angie Haney had a story to tell, and she was itching to tell it.

The third is the opposing counsel. In this case, it was David Hogue, the school district's lawyer.

The fourth player is the court reporter. The court reporter is a neutral person whose sole job is to take down—that is, transcribe—every word said by everybody. Our court reporter that day was Veronica. In any conversation, Veronica managed to laugh pleasantly several times. She also had an extraordinary metabolism—the woman remained thin and fit even though she relentlessly consumed sugary drinks and junk food, like Cheetos. She did this at every break. I'd never seen her go more than an hour and a half without eating some kind of junk food.

Veronica and her partner, Laurence, were "machine" reporters. In depositions, their fingers were clouds of movement on the weird little transcription machine. The machine spat out a paper with alien-like marks; Veronica and Laurence, though, could read them and tell me instantly what had been said. I've been told that it is some kind of typewritten shorthand.

12. Building the Case

This is different than the "mask" reporters. Mask reporters type nothing, but instead use a tape recorder and repeat what everyone is saying into a mask. Later, at home, the mask reporters listen to their tapes and transcribe everything. A mask reporter cannot immediately read back what was just said; for them, the only way to find out is to rewind the tape and listen. That is almost always impractical in the rough-and-tumble of an ongoing deposition.

This makes a difference. Inevitably, at some point in the deposition, a witness would try to throw me off track by asking me to repeat a question or give me an answer that does not really answer my question. With a non-machine reporter, I would be stuck with having to repeat the question from memory. With a machine reporter, I can just have the reporter read the question back. Not only does this ensure that my exact question gets answered, it also checks difficult witnesses who think that non-responsive answers will allow them to evade hard questions.

Angie's deposition started out with the standard, preliminary stuff—her name, address, and so on—and then I started asking her about Pastor Hodges.

Pastor Hodges, she said, conducted classes about "different types of witchcraft and satanic cults." He did this "in his Wednesday sermons, and he was just trying to give us insight about how you need to be aware that it can be anywhere in your life, and you don't realize it. And it was right after that, that the Harry Potter movie was coming out. The kids at school were reading it, and it was on the A.R. list."

When Angie mentioned the "A.R. list," I knew that she was referring to the Accelerated Reader list—a list of books that children could read for extra credit.

Angie told me how she was inspired to action. "I got to thinking about it and it really bothered me, especially after we had talked in church about how things like the Harry Potter series are just an opening."

By "an opening," Angie meant that it led down the path of witchcraft. "They start real simple and it grows, and they build on it like you do anything, and then the next thing you know, six months down the road you have got a really big problem. And I kept thinking about the book and it bothered me, so I filled out a request form asking the school board to review its policy with that particular book.... I didn't like the book and I wanted to do something about it."

Harry Potter and the Cedarville Censors

Prior to this deposition, I had done a bit of research on Angie Haney. Googling her name had revealed an article in *Citizen*. *Citizen* billed itself as "a web site of focus on the family." The article quoted Angie at length—it described the Wednesday night sermons as well as the clear and present danger created by the Harry Potter books. "It demeaned everything I was trying to teach my kids," Angie told *Citizen*. "I do not want them taught witchcraft and the occult. That's not permissible in my house." The article also quoted Pastor Hodges. "Pastor Hodges said the books are sequestered in plain view on shelves.... 'We're not hiding the books,' Hodges said in the article, 'but the local media made it seem like we were the Taliban.'"

I thought the comparison apt, but didn't argue the point with Ms. Haney.

The *Citizen* article also revealed Pastor Hodges' unhappiness with Estella Roberts. "She called the local TV stations," complained Pastor Hodges, "who stuck cameras in our faces. She's a full-force liberal, and it's like she owns the library. As a Board, we can check on textbooks, but we're told the library is for the librarians. That doesn't make sense to me."

The *Citizen* article really did have some good stuff in it, and I was glad to have found it. Thank you, Google. The article became an exhibit to Angie's deposition.

At this point, I still did not know if Pastor Hodges, in his own deposition, would fess up and admit to his real (and impermissible) reason for sequestering the Harry Potter books. So I asked Angie several questions about what Pastor Hodges had told her. And after I got that information, I asked the questions again to have them clearly and concisely on the transcript.

"Is it fair to say that from your conversations that Mark Hodges disapproves of the Harry Potter books because of the presence of witchcraft and magic in the books?"

"Yes."

"Is it fair to say that Mark Hodges' objection was that the books would expose children to the notion of magic, good magic and bad magic?"

"Yes."

The case law that I had researched before Angie's deposition used the words "message" and "viewpoint" in describing impermissible reasons for targeting books. I tried to include these same words in my questions. "And is it fair to say that Mark Hodges told you that a lot of his concerns

12. Building the Case

about the books were religious concerns because the books contained an anti–Christian message?"

"Yes."

"Is it fair to say that Mark Hodges' objections to the Harry Potter books is that the messages and ideas in Harry Potter are different than the messages and the ideas in the Bible?"

"Yes."

With those answers, Angie Haney had given me a good record as to what Pastor Hodges told her.

But having Pastor Hodges' impermissible motives wouldn't be enough. I had to prove the "motive" of the school board, which meant that I'd need more than one man's view. I'd need to prove improper motives from all three of the Board members voting against the books.

I tried to see if Ms. Haney could testify that the other two school board members thought the same as Pastor Hodges.

"Does Mr. Shelly believe that?"

"I don't know," Angie said.

I asked about the third anti–Potter school board member. "Does Gary Koonce believe that?"

She gave the same response. "I don't know."

I frowned. If I were going to decisively prove an improper school board motive—one held by all three school board members—I was going to need more than Angie Haney's testimony.

13. "There are schools of magic"

> *"Of course it is happening inside your head, Harry,*
> *but why on earth should that mean that it is not real?"*
> —J.K. Rowling, by the character Albus Dumbledore

I had allotted two hours for Angie Haney's deposition. It ended an hour early. While we waited for the school board members to arrive, David called his office for some ongoing client emergency, and I let him set up shop in our conference room.

Psychologically, depositions should be one-on-one, mano a mano. Properly done, the questioner should set the stage so that the person being deposed focuses only on the lawyer asking questions. The other lawyer and the court reporter should be ignored.

But in this case I needed to make an exception. My proof required that I show the motives of a majority of the school board.

The motives of the majority? There were three of them. What if they each had different motives? What if one of the board members had an improper motive, but two of them had an acceptable motive (for example, if the book caused "disruption" in the school)? In that event, I couldn't really ascribe the same motive to all three voters and, by extension, I could not portray the school board 3–2 majority as having a single, improper motive.

My depositions needed to lock the board members into an improper motive, and that same improper motive had to be endorsed by all three.

I had thought about how to handle this for several days. Deposing each of the three separately and asking them the same set of questions would not only be tedious, but treacherous. I needed them to agree with each other. The most likely way to make that happen was to have their depositions done together.

I tried to make this happen without alerting the other side what I was up to.

13. "There are schools of magic"

"David," I said to the school district's lawyer, "I'm just going to ask these guys the same things. Why don't we just have all three there—I'd start with Hodges—and then if he says anything different than what the other two think, they can speak up. It's my understanding that Hodges was kind of the driving force behind all this anyway."

Luckily, David agreed. When we started the deposition, I got it on the record.

> MR. MEADORS: David, just to reiterate what you just said, my understanding of the conduct of the proceedings is that I am initially going to depose Mr. Hodges. And Mr. Shelly and Mr. Koonce are both here and they are going to listen to the proceedings and take notes. And then I am going to ask Mr. Shelly and Mr. Koonce if they have anything to add or subtract from what Mr. Hodges said. And so we are going to do this so that it will go more quickly and more efficiently, and they are going to take notes to make sure that they haven't missed anything or that I am trying to put words in their mouth with Mr. Hodges. Is that your understanding?
>
> MR. HOGUE: Yes.

I suppose, in saying that, I was guilty of a lie of omission. Efficiency wasn't my real motive.

"Can I ask one question?" Mr. Shelly asked.

"Sure."

"What is the purpose of this deposition?"

The question took me aback. Had no one told him? Was he showing up cold?

I explained to Mr. Shelly what "discovery" was, and how I was entitled, under the court rules, to ask witnesses questions so that I would know, well in advance, what their court testimony would be.

"All right," he said, not appearing particularly satisfied with my answer.

David chimed in. He pointed out that depositions were also used to lock witnesses into their testimony, so that if they said different things in court, they could be made to look like liars. David's on-the-record explanation convinced me that Mr. Shelly had not been previously prepared.

I began the deposition like most, asking Pastor Hodges for his name, its spelling, where he lived, and so forth, all the while nursing a cup of my firm's mediocre coffee, spiked with two little French vanilla flavoring tubs.

Next, I wanted to know his version of events. How did all this start? His testimony pretty much matched Angie Haney's.

"Did you tell Angie that you would support her if she filed a formal written complaint about the book?" I asked.

"Yes, sure did."

At this point, I shifted to the notes I'd made. Item one: show a "restriction."

"Would you agree with me," I asked, "that there are restrictions on a child's ability to read the Harry Potter books in the Cedarville schools' library?" I purposely used the word "restrictions." I wanted testimony that matched the exact words used by case law.

"Yes, sir," Pastor Hodges answered.

"What other books have been restricted or removed from the library besides the Harry Potter books?"

"I have no idea. I would imagine not very many of them."

I knew that the answer to that question was actually "None," so I followed up. "If I told you that a book had not been removed from that library in the last eleven years, would that surprise you? Do you have any reason to doubt the truth of that statement?"

"No, it wouldn't surprise me if you were to tell me that."

"In your three years on the school board, has the school board ever removed any other book?"

"No," Pastor Hodges said. "No book has ever come up before us."

"All right. Please tell me your exact objections to the Harry Potter books."

Pastor Hodges answered without hesitation. "It produces a rebellious attitude in the kids. We live in an age of the Columbine and all that. That book actually testifies to the kids that they shouldn't be obeying any teacher. They should not be obeying rules. The teacher doesn't matter. He gets rewarded for doing wrong. That is one basis."

I made some notes on my paper, "Causes disobedience."

Pastor Hodges continued. "The other basis is it is witchcraft."

"Witchcraft—religion," I wrote.

"The other thing it's not fiction."

My eyes widened. Did I really hear that? Then, out loud, "I beg your pardon?"

"It's not based on fiction."

I did hear it. "It's not based on fiction? What do you mean it's not based on fiction?"

13. "There are schools of magic"

"If you know the occult, it's not based on fiction."

"Well..."

Pastor Hodges cut me off. "Like I said, I study occult. I studied J.K. Rowling."

I looked down at my notes and wrote the third basis Pastor Hodges identified. "Not based on fiction."

I took a drink from my now lukewarm coffee, taking the opportunity to collect my thoughts. "I am going to ask you questions about those three things, and I am going to take them in reverse order. Let's talk about the 'not based on fiction portion.'"

Surely, I thought, he must be referring to the fact that J.K. Rowling used the names of actual alchemists and self-proclaimed, historical magicians. "Is part of your reason for saying that is because it uses some of the names of wizards or names of past occult figures, like Flamel?"

"Yes."

"Is that one of the bases that you are saying that it is not based on fiction?"

"That is part of it."

Part of it, I thought. Just part?

"What are the other parts? What are the other parts of this book that you think are not based on fiction?"

"Are not based on fiction? The whole premise is not based on fiction. Occult is not fiction. Witchcraft is not fiction. Witches are not fiction. Wizards are not fiction."

The smartass in me kicked in. "What about the Hogwarts School of Magic?"

"There are schools of magic," Pastor Hodges replied with all seriousness.

"Is there a Hogwarts School of Magic?"

"Not necessarily by that name."

"The schools of magic that you are referring to, are they very similar to the Hogwarts school as described in the Harry Potter book?"

"Similar in content. They teach them how to be a witch."

I paused.

Time to funnel, I thought. I had to get each of his "objections" clearly identified.

"So one of your objections to the Harry Potter books is that—and I am going to do this in two steps—it's your testimony that witches and magic and wizardry of the type that are described or discussed or portrayed in the Harry Potter books have a basis in real life and are more or less real?"

"They are real and it has a basis down to Columbine."

That was nonsensical to me. I tried to clarify.

"So your objection to the Harry Potter books is that it is exposing children to witches, wizards, and so forth?"

"It exposes them to that, yes, that is one of my objections."

"Okay," I said. I had this terrible habit of saying "Okay" in front of all my questions. The court reporter mercilessly recorded them all. "Okay, you said one of your objections is that the notion of witchcraft. Is it your belief that witchcraft is a religion?"

"Witchcraft is a religion and it is documented."

"Witchcraft is a religion?"

"Yes."

"And your objection is that these books expose Cedarville students to the witchcraft religion?"

"Yes."

Perfect. One objection, witchcraft-as-religion, was identified. And that's an unconstitutional objection.

I went back to my list of objections that I'd written earlier. "Pastor Hodges, I would like to talk about the first objection that you mentioned about the books which is about the rules and so forth, but before I get there, I want to ask, have you ever read the Harry Potter books?"

"I read the first one."

"When did you read it?"

"Shortly after she gave it to me."

"After who gave it to you?"

"Sister Haney."

Angie Haney is not really Pastor Hodges' sister. Among evangelicals, "Sister" or "Brother" in front of someone's name indicates that the person is a "Brother in Christ" or "Sister in Christ." The sibling in Christ honorific is usually reserved for people who go to the same evangelical church. People at Grand Avenue Baptist aren't calling the folks at First Presbyterian "Brother" or "Sister."

"When did Angie give you the book?"

13. *"There are schools of magic"*

"Probably that one Wednesday night. I would not go and buy the book. She said, 'I will go buy the book.' She read it, read it all the way through and I said, 'let me have it. I will go ahead and read it.'"

Now that I knew he had read the book, I could chase down the "obscenity" angle. Under the law, books could be banned for that reason. Obviously Harry Potter books were not obscene. Nevertheless, I wanted the school board members to admit this, rather than getting bogged down in a fight about particular passages in the books.

"Is there anything in the book that you would consider obscene?"

"Obscene?"

"Yes, meaning are there any bad words or strong sexual situations? Are there any vulgarities or any profanities in there?"

"You mean like drinking unicorn blood? The book has that in there."

That was not an answer I was expecting. I didn't really consider drinking unicorn blood "obscene" in the true definition of that word. On the other hand, I recognized that my worldview was quite different than Pastor Hodges'.

"Okay," I said, "it has drinking unicorn blood. But are there any bad words in there? Are there any words in the book that I can't say on television during the daytime?"

David Hogue spoke up. "This is not an objection, but those are two different questions."

I didn't understand. "Fix me," I said. "What did I do?"

David explained. "You asked if there were any bad words or words that you can't say on the T.V. Those are two different things. A lot of people think that there are a lot of bad words said on T.V."

He had a point. I remembered how, back in the early 90s, the Fox show *In Living Color* broke the "bitch" and "ass" barrier on broadcast television.

"That is well-taken," I said, "because Fox has just ruined T.V." I turned to Pastor Hodges. "Answer the first question, please. Are there any words in that book that cannot be said in children's cartoons that currently air on public television?"

He said no.

"Are there any particular words or swear words or anything in this book that you find objectionable?"

"Swear words?"

"Right, profanity or swearing or cussing?"

"Offhand, there might be a few off color objectionable ones."

"Can you think of any of them right now?"

"Not right this minute. I am not going to say. I am just going by my recollection."

"Are there any inappropriate sexual situations in the Harry Potter books?"

"Inappropriate sexually? Not offhand that I remember."

"Just so I am clear, you have several bases or you have several objections to this book, but one of the objections is not that the book is too sexual?"

"Right, not this book."

"And of all these different objections that you have about the book, one of your objections is not that it needlessly uses profanity or cussing?"

"True."

I felt like I had the "obscenity" category down and moved on to the "decisive factor" test.

"What would you say is the decisive factor as to why you object to the Harry Potter books and placed the restrictions on them?"

"Because it's going to create problems in the school. It is a book that promotes you do whatever you want to do, if it's the way you want to do it. Don't listen to your parent. First of all, don't even listen to your parent. Call them offbeat names. If you are a parent that does not agree with Wiccan, this book suggests that you have a raunchy set of parents. That is wrong. That is not something we need to be promoting in the school."

That's it, I thought. A clear statement that the religious and social message itself is the "decisive factor." I wanted a clean record, good for quoting to the judge, so I followed up with a question using the same terms that were used in the case law.

"So the decisive factor in your objection to the Harry Potter book is the message that is communicated by the book?"

"Right, it presents that you are not going to listen to the teacher; you are not going to listen to anybody in authority. I don't think we need that in the schools, especially handing it out to kids in school and they go home and read that, and they come back saying, 'Harry did it, I could do it.'"

I wanted to make sure that the court reporter's transcript matched what I thought I heard. I turned to Veronica. "Let's go off the record. Please

13. "There are schools of magic"

read me the last question and answer." She read it back to me. Yes, I think I had it. But for good measure I locked it in more.

"So I understand you have got the issue with the books not based on fiction, it's based on real witchcraft; that the book promotes other religions, namely witchcraft; and that the book promotes poor behavior in children. Is that right?"

"Yes, sir."

Perfect. None of those reasons were legitimate, except, possibly, the supposed behavior problem. I explored that.

"What behavioral problems, if any, were created by the Harry Potter books?

"That I know about right now presently?"

"Right. If any."

"At our school, nothing, that I know of right now."

"And were there any that you knew of when you voted to restrict the books?"

"No."

Whew. I liked that answer. A more troubling answer would have been something along the lines of "The book makes kids disobey the teachers. Just last week we had to expel three students who refused to obey the lunchroom rules. Those students said that Harry Potter did not have to follow rules, so they did not either." An answer like that would have been more troublesome. Under existing Eighth Circuit case law, a school would probably be allowed to ban a book that exhorted students to actively disobey authority.

But here there was no allegation of any actual disobedience. There was only this ethereal, speculative notion that the books may cause disobedience. The case law said that wasn't enough to justify restricting books.

I mentioned earlier that I was "funneling" Pastor Hodges with my questions. Lawyers are trained to "funnel" deposition witnesses. "Funneling" starts with broad questions. The broad questions identify the scope of topics; the lawyer then follows up with more narrow questions, item by item by item. With Pastor Hodges, I had done this with the broad question of asking him to identify all his objections to the books; then I'd followed up on each one. Now, to ensure that I had completed my funneling, I asked the closing question. "Are there any other reasons besides the reasons we have talked about that you restricted the Harry Potter books?"

Harry Potter and the Cedarville Censors

Pastor Hodges said that there were not.

In retrospect, I should have ended Pastor Hodges' deposition right there. I had what I needed. But at this point in my career, I was green, perpetually indignant, and loved to hear myself talk. I spent the rest of the deposition asking Pastor Hodges about particular passages in the Harry Potter books, his notions of witchcraft, and I re-asked, probably four more times and in different ways, the "decisive factor" and "message" questions, one of which produced this little gem.

> Q: And I don't mean to offend by this analogy here, it is a rough analogy. Just as Jesus tried to convey a message with his parables, so too does J.K. Rowling try to convey a very different message with her books?
>
> A: Yeah, she leads you right down the road to evil.

I also used the deposition to simply argue with Pastor Hodges. Again, that really wasn't necessary, but I couldn't resist. I asked him questions about the *Chronicles of Narnia*, *Macbeth*, and *A Christmas Carol*. He distinguished these by pointing out that they did not actively teach witchcraft the way Harry Potter did; it's a distinction I could not quite grasp. We talked about these nuances for about half an hour, at which point, exasperated, I ended the deposition.

* * *

I moved on to the next board member. "All right. Mr. Shelly, please state your name for the record."

He did.

"How long have you been a school board member?"

"Twenty years."

"What is your educational background?"

"I don't have one," he said. "Ninth grade."

"Do you have any training in children's literature or education or anything along those lines?"

"Twenty years." Mr. Shelly had looked irritated throughout Pastor Hodges' deposition, and that look continued.

"Twenty years on-the-job training?" I asked.

"Yes."

I asked Mr. Shelly whether he agreed with Pastor Hodges' testimony. He did. But for good measure, I asked some "message" and "decisive factor" questions.

13. "There are schools of magic"

"Let's assume for the sake of argument that J.K. Rowling is an occult author, she has ties to the occult and she has an occult message. Should her books be excluded because she is related to the occult?"

"Yes, if they are related to the occult."

I also asked Mr. Shelly to enumerate his objections. "Please tell me your exact objection to the Harry Potter books."

"There are lots. They teach witchcraft. They have the Hogwarts school that teaches witchcraft. And then they do drink the unicorn blood. And that is enough."

"Is there anything else?"

"Well, teaching witchcraft, sorcery."

"So it teaches sorcery, it teaches witchcraft, and there is an instance of drinking unicorn blood. Is there anything else in the book that you find objectionable?"

"I wished I would have read it," Mr. Shelly said. "I can't tell you."

"What would you say for you was the decisive factor in voting to restrict the Harry Potter books?"

"Hogwarts school and the teaching of witchcraft and the unicorn blood. There are other things, but I don't remember them."

"If this book had instead of being at the Hogwarts School of Magic, if it had instead been set at the Assembly of God School for Children, and instead of teaching witchcraft had taught Christianity, would the Harry Potter books be okay? In other words, the same plot line, but instead of there being magic and witchcraft, there would be Christianity at a Christian school."

"If it teaches Christianity, I would be for it, yes."

I tried to lock in Mr. Shelly's purely religious objection to the Harry Potter book.

"So teaching witchcraft instead of teaching Christianity is really your objection to the book?"

"No, sir."

"Then explain to me what I am missing."

"At a Christian school, that is what they are for is to teach you Christianity. I have two grandchildren that go to a Christian school. And this don't. I don't like it, witchcraft and stuff."

"Right. But let's say that instead of *Harry Potter and the Sorcerer's Stone*, okay, let's say it were called *Harry Potter and the Communion Cup*, and instead of being at the Hogwarts School of Magic, it was set at the Brean Assembly of God School for Children, so same general plot line, but instead of it promoting witchcraft, it promoted Christianity. Under those circumstances would you have any objection to this book?"

"If it promoted Christianity, I wouldn't have an objection to it."

Two down, one to go. Both Hodges and Shelly had, now, for the record, confirmed that their real reasons were religiously motivated. Before ending Mr. Shelly's deposition, though, I had, just as a matter of curiosity, to ask a few more questions. "Do you believe that witches and wizards are real?"

"Yes, I believe there are real witches."

"Do you believe there are schools of magic?"

"Yes, I believe there is."

"Do you believe there are schools of magic that are on par or like the Hogwarts School of Magic that are in the Harry Potter books?"

"Yes."

"Besides the message of the book, was there anything else about the book that made you think that the book was a problem?"

"No."

Bingo. I was done with Mr. Shelly. "That is all I have for Mr. Shelly," I said.

"No questions," David Hogue said.

We took a short break. I stood up.

"May I have a drink?" Pastor Hodges asked.

"Sure," I said. One of the firm's runners happened to be passing by the conference room at that moment. I stopped her and asked her to bring him a Coke. "Anybody else want anything?" One of the other board members asked for a Sprite. The runner nodded and went to the break room.

The runner should have returned quickly with the drinks, but did not, and after several minutes I looked around, irritated at the delay. Then I saw my secretary Donna waving at me, furtively, trying to get my attention. "The runner needs to see you in the break room."

"About what?"

"She needs to talk to you."

"She can talk here. Let's get our guests their drinks."

"No," Donna said, "go see her in the break room."

13. "There are schools of magic"

When I arrived, the runner showed me the problem. "See," she said, showing me a Coke bottle. "Do you really want me to give him this? I've looked around, and they're all the same."

She held up a glass bottle of Coke. All our Cokes are in glass bottles, a pleasant throwback to yesteryear. It's one of the benefits of having a Coca-Cola bottling plant in the city. The bottle displayed the Harry Potter logo, with its magicky-looking letters and lightning bolt symbol. At this time, Warner Bros. had teamed up with Coca-Cola to market the movie *Harry Potter and the Chamber of Secrets*. Every Coke bottle in our refrigerator had the promotional on it.

I went back to the conference room. "Are you sure you want a Coke?" I asked. "I have Dr. Pepper."

"I'd like a Coke, if you have it."

"Well, we have it, but..." And I explained.

"That's fine," he said.

So I brought in the Coke, logo and all, and Pastor Hodges drank it in stride. He even laughed about it, too.

※ ※ ※

Having resolved the Coca-Cola crisis, I started Mr. Koonce's deposition.

Of the three anti–Potter board members, Mr. Koonce had the greatest amount of formal education—an associate's degree in mechanical technology from the local community college. He had seen the Harry Potter movie and read about a quarter of the book. His reasons for restricting the book matched the other two's.

"Let's say that the Harry Potter books, instead of promoting witchcraft, promoted Christianity, would that make them more or less acceptable in your eyes?"

"It would make it more acceptable, and I will tell you why. I have seen people that get involved in witchcraft. People who get involved in Christianity don't burn the couches in their houses trying to get the demons out and then burn their houses down and end up in prison for arson. People that get involved in witchcraft, they do this."

How strange, I thought. Let's make sure that none of the Cedarville students are doing these things. "Are you aware of any children that did this as a result of the Harry Potter book at the Cedarville school?"

"That did what?"

"Burn their couch and get thrown in prison for arson."

"No, it's just a start. Harry Potter books are just a start."

"Is it fair to say that your restrictions on the books were a preventative measure to stop these bad things from happening?"

"My intentions was to make the parents aware of what the books had in them so they could be accountable for their kids like they should be."

"So what motivated you wasn't bad things that the children were doing at that time, but it was bad things that the children might do later?"

"Yes."

With that, Mr. Koonce, having already adopted the reasons given by Pastor Hodges and Mr. Shelly, confirmed that the books were not causing any actual disruption in the school. I ended the deposition.

But it was David's turn. "Question," David Hogue said, leaning forward. "If a parent refuses to sign the slip to let their child read Harry Potter, who restricted the book from the child, the school board or the parents?"

Mr. Koonce answered. "The parents."

David sat back in his chair. "I have nothing further."

14. Dakota Counts

"Truly wonderful, the mind of a child is."
—Yoda, *Star Wars Episode II*

Dakota's and Bill's depositions were next, but they were scheduled on a day several weeks later. A few days before their deposition, I asked them to come to my office to prepare.

I almost didn't. I had thought, in a moment of laziness, that whatever they had to say was so straightforward that no preparation was needed. But, out of (good) habit, I did call them in to prepare.

And I sure am glad I did.

"Dakota, pretend that I'm the school's lawyer. I'll ask you questions."

"Okay."

"Miss Counts, you were on the library committee, right?"

"Yes."

"What was the purpose of the library committee?"

Dakota gave me a blank look.

"What was the library committee supposed to do?"

"We were supposed to approve the book."

"What?"

"We were supposed to approve the book."

I looked at Bill. "Surely you were not instructed to approve the book. You were told to evaluate the book."

"Yes, we were," said Bill. "I don't know where she's getting this."

"Right. I don't either. We've got to fix this."

I needed to have the library committee be neutral. Or, if it was not neutral—and I strongly suspected that many of those selected were not, as they were hand-picked by the librarians—then the library committee had to at least appear to be neutral. I couldn't have Dakota saying that the library committee's role was to "approve" the book when its official function was to "evaluate" the book.

And this is where I walked right up on the fine line between "preparing" your client for a deposition and "coaching" your client. Preparing is legit; coaching is not. Proper preparation means meeting with your client beforehand, telling the client what to expect, and practicing questions with the client. Coaching, on the other hand, is simply telling your client what to say. That's dangerous ground—it potentially leads a lawyer to suborn perjury or tamper with witnesses.

"Dakota," I said, "the library committee's job was to evaluate the book. Not approve it."

"Okay."

"Let's try again. What was the library committee supposed to do?"

"We read the Harry Potter book."

"Why?"

"Because it was taken from the library, and that was wrong."

I looked at Bill and frowned. "Let's try again."

After about half an hour, we had Dakota on track. Her role on the committee was to evaluate the book and, after evaluation, they approved it.

I also knew that standing was going to be an issue, so we talked about that too. (You remember standing—the concept that a person suing has to "have a dog in the fight" or some other stake in the matter.)

I asked Dakota questions about how she had to get parental permission, and how even with that permission special efforts had to be made to check the book out. Dakota well understood this point. Like her father, she understood and objected to censorship.

I also spoke with Bill about his standing. All we could come up with was that, as a library committee member, his vote was overturned by the school board. I doubted if that were enough to satisfy the standing requirements, but maybe the school's lawyer would overlook that point.

After Bill and Dakota left, I shut and locked the front door after them. I walked the firm's green carpeted halls, checking that windows and doors were locked, turning off lights and copiers, and drove home in the dark.

* * *

David Hogue's deposition of Bill Counts went quickly.

Bill Counts explained how he got involved. "I was asked one day by

14. Dakota Counts

Mrs. Franklin, the librarian, if Dakota and I would be on a book committee. She said they'd had a complaint about a book and needed to review it. And I said yes, I didn't have a problem doing it, and then she mentioned what book it was, and I told her I'd already read it.

"We had our meetings, discussed the book. She gave us a copy of Ms. Haney's complaints with the book, and we, you know, looked through her complaints, looked through the books, tried to verify any of her complaints. We found most of her complaints to be baseless."

"Okay," David said, "what happened from there?"

"If I remember right, we had two meetings at the elementary school, and I think, if I remember right, two meetings at the high school. In the final meeting, everyone voiced their opinions of the books, any objections the books."

David nodded. "And I know the vote. What happened from there?"

This, by the way, is good deposition technique on David's part. He asked broad, open questions like "What happened next?" This draws details out of the witness that would not otherwise be discovered.

"Once you found out about the ban," David asked, "what happened?"

"Well, that's when this whole thing started. We had to sign a permission slip, and I thought, you know, 'this is not right.' They should not ban a book, especially on the grounds which I was told. Rumor was it was banned for religious reasons. And religion is not a reason to ban a book in a public school."

"So, okay, at some point you found out that the school board voted the way they did, and the story continues. What did you do then?"

Inside, I cringed. David was about to ask how Bill Counts got the idea to sue. I preferred my borderline ambulance-chasing to remain unspoken.

"Ms. Franklin, the librarian, called us," Bill said. "She told me what had happened, and we were given the opportunity to bring suit against the school for ignoring our wishes and, basically, censorship, or had the chance."

The passive voice. Gotta love the passive voice. Bill "was given the opportunity" to sue. Who gave it to him? That was unsaid. Would David follow up on that?

He did. "When you say you were given the opportunity, what do you mean? Who gave you the opportunity?"

"I was told that I could call Mr. Meadors, and that he would be willing to take the case."

I tried to keep my poker face at this point, but I really didn't like this line of questioning.

David pursued the topic. "Who told you that you could call Mr. Meadors?"

"I believe it was Mrs. Franklin, I believe, if I'm not—I'm trying to remember at this point."

"Did she just already know that Mr. Meadors was interested in that type of case, or do you know?"

"I don't know."

"Okay. Ms. Franklin just said to you, 'This is what has happened, and hey, if you'd like to file a lawsuit, Mr. Meadors would be interested?' What did she say to you? I'm just trying to figure that out."

I couldn't stand it any more. "I think we're getting perilously close to attorney-client privilege here," I said to David. Truth be told, David had not yet crossed that line. Attorney-client privilege only applied to conversations between Bill and me. Bill's conversations with Ms. Franklin would not be covered. Nevertheless, I raised the objection and tried to nip this line of questioning.

"As soon as we get there..." David said, indicating he knew full well he had not yet crossed the line. David turned to Bill, expectantly, and awaited his answer.

"I could not give you Ms. Franklin's exact wording, really. It was just basically what you have just said, that if I wished to, you know, do something about this, here was my opportunity."

David paused, looked up for a bit, and then said, "Were you encouraged to file the suit, or just told that if you want to, here's somebody that will—"

"I was just told," said Bill, "that if I wanted to do it, here, here was a lawyer."

"And so at that point you came and hired Mr. Meadors yourself."

"Yes."

And then, thankfully, David dropped the subject.

David made a check mark on one of his papers and read the next line in his notes. "Okay. Please tell me why you chose to file this lawsuit."

"I do not believe in censorship," Bill said solidly.

14. Dakota Counts

"And this is censorship?"

"Yes, it is."

"Define censorship for me."

"The removal or prevention of material to be used. The school board ignored the book committee's wishes."

"Do you believe that you have some particular right not to be ignored on that committee?"

"Yes."

There's a nuance here that bears explaining. It goes back to standing. Dakota, as a student at the school, was actually affected by the school board's actions. She used to be able to check out the books without restriction. But Bill was not, in a legal sense, truly affected by the school board's actions. He could not have checked out the books anyway—he did not attend Cedarville schools. So his "injury" was, at best, that the school board overrode his vote on the library committee.

And David knew this. "Do you have any documentation or anything that says that the school board does not have the privilege of ignoring your wishes?"

Bill was at a loss. "No."

David moved in for the kill. "So how are you injured in this case?"

"By the book committee being ignored."

David's eyes narrowed, and he smiled slightly. "Your only injury is that you were ignored?"

"Yes."

And having successfully cemented the virtually non-existent nature of Bill Counts' "injury," David ended the deposition.

I sighed, knowing we'd lost on Bill Counts' claim. He had no standing.

* * *

Dakota arrived at my office with her father. We had arranged an afternoon time to minimize the amount of school Dakota would miss. I tried to imagine the note that her parents may have written excusing her from school. "Dear principal, please excuse my daughter Dakota from afternoon classes. As you know, she is suing your school and has been subpoenaed by your lawyer." I feel certain that's not what the excuse note said, but it would have been fun if it did.

Dakota's role in the suit was well known among the teachers and students at Cedarville. Many students began reading the Harry Potter books at around that time, curious to see what the fuss was about. They carried their copies to school. Parents made a mild protest by asking for and signing the Harry Potter permission slips. The teachers, for the most part, were circumspect; they feared reprisal. One exception was Dakota's teacher for her gifted class—she taught several classes about censorship.

Dakota took the "hot seat" by the court reporter and across from David Hogue. I sat beside her. Her father Bill sat further down the table, out of Dakota's line of vision—typical deposition set up. David had selected a different court reporter for his depositions. She was a mask reporter who was notoriously slow in getting her transcripts completed.

David had previously mentioned to me that Dakota was going to be the youngest or the second youngest witness he'd ever questioned. There's no minimum age for witnesses, just a general "competency" test. Does the witness know what it means to be truthful?

David started right in on that topic.

"Dakota, I need you to explain the difference between telling a lie and telling the truth."

"The truth you can just get out all at once, and a lie you have to keep going, keep lying, and later on it's going to result in something."

Dakota had certainly internalized one of the rationales for not lying, but she had not really identified the difference. David, recognizing this, followed up.

"Okay. The truth—either telling the truth or telling a lie is bad, right?"

Dakota nodded.

"Which one is?" David asked.

"A lie is bad, and the truth is good."

"If I were to tell you that this table that we're sitting at is purple, would that be the truth, or a lie?"

"A lie."

"If I were to tell you that your dad is wearing a green shirt, would that be the truth, or a lie?"

"A lie."

"And it would be bad for me to say those things," said David, "because that would be a lie. Okay?"

Dakota nodded.

14. Dakota Counts

David turned towards me. "Do we have any issue with her competency to testify?"

I shook my head. "No, we don't."

David turned back to Dakota.

"Where do you go to school?"

"I go to Cedarville Elementary School."

"And what grade are you in?"

"I'm in the fourth grade."

David turned on more charm, smiled, and tried to seem friendly. He succeeded. "Fourth grade? I'm trying to remember—what do you learn in fourth grade? What kind of classes do you have?"

"We have math, language, reading, science, and social studies. And spelling."

"Spelling? I remember spelling." David then quizzed Dakota on some of her spelling words. He also asked her to spell some of the Harry Potter words. "How about Gryffindor? Can you spell Gryffindor?"

"I'm pretty sure."

"Okay, try it."

"G-r-i-f-f-i-n-d-o-r."

"As close as I think anybody would be expected to get. The first syllable has a y in it, so it's G-r-y. But pretty good."

I thought that was pretty good. I had known about the "y," but had mistakenly thought there was one "f," not two.

David smiled at Dakota again. "Have you read the Harry Potter books?"

"Yes."

"Which ones have you read?"

"The first and the second."

"And do you remember the name of the first one?"

"Yes. *Harry Potter and the Sorcerer's Stone.*"

"And do you remember the name of the second one?"

"*Harry Potter and the Chamber of Secrets.*"

"Okay. Did you like them?"

Dakota indicated that she did.

"What do you like about them? Why do you like them?"

"They're really adventurous. He does a lot of things that are fun, and just—pretty much things that I like to read about."

"And do you have those books at home?"

"Yes."

Now, notice how David just slipped that in. He really did this very well. To a less than fully-informed observer, David was just having a pleasant chat with Dakota. But there was a reason for that question, and I knew full well what that reason was. If Dakota has the books at home, David would argue, then the school library's restriction would not affect her—she could just read her own books. Thus, David would argue, Dakota has no standing to bring this lawsuit. She is not affected by the school board's actions.

I knew that was what he was doing. But I could say nothing. It was his deposition, and he was entitled to question my client. The fact of the matter was that she did have the books at home, and nothing I did could change that. I would just have to deal with the standing argument when it reared its head.

David continued asking Dakota about her Harry Potter collection. "What books do you have at home?"

"We have the first book, the second book, and the third book."

"But you haven't read the third book yet?"

"No."

"Are you saving it?"

"I started, but I haven't finished it yet."

"Of the first two books, do you find anything in them to be a little scary?"

"No."

"Where did you get the books that you have?"

"We bought them."

"From?"

"Walmart."

David then changed topics. I think he remembered that he should have asked this initially, but had forgotten. "Where do you live?"

Dakota, with a practiced rapidity, gave her house number, street, city, state, and zip code. I could not have given my own address with as much efficiency as she did.

David and I laughed. "Man," David said, "that's the best answer on a deposition I've ever gotten to a single question. That was good."

I nodded. Dakota just sat there. I don't think she knew that she had been funny. Knowing your address was serious business.

14. Dakota Counts

David got back to questioning. "Do you know, are the Harry Potter books in the library where you go to school?"

"They are off the shelf. You have to have a permission slip from your parents to read them."

"And do you need the permission slip?"

"No."

"Why not?"

"Because my parents already turned one in."

Standing again. I knew David would quote this in some future legal brief.

David knew it, too, and cleaned up the record by re-asking the question in such a way to get a simple "Yes" or "No" on the transcript. Lawyers love a clean record. "Okay," said David. "You have the books at home if you need them?"

"Yes."

I grumbled silently.

"What other books have you read recently—in the past couple of years, I guess. That's not very recently for you, probably. What books do you like besides Harry Potter?"

Dakota mentioned the Sweet Valley High books. I hadn't realized that those books were still around. Sweet Valley High books, for those of you who don't know, are what I call "gateway" books. Sweet Valley High books are a gateway to trashy romance novels, just as marijuana is an alleged "gateway" to harder stuff, although I'll concede that addiction to trashy romance novels is far preferable than addiction to heroin. Growing up, my sister loved the Sweet Valley High books and has no apparent ill effects from reading them.

"How much do you read?" David asked Dakota.

"I read a lot."

"How many times a week would you say you get the chance to read?"

"Maybe once a week."

"Maybe once a week. Okay. And how often would you say your parents do the same thing?"

"My mom reads every night."

Good for you, Mary, I thought.

"What does she read?"

I was curious to hear this answer. But Dakota kept it vague.

"She usually reads one book every two nights, and so I don't really know what she reads."

"You don't know the names of them or anything?"

"No."

"What about your dad?"

"He reads. He just doesn't read all the time."

"Do you know what he ever reads?"

"He reads Harry Potter."

He and several million other adults, I said to myself.

David then started asking about the Harry Potter movies and asked Dakota about scary parts. Again, I knew what he was up to. If the books are really scary, then maybe they are not appropriate for young children. David wasn't saying any of this out loud, of course, but I felt certain that was his strategy in the deposition.

"Have you seen the Harry Potter movies?"

"Yes."

"Both of them?" At that time, only the first two Harry Potter movies had been made.

"Yes."

David continued with his friendly, Mr. Rogers voice. "What did you think of them?"

"I liked them."

"Was there anything scary in the Harry Potter movies?"

"No."

Good answer, I thought. I didn't want to hear anything about unicorn blood or nightmares.

David switched topics.

"Do you have a lot of friends at Cedarville?"

"Yeah."

"How big? Do you know how many people are in your class?"

"Yeah. Nineteen, right now."

"Is that all of fourth grade, or are there different fourth-grade classes?"

"There's three. We switch classes. That's my main class, and there's nineteen."

"Is each class about the same size?"

Dakota nodded yes.

"Do the other kids in fourth grade seem to like the Harry Potter books?"

14. Dakota Counts

Oh, I saw where this going.

"There's some," Dakota said.

"Have you heard of anybody in the fourth grade that is just not interested, doesn't want to read the Harry Potter books?"

"Yeah, there's some people who aren't interested in stuff like that."

David was going after my "stigmatization" argument—the argument that I'd made that requiring parental permission would unfairly stigmatize children who wanted to access the books.

"Have you heard of anybody in the fourth grade that is basically afraid of reading the Harry Potter books because of what people might think about them if they do?"

"No."

"Do you think that if you went to the library and checked the Harry Potter books out that people would criticize you, or think you are a bad person, or anything else, because of that?"

"No."

Ouch. That hurt my stigmatization argument.

"Okay. Do you know any third graders?"

"No, I don't really know that many third graders."

"Do you know any of the fifth and sixth graders?"

"I know a few, but not that many."

"Do you know if any of them read Harry Potter?"

"I don't know."

There we go, I thought. Maybe I can use the stigmatization argument with those other unnamed children.

David and Dakota then chitchatted about the books themselves. Dakota liked Harry the best, even better than Hermione. "I like Hermione," Dakota said, "but not as much as Harry, though. Hermione is really smart. She always comes up with the things that they should do. She's always trying to get them to stay out of trouble."

Harry, Dakota explained, was much more exciting. "Harry gets to do all the adventuring, and he's the one who goes on to the Sorcerer's Stone, and he's the one who figures out the chamber's secrets. And he gets to do all that."

Snakes were cool too. "I like the animals and all that stuff," Dakota said.

"You do not."

"Yes, I do."

"You like snakes?"

"They're cool. I don't like getting up close to them, but they're cool."

"Do you think you'd like a big snake that was the size of this room?"

That would, by the way, be a super-large snake. The conference room was about twenty feet long.

"If I didn't have to touch it, yeah."

"Do you think it would be neat to talk in Parseltongue?"

"Yes," Dakota said.

Parseltongue is snake language. In the books, Harry Potter had the magical ability to speak with snakes. He spoke Parseltongue. I looked at the court reporter. Surely this was the first time she'd had to record "Parseltongue."

David leaned forward, calmly, but with earnestness, and asked, "Do you think anybody actually can speak Parseltongue?"

Dakota laughed out loud. "No."

"You don't?"

"I can kind of remember some of the words from the book, but—no."

"Okay. Do you think that if you read enough of the book you might could try, and it might would work?"

Dakota kept laughing. "No. I don't think it would work."

"Is there any—do you think that any of this magic stuff that's in these books, do you think any of it actually happens in real life, ever?"

Dakota looked at David incredulously. "No."

"Do you think witches really exist?"

"No."

"Do you think there's actually schools of magic?"

"No."

This, by the way, is exactly why I like to have something to drink at a deposition. I can take a sip when I need to hide reactions like, for example, my own laughter. I did so here.

David continued. "Let me ask you this. What is it that the magic people, the wizards and witches—what do the people at Hogwarts call—what would they call me?"

"A Muggle."

"A Muggle. Why would they call me a Muggle?"

"Because you're not magic folk."

14. Dakota Counts

"And what would they call you?"

"A Muggle."

"What would they call your dad?"

"A Muggle."

David pointed at me. "What about him?"

"A Muggle."

"Are you sure?"

"Yes." Dakota did not have to think very long to be sure that I had no magical powers.

"Do you know anybody that is not a Muggle?"

"No."

"Okay. Kind of a silly question, isn't it?"

Dakota laughed and nodded. "Like I don't believe in Santa Claus."

"You don't believe in Santa Claus?"

"I know he's the parents. They told me."

"Do you believe in the Easter Bunny?"

"No."

I leaned back in my chair. This was a fun deposition.

"Why don't you believe in Santa Claus?"

"Because I know he's not real."

David asked her more questions about the plot of the books—why he asked, I don't know—and then wrapped up the deposition.

"All right. We started out with this, and this will finish this too. We started out by talking about the difference between telling the truth and lying, right?"

Dakota nodded.

"Are there some situations that you know of when it's okay to lie?"

"Yes."

"Like when?"

"I'm trying to think of one."

I leaned forward, cupped my hands around my coffee, anxious to hear the example she would come up with.

"Like when—if your friend tells you that their parents are beating on them or something, and you promise them you won't tell anyone, but you need to tell someone. So you tell."

David nodded. "Good example."

Now, David had said that was going to be his last question. But that was not true. He lied about that. Not intentionally, mind you—he couldn't help himself. "This is my last question" or "Just one or two more minutes, your honor" are classic lawyer lies. These promises of a soon-to-come conclusion are uttered every business day in conference rooms and courts across the nation. None of them are true. The lawyer always takes longer than promised.

Here, David succumbed to the temptation to ask more questions about standing. And how could he resist? It was his best, if not only, argument.

"Do you know where the Harry Potter books are in your library now?" David asked.

"They're on the shelf that only you can get to—our librarian can get to—and she'll get them for you if you have a permission slip and you want to check them out."

"And you have a permission slip?"

"Yes."

"And so you can go in and get the books when you want."

Dakota nodded.

"Let's say, pretend for a minute, that you didn't have a permission slip. Okay? And you go in and get one of the books, okay? First of all, is that an okay thing to do?"

"No."

"Okay. Why not?" David asked.

And then Dakota, who had already done a great job throughout the deposition, really shone. "Because they're on a shelf that is supposed to be only where the librarian can get to. But here's what I think," Dakota added. "Children should be able to go into a library and get whatever book they want without anything like a permission slip."

I beamed. I wish all my clients were that articulate.

15. The Expert

"An expert knows all the answers—if you ask the right questions."—Levi Strauss

I needed an expert.

An expert witness, that is. "Expert," in the litigation world, is a term of art. It is a special kind of witness. Normally witnesses can only testify as to what they saw, smelled, tasted, felt, or heard. For example, a witness could say, "I saw the doctor take the scalpel, make an incision, and take out a pink lung." But a witness could not say, about the same event, "I watched that doctor operate, and I think he committed malpractice." The first example is just a fact. That's okay. The second example is an opinion. That's not okay.

But an "expert witness" is an exception to the rule. Experts can give opinions, if they're qualified to do so. So a doctor can opine about another doctor's surgery. One engineer could criticize another engineer's work. And so forth. Lawyers, as lawyers are wont to do, have creatively used the expert witness rule to classify people as experts in all sorts of things. I've done the same. In one case, I had to litigate whether a pet bobcat was a "domesticated animal" according to the neighborhood covenants. I got a veterinarian as an expert witness to say, in her opinion, it was not. The other side hired their own expert to say the opposite. In another case, I had an engineer give an opinion about whether future rains would flood someone's property.

Experts are great devices for getting good testimony that other witnesses cannot give.

In the Harry Potter case, I wanted testimony about how wonderful the Harry Potter books were. I decided that my best bet was Louise Turner.

Louise had been a Fort Smith children's librarian for more than thirty years. Back when the library was in the old Carnegie building downtown, the children's section was in the basement. It had tall metal shelves, bright, buzzing fluorescent lights, and a shiny, institutional floor. Children like me spent hours there, browsing the stacks, checking out everything from the Burgess animal books to the history of the Nazis. Louise Turner had been a gentle presence in those elementary school days; she let older children work behind the desk, checking patrons' books in and out and reshelving.

Louise loves children, but she never had any of her own. Growing up the oldest of five siblings, Louise was the daughter of a Fort Smith factory worker with a grade school education and a housewife who kept up their modest home. Though her parents lacked any formal education, they were both readers, and young Louise was encouraged to read aloud to the family each evening after supper. She would spend hours at the local library; entertainment in the form of books was free. It was there that she began appreciating the public library as the most democratic of institutions, a place where people from all walks of life were welcome.

When it came time for Louise to go to college, she worked at the library to earn money to pay tuition. Even after she became an elementary school teacher in the rural public schools of eastern Oklahoma, she would always come back to Fort Smith for the summers. She worked in the quiet library stacks, helping patrons find books and organizing the shelves. When offered the position of children's librarian, she immediately accepted.

The job was perfect for Louise—she felt as though she had autonomy and respect, and she could work with her beloved books. The fact that the job required little to no confrontation with anyone was a plus too. Louise is conflict averse and has structured her life to avoid friction. In her youth, she had been engaged twice, both times to budding young pastors, and both times she got cold feet and broke off the engagements. Louise was concerned that she would have to hide her true self if she became a pastor's wife—or anyone's wife, for that matter.

A person first meeting Louise would think her the very cliché of a spinster librarian. She looked older than her years, with gray hair, small, intelligent blue eyes, and a jutting chin under thin lips. She wore turtlenecks and cardigans in the library, even when the weather outside was mild, and she walked carefully, with measured steps and a slight stoop.

Seeing her perform a children's story time was startling. As children

15. The Expert

sat in a semi-circle at her feet, she stood before them, holding only a book, and the quiet space transformed into a Broadway stage with Louise the star of the show. Sentences with exclamation points were screamed; witches' dialogue got an evil cackle; monsters roared. It was a loud, dramatic affair, and it made cartoons on television seem subdued by comparison.

Story time was the only time I've seen Louise so animated. In all other contexts, her speech was measured, words carefully chosen. She considered herself a good Democrat and Christian, sincere and dedicated in her work ethic.

Louise had read every children's book in the library. Tables in her office were stacked with new books; they awaited her review before being released for cataloging. Her encyclopedic knowledge of children's literature gave her the ability to instantly identify books tailored to a particular child's interests. "Once I know a child," Louise told me, "I can choose a book that child will love."

I was sure that from an experience point of view, Louise had no match. She had been "the" children's librarian in Fort Smith. Not just for my generation, but for my own children as well.

Louise, along with the rest of the Fort Smith library, had moved to a shining new jewel of building near a city park. Two stories of clean red brick mounted itself on the side of a green-grassed hill. Green roof, green trim, and stained glass added the finishing touches.

Funding for the new library came from an unusual benefactor—Leah Arendt, a rich, ninety-seven-year-old eccentric. Not that anybody would have known that she was rich; she lived in squalor with her two hundred dogs and cats. While Ms. Arendt was alive, neighbors had contacted county health authorities many times to complain about the stench. After she died, one of her friends presented a typewritten will that just so happened to benefit that friend. Another person presented a competing handwritten will that divided the $3-million-estate between the library and Ms. Arendt's two hundred animals. Distant family members, including an alleged illegitimate nephew, joined the fray. The case ultimately settled, and the library's share funded its endowment.

The children's section of the library occupied an L-shaped area on the ground floor, with Louise's office in the inner corner of the L-shape. I found her among the children and the shelves, identified myself (I didn't expect her to remember me), and told her about the case.

Harry Potter and the Cedarville Censors

Louise spoke slowly. "Oh, yes. I know about that. I would be delighted to help."

I didn't think that Louise fully knew what she was getting herself into—the ramifications of being an expert witness are not common knowledge—but I wanted to first see if she could help me with the case, and what that help would be. I gave her copies of the school board members' depositions, and we set an appointment to meet a few days later.

At our next appointment, Louise was ready.

"Let me show you some things." She led me to her office. "This is the American Library Association's *Booklist*, and this is the *School Library Journal*." She pulled two thick books off of a shelf. "They are summaries of books. They list and review them. We use these to order new books." She set them on a table, opened them, and showed me.

"The real shame in all this," she said, "is that the Harry Potter books, more than others, encourage children to read. I have heard so many children tell me that reading Harry Potter made them start reading for fun."

I spent more than an hour with Louise, discussing how libraries selected books, what "age appropriate" meant, and how the Harry Potter books fit into all this. Louise had three main points to make.

First, when selecting children's books, the test is "age appropriateness." For example, the Stephen King novel *Misery*—about a person who is tied up and tortured—would not be age appropriate for elementary school children. Themes, language, topics, and message are the factors to determine age appropriateness. Louise's opinion was, not surprisingly, that the Harry Potter books were age appropriate.

Second, library books must be open and available to all patrons for reading, browsing, and check out without stigmatization or other impediment. Cedarville's policy of requiring special parental permission, opined Louise, violated this principle.

Third, fantasy and imagination are a necessary and integral part of children's literature. In Louise's opinion, the Harry Potter books got children involved in reading—sometimes children who would not have otherwise read for fun.

After our meeting, I went back to the office and prepared the first draft of the "Expert Report of Louise Turner" based on the notes I took. Court rules require experts to create "expert reports" summarizing their opinions. A few days later, I showed Louise the report I'd created based

15. The Expert

on what she'd told me. She made some changes, and we finalized the report.

Prior to this case, I never knew that people wrote books and magazines about how to buy books and magazines, but apparently they do. Louise was well versed in these books. Her expert report listed them too—in addition to things like ALA *Booklist* and the *School Library Journal*, we also listed other book reviews, like *Horn Book, Bulletin of the Center for Children's Books*, and the *New York Times Book Review*.

Louise's report took issue with Pastor Hodges' belief that the books described real events. "I do not think J.K. Rowling ever intended the reader to believe that Hogwarts and all its witches, wizards, and mythical beasts are real." And Louise honed in on the real censorship/restriction issue. "One of the board members said the school board had not banned the Potter books, but had only restricted them. To me, this is only a matter of semantics. Whatever it is called, by placing restrictions on books, a form of censorship has taken place." In Louise's view, censoring a book merely because a patron finds it "offensive" defeats the purpose of a public library. The public is made up of people with many different experiences and points of view, so what is objectionable to one may not be objectionable to another. Instead of censoring a book and depriving others from reading it, a librarian should simply direct a disgruntled patron to the vast selection of other books on the shelves. With so many options, there are bound to be many books that are not "objectionable."

Louise's report closed with an inspired message. "Each Good Friday I read the chapters in the 'The Lion, the Witch, and the Wardrobe' dealing with the death and resurrection of Aslan, the fictional character C.S. Lewis uses to symbolize Christ. I mention this only because it reinforces my belief that two people, even two people who are Christian, bring to their reading their own personal values, prejudices, and life experience. Therefore, it is not only possible, but probable, that they may form entirely different opinions about the same book. That is why it is wrong to let one person, or even a group of people, be the deciding factor in determining which books should be freely available on the library shelves."

The finished product was eleven pages long. In the interests of transparency and fair play, I also included a fifty-page addendum containing earlier drafts of the report and excerpts from books and review periodicals. David Hogue was entitled to those under the court's "discovery rules." I put it all in the mail for David, and by doing so, fired another shot in the censorship war.

* * *

A bright February sun shone on Louise Turner as she came to my office for her deposition. The firm's heating units puffed quietly against the mild Arkansas winter. Louise kept on her gray button-up sweater even after coming inside.

We met briefly in my office. I had asked her to bring any notes she may have made. Under the court rules of "discovery," the school's lawyer was entitled to see them. Louise handed me a fistful of yellow notepad pages. I smoothed, skimmed, and bates-stamped them. We then went to the conference room where David Hogue and the court reporter were already waiting.

"David, I told Louise that every scrap of paper that she touches or looks at in connection with this case is discoverable, and she made some notes." I handed him the yellow paper. "This is actually the first time I have seen them, but I have gone through them and I have bates-labeled these LT-70 to 96, and we can make those Deposition Exhibit No. 1."

David studied the notes. I directed Louise to the hot seat. The maroon high-back executive conference room chair dwarfed her small frame. I slouched in the chair next to her.

David looked to see if Veronica as ready. She nodded and turned to Louise. "Ma'am, I need to put you under oath." Veronica raised her right hand and Louise followed suit.

"Do you solemnly swear to tell the truth, the whole truth, and nothing but the truth?"

"Oh, yes, I certainly do," Louise said meaningfully.

David started out with the usual—getting Louise's name and background. If there had been any doubt that David and I were babes compared to Louise, it was soon removed by her responses.

"I think it's thirty-two years that I've been with the library, but I forget exactly. I have been the head of the children's department for thirty-two years. Part of my job is selecting the books that go in the children and young adults section." In other words, Louise had been selecting children's books almost as long as David and I had been alive.

David continued to quiz Louise on her educational background and

15. The Expert

explored whether she'd ever published anything. Standard, boring deposition stuff. I sat motionless except for an occasional slurp of coffee.

Then David got to the nitty-gritty. "What I would like to do is have you define a few things for me."

"Okay."

"Give me a definition of age appropriate. In the context of this case, what does that term mean?"

Louise waited for about half a beat—I figured that she was choosing her words—and then said, "It means that the book is within not only the language understanding of a child, but the themes of the books—the issues discussed in the books—are appropriate to the age of the child reading it."

A practiced witness would have stopped there, having answered the question, and not volunteered further. But Louise, bless her heart, was not a practiced witness but was instead a genuinely nice and helpful person which, frankly, is not a good a thing in a deposition. So she continued talking, trying to be helpful. "For instance, I was thinking of—stop me if I am telling you more than you want to know—"

Stop, stop, I thought to myself, make him drag it out of you. But I only thought that; I didn't say it out loud. I did sit up, though. Slouch time was over.

"—but like Hansel and Gretel, I have been thinking about that story in terms of Harry Potter and witches and so forth. That is a book that disturbs me or a story that disturbs me. I would never use that with very small children. In fact, I don't use it at story time at all, not because it has witches in it, but because it has parents who don't care enough for their children. In some versions it's a stepmother who is causing the problems. A lot of children are living with stepmothers, and I don't want to bring them sorrow. So I would leave that on a shelf and if kids want to discover it and read it, okay. But in the story times I have, which are basically for very young children and preschool, I would never use that; that would not be age appropriate."

David pressed her. "So Hansel and Gretel is not age appropriate for exactly who?"

"It is not age appropriate for preschoolers, I don't think."

"What about first graders?"

"Depends on the first grader. Third and fourth grade, maybe. You know, a lot of these Grimm's fairy tales were originally written for adults anyway."

Ouch. I didn't like where this was going. I privately agreed that Grimm's fairy tales were, well, grim, but did we really need to be focusing on that?

David tried to get Louise to draw a bright line as to "age appropriateness," but Louise resisted. "Once children are able to read for themselves," she explained, assigning particular books to particular ages was not practical. "Children progress differently. The Harry Potter books, for instance, might be a little much for third and fourth graders, but I have fourth grade kids in my Sunday school class who are reading them and loving them. It's difficult to say because children mature at such different ages."

David wasn't going to let Louise off the hook so easily. "My issue here is trying to take the term age appropriate and take the fuzziness and mushiness out of it. You said that Hansel and Gretel may not be age appropriate for preschoolers because of the way parents are depicted in it."

"And they are violent, some violent things. For young children, I guess I tend to want them to have a rosy world, a world where life is fun. And it isn't that they can't have books that have sad things in them, but I don't do violence. I don't do—I want them to feel the joy of a loving family...."

We were getting too far astray, and no good was going to come from talking about Hansel, Gretel, witches, ovens, violence, and stepmothers. I tried to derail Louise's tangent under the guise of "seeking clarification." "I'm sorry, I am going to interrupt. Are you talking about books that you are selecting for kids or are you talking about books that kids can and cannot have access to or to be removed from the shelves?"

"I said I have a problem with Hansel and Gretel using it in a story time, but I would never remove it from the shelf. It's a classic," Louise said.

My "clarification" irritated David, and he rebuked me. "Brian," he said, "if you have questions, you can ask them on cross-examination."

He turned toward Louise and cleaned up his record. "I understand you may have an issue with Hansel and Gretel being age appropriate for preschoolers or questionable maybe for first or second graders, but you are not saying that it should be pulled off the shelves and placed on restriction. Is that right?"

"Absolutely."

"And what I am getting from you is that you probably would not pull

15. The Expert

a book like that off the shelves so much as you would let them discover it and let them find it, you just may not lead them to it?"

Louise agreed.

David then asked about Harry Potter's "age appropriateness." Louise gave the same kind of answer. "Each child is different," she said, "and I tell parents when they come in and ask my help in finding a book, I say, now, this is the age I think, you know, they have a second grader and they are looking for something for their child to read. I said I think he can handle this, but you know your child better."

And, hearing Louise mention parental involvement, David moved in and did some damage. "So are you saying that a particular book may be age appropriate for that parents' child, but then it's up to the parents from there?"

Louise nodded yes.

This weakened my case. Or, at least, it weakened Louise's testimony, which could now be used to support parental control of library books.

Louise tried, though, to make a distinction between parental involvement in library books and parental control. Just because a book was or was not age appropriate, she said, it would still be freely available on the shelf.

David asked about the set up of books at Louise's library.

There are different sections, she responded. "The teen books are in a separate section, young adults." There was also an adult section as well as a children's section.

"Let's pretend," David asked, "that we have a library that isn't compartmentalized, they don't have different categories. They just have a room like this and shelves all the way around it with all the books mixed up. Any given child, regardless of age, has access to that library and walks in. A first grader may walk in and see books that are age appropriate for a teen. Now at that point, should that book still should be available for discovery and browsing by that first grader?"

Louise held her ground; she answered yes. "Scary, isn't it," she said, "but that is the way it is."

David moved on to the topic of profanity and whether it should be in children's books. Louise responded as she had before—such things ought not be recommended for children, but they should be available on the shelf. Besides, Louise pointed out, grown-up books—big, thick books with bad words, but without pictures—were less likely to even attract the interest of children.

"Can you name a book that is not age appropriate for first through twelfth grade?"

"*Playboy* magazine," Louise offered. "I wouldn't want to see that, and it's not in the library, for instance."

"Is that age appropriate for anyone?" David asked.

I thought back to my Navy days and my lonely shipmates on day 50 of a 78-day run. *Playboy* was certainly age appropriate for us. If anything, it was way too tame.

Louise thought *Playboy* had a place, although she declined to give specifics. "Well, I am sure it is age appropriate for someone, but given the limited amount of library funds, we are not likely to have it at the Fort Smith Public Library for anybody."

David loved this answer. If Louise's own library wouldn't stock certain books, how could Louise criticize Cedarville? "Such a great example, *Playboy*," David said. "*Playboy* is age appropriate for some people, but because of lack of funding or lack of space, someone chooses not to select it for the Fort Smith Library, how do you decide that it is not going to be available for the patrons of the Fort Smith Public Library?"

With this question, we had, interestingly, drifted into a slightly different topic. It's one thing to restrict a book once it is in the library. But it's another to choose not to buy it. The Cedarville case focused on the former; the latter was truly uncharted territory in the law, and was probably a winner for the schools. In other words, once a school bought Harry Potter, it had to allow unfettered access. But it was doubtful, under current Supreme Court law, that a court would make a school buy it.

Louise answered David's question about selecting books, and I sat back, relatively unconcerned. A discussion about selection criteria wasn't going to affect this case. Or at least, it shouldn't.

The deposition drifted over to Louise's expert report. David asked Louise about how the report was drafted, and then moved into specifics. He asked Louise about her praise of the Harry Potter books. "You give a specific example that Harry Potter books are getting children involved in reading, including children who would otherwise not read. Have you seen this happen?"

Louise nodded. "I know a lot of kids, and it isn't that they don't have

15. The Expert

the capability of reading, they just don't love to read. And I have seen children become very enthusiastic about books and about reading itself. Then, going from the Harry Potter books, it was so long between *The Goblet of Fire* and this next one that is coming out that they are looking for other titles and other authors to read. And it's so nice to be able to hand them the *Redwall* series or some of the other books that they might enjoy and see them continue on."

"This never happened before Harry Potter?"

"I am not saying that," said Louise. "But I am just saying I have never seen it in such a great mass. In all my years of being a children's librarian, I have never seen such a phenomenon. We have copies of Harry Potter in every section of our library and sometimes they are all out."

Louise also gave evidence, albeit anecdotal, of the inter-generational appeal of Harry Potter. "In my church, for instance, it's been almost like a Harry Potter club. Several adults and children who are reading the books at the same time, and on Sunday morning before going to Bible class or such class, they are talking about what they have read. These are adults and children talking together. And that is the inter-generational thing."

She continued, "At Christmastime, in my family—I guess it was the year *Goblet of Fire* came out—we were sitting at the table and all of us were enjoying dinner together and conversation. My brothers, who are younger than I, had read Harry Potter. Their children and grandchildren had read Harry Potter. And all of us were sitting around talking, all these different generations talking about Harry Potter and what fun he was. And I see this, parents reading with their children too, the Harry Potter books and talking about them."

David then went back to *Playboy*—what if there was a copy of *Playboy* in the Fort Smith Public Library's collection? What, if anything, would be done to protect children from the evils of naked women? And after a great deal of verbal dancing, Louise came out on the only side she could while maintaining intellectual consistency. "Back to the *Playboy* thing, I can't imagine it happening in Fort Smith, Arkansas, quite frankly that there would be a *Playboy* magazine in the public library, but if there were, I would have to come down on the side of supporting it being on the shelf."

It was, truly, the only thing she could say. Any other response would have been a chink in the armor—it would have conceded that restricting books would be acceptable based on their content.

Harry Potter and the Cedarville Censors

By the end of Louise's deposition, David exposed the squishiness of the "age appropriate" test and developed interesting conundrums on the *Playboy* questions. That was actually a nifty trick on his part—the unspoken equating of J.K. Rowling's children's books with Hugh Hefner's periodical. I thought that David did as good as a job as could be expected with Louise's deposition, and, in fact, I told him so.

Which was a mistake. I should have kept my mouth shut, because when Louise heard me say that, she took it personally. She had been in the conference room for over two and a half hours, and it had worn her out. After my comment to David, she left abruptly, feeling that she had done badly. I ran after her and caught up in the parking lot outside the firm.

"Louise, why are you leaving so quickly? That went fine, we're in good shape."

"Oh, no, I didn't do well at all." She shook her head. "I've messed this up."

I assured her that was simply not the case, but she didn't believe me and remained sad. Louise drove off, distancing herself from the stress of the deposition. I felt bad (and still do) about the whole situation.

16. Legal Backstory: *Bystrom* (8th Circuit Adopts the *Pico* Plurality)

"We thought, because we had power, we had wisdom."
—Stephen Vincent Benét

About a week after the depositions, the court reporter dropped off a stack of binders. Donna put them in my inbox; a towering stack of paper greeted my next visit to her office.

"What's all this?"

"Cedarville depositions."

Each deposition came in a clear plastic binder with fasteners. I think that court reporters present them that way to make them look more official, much like I, when I was in high school, would put term papers in fancy bindings, hoping that the presentation would bolster the substance. As I always did when getting depositions, I removed and discarded the binders and stapled the transcripts together. Deposition transcripts don't need office supply glitz.

"Please pay this," I said to Donna, handing her the court reporter's invoice for $900. That was actually a fair price—as a rule of thumb, in Arkansas in the early 2000s, court reporters and the transcripts they made cost about a thousand dollars per deposition day. Donna cut a check, and my firm's accounting system recorded that, on the Harry Potter case, I'd bet another $900 on the outcome.

* * *

When I first filed the case, I filed in federal court because I figured it would be best to avoid locally-elected judges.

Harry Potter and the Cedarville Censors

But normally I avoided federal court. Litigating in federal court is much more frustrating than litigating in Arkansas' state courts. Federal courts impose unnecessary and niggling restrictions on the types and methods of filing. And each of the federal courts (and there are about a hundred throughout the country) has its own set of "local rules," so there's not even the advantage of uniformity from one federal court to another.

One thing that the federal courts have gotten right is the settlement conference. The court requires that the litigants get together, whether they want to or not, and talk about settlement. A magistrate judge is appointed to run the settlement conference.

In Fort Smith, at that time, the magistrate judge was Judge Beverly Stites Jones. She had been on the bench for years. Judge Jones was short, thin, had black hair, and could be, if appropriately provoked, mean. I have witnessed her, on several occasions, upbraid lawyers for engaging in typical lawyer silliness. She cared not about the stature or experience of the lawyer.

Quite simply, the woman did not suffer fools. I am aware of one case in which an esteemed lawyer with more than thirty years of experience did something to annoy her, and she chewed him out for several minutes. He deserved it. She once chewed me out. I deserved it too.

Judge Jones' no-nonsense style got the job done. A settlement conference with Judge Jones was not a feel-good chitchat. She put each of the parties in a room and spoke to them separately. Each side got straight talk from her about the weaknesses in their cases. Then she would go to the next room and talk harshly to that party. She kept people there for hours, oftentimes using her judge-ly powers to forbid them from leaving. After a while, tired and brow-beaten, the parties would inch their way to a middle ground, to a place where nobody was happy, and a compromise would be reached. Judge Jones' method got a lot of cases settled, which reduced the court's docket.

The Harry Potter case, as with all cases in federal court, was slated for a settlement conference. The court announced this in a letter sent to the lawyers.

But what was there to settle? It wasn't like most cases, where people were just fighting about money. In those cases, there can be a compromise. Money fights lend themselves to compromise, because it's very easy to divide by two.

16. Legal Backstory: Bystrom

Our case, though, was one of principle—we wanted no restrictions, period.

And I knew the school district would refuse to budge, too, because my earlier attempts to quickly resolve the case had failed. I had sent David Hogue a letter telling him that his clients were going to lose and so he should just give up. Predictably, that overture on my part was not well received; the school district declined my invitation for it to surrender. I asked, figuring that it was worth a shot. Also I was pretty obnoxious in those days and wanted to taunt the other side.

Thus, when we got the letter from the court setting a time for a settlement conference, I knew that it would be fruitless. Not even the ruthless efficiency of Judge Jones would make this case settle.

I asked her to release us from the conference:

> Dear Judge Jones:
> After evaluating this case, I am convinced that there is no chance of a settlement.... Defendant's school board members admitted in depositions that a decisive factor in their actions was based on their disagreement with their perception of the book's social and religious viewpoint and message. It is unconstitutional to [do that].... My clients are seeking very limited relief: they would like an injunction from the Court that removes the restriction on the Harry Potter books.... This lawsuit is based on the principle of the matter; it is not a suit to recover an economic loss. Therefore, a compromise settlement is simply not possible.... Any restriction—even a light restriction—is too much when it comes to free speech.

After getting my letter, Judge Jones demanded that David Hogue and I get on a conference call with her. We did, and she confirmed that each of us were entrenched in our positions.

"Then I agree," she said. "There's no point in a settlement conference. Goodbye." And she hung up.

As I said, Judge Jones was very efficient.

* * *

Not all cases are decided by people going to court, taking an oath, and giving testimony. That only happens if the witnesses' testimony will be conflicting—the jury will have to pick which version of events to believe.

But sometimes, everybody pretty much agrees on what happened—they just disagree as to who is in the right. In that kind of case, no trial is necessary. The lawyers need only write briefs, tell the judge what the facts are, and then let the judge decide what the law is. This is called "summary judgment."

* * *

The summary judgment stage required me to match my legal research to the facts I'd developed. The *Sund* case (can't hide a library book in a different section) was helpful, but it was in a different jurisdiction.

The Supreme Court's *Pico* case was helpful, but was won only by plurality (fewer than five justices). What happens with Supreme Court cases, and more so with Supreme Court cases that only have a plurality, is that each of the thirteen circuit courts of appeal implement Supreme Court precedent in their own way. Sure, they're following the law as pronounced by the Supreme Court, but since each case before them is a little different, how that law is applied—rigorously, liberally, with a twist, etc.—varies. Thus, a Supreme Court case's holding will, invariably, evolve over time based on how the circuit courts are implementing it.

A well-known example of this is abortion cases. *Roe v. Wade* is commonly known as the case that made having an abortion a right. That seems clear, but after that, circuit courts were put to the test. Can abortion be restricted to only the first trimester? Can we require parental permission? Can we require the abortion only be done in a hospital? And so forth.

Almost all Supreme Court case holdings get molded and bent and evolve in this manner.

So when it came to *Pico*, my research needed to discover if the rule announced by the *Pico* plurality had been adopted by my local federal courts. I started with the federal appeals court that governed Arkansas—the Eighth Circuit—and found the *Bystrom* case.

* * *

When I was a kid I used to play a game called Dungeons & Dragons. D&D is a fantasy role-playing game set in a medieval world with wizards, knights, dragons, and so forth. Players start out with low-level, low-ability characters and then, as they play the game, the characters advance in power and prestige. My favorite character was the wizard. Powerful wizards, after many successful adventures, retired in tall towers where they would research new magic spells, create wands, make potions and artifacts, and govern the various serfs that toiled on the lands around the tower.

I mention this because I think it is a good analogy to the Eighth Cir-

16. *Legal Backstory:* Bystrom

cuit Court of Appeals. Like D&D's wizards in their towers, Eighth Circuit judges are housed in a tall, thirty-story building in downtown St. Louis, Missouri. From its green marble and ivory-granite tower, they oversee the federal courts in a seven-state area. The judges are all lawyers at the zenith of their legal careers. They started out in the trenches of various law firms, dealing with pedestrian matters such as divorces, will contests, and car wrecks, and through years of hard work, perseverance, and significant political connectedness, managed to get an appointment to the federal bench.

Eighth Circuit judges write opinions affecting the legal rights of twenty million people. They are thoroughly protected from interactions with those people. Anti-vehicle concrete posts surround the building. The lobby has airport-like security. Fancy, gleaming metal detectors and X-ray machines must be navigated. Federal guards direct visitors to remove metal, empty pockets, and open bags. Once past security, the visitor is faced by three banks of elevators, each to a different decade of floors.

The Eighth Circuit is on the twenty-fourth floor. The elevator empties into an unfurnished, unoccupied lobby with a floor-to-ceiling window overlooking the Eighth Circuit's domain. Even at this point no judges can be accessed. Their offices, called chambers, are walled off behind an additional set of locked doors, cameras, and intercoms. I managed to visit one of these offices once. It was very nicely furnished. The window revealed a breathtaking, far-reaching, view-from-above of St. Louis and its surroundings.

It takes a full ten minutes, at least, to go from the city streets into an Eighth Circuit judge's chambers. And that is only if the visitor has been invited and is expected.

From their tower, the Eighth Circuit judges write, rewrite, revise, and issue their pronouncements. While they, in theory, decide just one case at a time, their decisions in each case affect future cases, and their pronouncements are read with care by the unlearned and not-so-accomplished members of the bar beneath them.

One such case is *Bystrom v. Fridley High School.*

* * *

Mr. Wenholz, the math teacher for Fridley High School (Minneapolis), finished his lesson early, shut his book, and looked at the clock. "There's about five minutes left. You can talk, but keep it down."

Harry Potter and the Cedarville Censors

Jeremy Saperstein, slouched in his desk, suddenly perked up and pushed his bushy brown hair out of his eyes. "God, I can't wait to graduate from here and get out of this cookie-cutter, bullshit, bureaucratic institution."

His friends agreed, and in the time remaining before the bell, they griped, quietly and to themselves, about the conformity of their classmates and school. The official school paper, more than anything else, exemplified their complaints. It was not a "newspaper" in any meaningful sense of the word. There were no up-and-coming Woodwards or Bernsteins on the staff of Fridley High's official rag. The staff of the school paper—populated by a score of obsequious lackeys who would say or write anything to curry favors and grades—acted as nothing more than a propaganda arm for the school administration.

"You know what I'd like to see?" said one of the boys. "I'd like to see a story done on the lunchroom. God knows that place needs a good investigation." The others nodded, and the conversation turned briefly to the unfairness accompanying a recent menu change. Students opting for the hamburger and fries instead of the main course would, as a result, not get the main course's sides, such as "cowboy bread," which was some sort of dessert pastry. This was particularly distressing, as cowboy bread was one of the very few edible things to come from the cafeteria.

"If I avoid that poisonous turkey pot pie, I have to give up cowboy bread. Man, that pisses me off."

"Forget the lunchroom. What's up with the 'Letters to the Editor'? Did you see the letter in the last issue? It was written by the Editor. The Editor wrote a letter to himself and put it in the 'Letters to the Editor.' How stupid is that? And it wasn't even about anything that should even be in the school paper; he was just advertising his Bible class."

"You're right," Jeremy said, rolling his eyes and shaking his head. His hair flopped down in front of his eyes, and he pushed it away again. "God, I can't wait to get out of this place."

Jeremy does not remember—as it's been decades since that conversation in Mr. Wenholz's math class—who first came up with the idea. He does not know if the concept of *Tour de Farce* was the brainchild of Cory Bystrom, John Collins, or one of his other friends in the AP math class. But one of them, in this particular informal bull session, suggested they do something more than complain.

16. Legal Backstory: Bystrom

"You know, we really should just put out our own paper. That would kick ass."

And with the seed planted, the boys got to work.

This was in the days before everybody had a personal computer. To make their own newspaper, each of the boys handwrote their articles and gave them to Jeremy. He pulled out the typewriter and typed them up. And actually, gauging by the very few typos in the final product, whatever failings the Fridley school system had, it had succeeded in teaching Jeremy good typing skills.

After finishing the articles, the boys created the newspaper by physically cutting and pasting the contents together. The boy using the nom de plume "Vince Jism" made copies of the proofs at his dad's work. Vince and the others then got together at Wayne Hlavac's house to staple the seven-page initial edition of *Tour de Farce*. Vince's dad (who I assume to be the "Mr. Jism" listed in the credits) received appropriate recognition for his contribution of the free copies. The front page of *Tour de Farce* recognized other contributors as well.

TOUR de FARCE was skillfully crafted by:
AUTHORS
Anonymous Bosch
Touche'
Teeley McDaggert
Vince Jism
CARTOONISTS
Kilroy
Dr. Doodler
Typing and Layout: Touche' & Mr. McDaggert
Reproduction: Mr. Jism

And, of course, in identifying itself, *Tour de Farce* gave a nod to the fine institution that inspired its creation.

TOUR de FARCE
Fridley Detention Center
6000 West Moore Lake Drive
Fridley, MN 55432
Dictator: Richard Stanton
Assistant Dictator: Brian Ingvalson

Messrs. Stanton and Ingvalson would likely tell you that their actual titles were "principal" and "assistant principal."

Harry Potter and the Cedarville Censors

On page three, *Tour de Farce* had a rather prescient filler ad:

> Fridley High School
> over 20,000 incarcerated
> visitors, please leave personal liberties at door

And *Tour de Farce* asked the tough questions of the day—questions never addressed by the official, wet-noodle school paper. "Why," started an article entitled "Screwed-Up Priorities," "does school suck? Why are the teachers idiotic fools? Why aren't there any exciting classes besides Masturbation for You? Do you constantly ask yourself these and other questions while you waste six and one half hours of your day? I've taken some time to answer these complex and thought provoking questions..." The author of this piece went on to give his insights into the educational system in America and also expressed his moral indignation that an "A" in the advanced college-level classes got treated the same, for grade point computational purposes, as an "A" in Woodworking. The "Screwed-Up Priorities" expressed all this in about 350 words, only ten of which were "suck," "fuck," "shit," "bitch," "asshole," or variants thereof, and were, in my opinion, used in an appropriate way. But then I used to be a sailor in the Navy, so my view of appropriate swearing should be treated with suspicion.

Swear words aside, the essay closed with a criticism of the public schools: "This beautiful system rewards mediocrity and perpetuates it, while it ignores the potential of high achievers. All we need is a change of these fucked-up priorities!"

Other *Tour de Farce* essays addressed less pressing matters: "Why are the bathrooms so damn cold?"; another explored the idiocy of the hall pass requirement. The article called "Lunch Scam" took the school to task for denying burger-eaters their cowboy bread.

All in all, *Tour de Farce*, sprinkled with two dozen swear words, was the product of adolescent minds rebelling by writing. It targeted nobody in particular, only "teachers" and "school" in general. And that targeting primarily criticized them for being "oppressive," "idiotic," and, as the boys would say, generally sucking all around.

The boys distributed *Tour de Farce* in the lunchroom on a gray, January day; they gave stacks of copies to friends to distribute further. The school's lawyers would later concede in court filings that there was no "material or substantial disruption of the orderly educational process at Fridley High School as a result of the distribution of *Tour de Farce*."

16. Legal Backstory: *Bystrom*

In reacting to *Tour de Farce*, the school administration had many options. It could have ignored *Tour de Farce*, since its distribution harmed nobody. It could have praised *Tour de Farce*, on the theory that it is preferable for teenagers to spend their Friday nights writing essays rather than drinking and fornicating. Or it could have actually addressed the boys' concerns by having some intellectually fulfilling classes, encouraging an independent student press or, at the barest minimum, not being so stingy with the cowboy bread.

But the powers that be at Fridley High School did none of these things. On the day after the distribution, Dictator Stanton summoned the boys to his office and told them that *Tour de Farce* violated school policy. "You can't distribute this, or anything else, unless you get permission first."

"And if we do?" the boys asked.

"Then you'll be punished." And the principal dismissed them.

Having gotten the kibosh on their underground newspaper, the boys gave up hope on any further editions until, several months later, the Honor Society hosted a speaker—attorney Matthew Stark, the head of the Minnesota Civil Liberties Union. Inspired by his rah-rah talk of constitutional rights and liberties, the boys collared him after the speech. "Can you help us?" they asked.

"Send me a letter," Matt Stark said. "Before we can help anyone, we need a letter formally asking for assistance."

The boys sent a letter in short order, and Stark set up an appointment. Late in the day, after school and after most businesses had closed, the boys and their parents ventured into a quiet and empty downtown Minneapolis to the Minnesota Civil Liberties Union headquarters.

The MCLU may be long on fervor, but like all non-profits, it is perpetually short of funds. Its "headquarters," such as they were, had no signs. If the boys and their parents hadn't had the address, they never would have found it. "I guess that's it," said one of the parents, pointing to a nondescript door with only a street number. The late hour allowed easy street parking. They knocked timidly, opened the door, and crowded into the small office.

Their meeting with Matt Stark was the first of many. At this first meeting, Stark took down their contact information, discussed their case briefly, and looked the parents in the eye to make sure they were committed to their children's cause. He followed up in other meetings, some of them at their homes. After working up the case a bit, Stark prepared his referral forms, checked his MCLU supporter list, and ultimately located a ritzy, white shoe law firm that agreed to take the case for free.

The boys and their parents met with the ritzy firm attorney, Steve Foley, in an upper floor of the IDS Tower, then the tallest building in Minnesota. At fifty-one stories, it dominated the Minneapolis skyline and for many years was seen nationally during the opening credits of *The Mary Tyler Moore Show*.

Twenty years after the fact, John Collins (who, in *Tour de Farce*, went by the pseudonym "Anonymous Bosch") a play on the name of painter Hieronymous Bosch, told me his recollections of the lawsuit. "Looking back on it now," John said, "I don't feel any particular animosity toward Principal Stanton and Vice-Principal Ingvalson. I think they were both decent men, but they viewed us as children who needed to be supervised. When I met with attorney Foley, I was struck by how different it felt to be treated as an adult."

That different feeling came in a discussion about "prurient interests."

"Let me give you some background on First Amendment law," Foley said. John and the other boys tried to focus on his face instead of the sweeping Minneapolis skyline in the conference room windows behind him. "Students don't lose their rights at the school steps. That's a paraphrase of a Supreme Court case. And what that means is that you still have First Amendment rights, even though you're students. The school can ban some speech, like if you were to advocate illegality, or libel people, or be obscene."

"What about all these cuss words?" someone asked. "Does that count as 'obscene'?" It was a good question; *Tour de Farce* hadn't pulled punches on the cuss words.

"It takes more than cussing to make something 'obscene,'" Foley explained. "Obscenity means that it only appeals to the prurient interest." Foley noted the confused look on his clients' faces. "A prurient interest means that it's purely sexual and nothing else. Basically, a publication has prurient appeal if it were something that you could masturbate to." Foley looked down at his copy of *Tour de Farce*. "Nobody's going to be masturbating to this."

John and the others appreciated attorney Foley's candor; the staff at Fridley High had never talked to them frankly and without condescension.

16. Legal Backstory: Bystrom

The lawyers drafted the lawsuit papers. Jeremy Saperstein and John Collins, being over the age of eighteen, could sue on their own behalf. The others—Cory Bystrom and Adam Collins—needed, and received, parental permission. The lawsuit named the principal, the superintendent, and the school district as defendants. The lawyers encouraged the boys to sue for money as well as a change in the Fridley school system's "Distribution of Literature" policy.

"Absolutely not," said Cory Bystrom's parents. "This isn't about money, and we're not asking for that." The other boys and their parents nodded agreement.

"Are you sure?" said Matt Stark. "I like to punish people by taking away their money."

They were sure. It was a matter of principle; they only wanted a change in the policy. Stark acquiesced.

The lawsuit papers—called the complaint—clearly identified the part of the policy being challenged: "Any written material distributed to students must be approved by the principal or assistant principal.... It must provide educational or informative material which is in the best interests of Fridley students.... It must pertain to the Fridley Schools.... It cannot provide information which would advocate a disruption."

The school policy also said violations would "subject [the student] to immediate suspension." The complaint attached a copy of *Tour de Farce*, and thus that publication is now a part of the nation's timeless and official court archives.

The wheels of justice began their slow grind. Lawyers prepared briefs and filed them with the court. After several months, the lawyers argued their case to the local Minnesota federal judge. Sitting in the courtroom beneath its twenty-foot ceilings, the boys had envisioned impassioned speeches about the value of the First Amendment. But the lawyers' arguments were not nearly that exciting; they were calm colloquies using legal terms of art like "prior restraint," "in loco parentis," and "likelihood of material disruption." The judge ruled against the school. Fridley High School's policy, he said, "is an unconstitutional infringement on the First Amendment."

The boys celebrated and issued another edition of *Tour de Farce*.

Here, again, the school had options. It could have accepted the judge's ruling and waited for the boys to graduate, thus ridding itself of *Tour de*

Harry Potter and the Cedarville Censors

Farce. Or it could have dropped its requirement that student literature receive prior permission.

But the school chose to spend money—ostensibly allocated for the purpose of educating children—to pay lawyers to put the case on appeal. Armed with the permission received from a four-to-one school board vote, the school took the case to the Eighth Circuit in St. Louis. There, hoped the school, wise judges would see how critical it is for public school administrators to be able to control the content of underground student newspapers. These four students, most of them at an age where they could be legally sent to war to die, simply could not be permitted to write their thoughts and distribute them, uncensored, to friends at school.

And the wise judges of the Eighth Circuit agreed. In the case of *Bystrom v. Fridley High School*, 822 F.2d 747 (8th Cir. 1987), the Eighth Circuit Court of Appeals reversed the Minnesota judge who ruled in the boys' favor.

Fridley High School had won.

* * *

The *Bystrom* decision, as it gave its reasons for allowing the censorship of *Tour de Farce*, listed the types of speech that a school could legitimately censor:

- obscene to minors (this is the "prurient interest");
- libel (telling malicious lies about people);
- pervasively indecent or vulgar (lots and lots and lots of swear words, disgusting images, and so forth);
- advertising of products or services not permitted to minors by law (for example, alcohol and tobacco advertising); and
- material that causes material and substantial disruption of school activities (and this has to be actual disruption, not just a fear of possible disruption).

The final words of the *Bystrom* opinion were so unusual, that I think they were meant as an apology by the Eighth Circuit—an apology that certainly should have been made, given the unfortunate result for the *Tour de Farce* authors: "Finally, we are certainly not holding that guidelines of the type we have upheld in this opinion are wise or advisable policy.... Our holding is only that ... [Fridley's] policy will not, on its face, violate the Federal Constitution."

After studying the *Bystrom* opinion, I got hopeful. True, the *Bystrom*

16. Legal Backstory: Bystrom

opinion was a victory for school censors. Students wanting to distribute underground newspapers could not do so without first getting their principal's permission.

But the language the Eighth Circuit used, ironically, helped students. *Bystrom* relied on, and cited, the Supreme Court's plurality opinion in *Pico*. As you recall, the *Pico* plurality would be exactly in Dakota's favor in Cedarville's Harry Potter situation. The problem was that I couldn't rely on the *Pico* plurality alone because only three justices had voted that way. But the Eighth Circuit, in its convoluted *Bystrom* reasoning, cited the *Pico* plurality with approval, and that made the *Pico* plurality good law in the Eighth Circuit, which included Arkansas.

I also took heart at the *Bystrom* opinion's list of things that can be censored. A fair read of *Bystrom* was that only things on the list—things that were obscene, libelous, vulgar, illegal, or disruptive—could be censored by the schools. And in their depositions, the Cedarville school board members had admitted that the Harry Potter books were not obscene, libelous, vulgar, illegal, or disruptive.

17. Summary Judgment

"Strike first, strike hard, no mercy."
—Motto of the Cobra Kai, The Karate Kid

The Cedarville case was a prime candidate for summary judgment. The depositions gave me what I needed to show that the school board members' motivations were, under *Pico*, unconstitutional. And I could show that the Harry Potter books didn't fall into any of the "censor-able" categories under the *Bystrom* case standards.

All I had to do was write this in a brief.

But it is impossible to write briefs during a normal lawyer workday—phone calls and interruptions stop any possible progress. So I came in on a weekend, starting on a Saturday morning, and ultimately spent twenty hours writing the brief, finishing on Sunday afternoon.

The brief began with a discussion of the free speech rights, such as they are, of high school students. "Students," I wrote, quoting the United States Supreme Court in *Tinker*, "do not shed their constitutional rights at the schoolhouse gate." Then I cited to *Bystrom* and said, "When speech to, from, and among children is restricted, the burden is on the school administrators to justify their actions."

Next, I addressed the issue of a "ban" versus a "restriction." I knew that Cedarville was going to make the argument, so I headed it off at the pass. School officials, I wrote, "may argue that their actions do not rise to the level of a First Amendment violation because they did not actually ban the books, but simply required parental permission to access the books. But this argument fails." And then I relied on *Sund v. City of Wichita Falls, Texas*—the case where the city council ordered the library to move the book *Heather Has Two Mommies* from the children's section to the adult section so kids couldn't find it. *Sund*'s facts were very close to my facts,

17. Summary Judgment

and so I read the cases relied upon by the *Sund* judge and quoted them back to Judge Hendren. I gave full credit to the *Sund* decision and my reliance on it—in a footnote I wrote, "Many of the legal arguments used in this brief have been all but plagiarized from ... *Sund v. City of Wichita Falls, Texas.*"

My brief discussed the *Bystrom* factors. I listed the "censor-able" types of speech—obscenity, libel, pervasive vulgarity, promoting illegal activity, and disruption—and walked the court through each of them.

Obscenity. In their depositions, the board members admitted that there was nothing sexually inappropriate about the Harry Potter books.

Libel. I had fun with this one. "There is no allegation by the anti-Potter board members that Harry Potter books are libelous. Indeed, Pastor Hodges claimed that Harry Potter books 'are not fiction.'"

Pervasive vulgarity. The only thing that the board members had complained about in their deposition that could possibly be considered vulgar was the drinking of unicorn blood. I argued that such a scene was not "vulgar," but even if it was, it was not pervasive vulgarity, merely an isolated incident.

Promoting illegal activity. This category mainly had to do with advertisements encouraging minors to drink and smoke. It was, obviously, not an issue in the Harry Potter books. At no point in the *Sorcerer's Stone* or any other of the Harry Potter books did Harry try to get Hermione drunk or persuade Ron to go to the back alley and smoke.

That left the "disruption" category. And on "disruption," the board members had made some complaints. They believed that Harry Potter books would lead children to not just mischief and disruption, but damnation and evil too. Nevertheless, the board members' fears were future and speculative—not present and concrete. "In order for the disruption exception to apply, the danger must be 'clear and present,'" I wrote. "Lawlessness must be imminent."

To support this contention, I cited several cases, such as *Bystrom*, that had said exactly that. I also cited myself as an authority. While in law school, I had written a paper on the topic of the "clear and present" disruption exception. I entered my paper in a national essay contest; it won first prize and was published in a magazine for judges called *Court Review*. It's a little over the top for a lawyer to cite to his own articles as a legal authority but, I figured, when else would I have that opportunity?

Harry Potter and the Cedarville Censors

I also invited Judge Hendren to read the books for himself. "All four Harry Potter books," I wrote in a footnote, "are included with this Motion for Summary Judgment. The Court can read them and decide for itself if the books are inappropriate for children. Plaintiffs also note that reading Harry Potter books is far more entertaining than reading legal briefs."

In closing, I wrote: "School boards may have control over the curriculum, but their power wanes in the school library. Libraries—even school libraries—aren't about a single viewpoint or message; they are about exploring different viewpoints and different messages. School libraries are, in the words of the *Pico* plurality, 'the principal locus of such freedom.' Indeed, how can we reasonably expect Cedarville schoolchildren to become critical thinkers able to defend their own ideas of right and wrong if they cannot, in their own school library, be exposed to ideas different than the ones promoted by their parents and teachers?"

* * *

Dan Mach, the East Coast lawyer who represented the American Library Association, was at work too. He began collecting "amici." Amici is a Latin word and is a shortened version of the phrase "amici curiae" or "friends of the court." Friends of the court are people who are not in the case—and likely could not be in the case, even if they wanted, because they would have no "standing"—yet want the judge to hear what they have to say. For example, suppose that there was an employment case between a worker and her boss, and their dispute involved some novel and unsettled legal issue. The court's resolution of that novel and unsettled legal issue would not only decide that one case—it would affect the resolution of other cases having that same issue. In this example, because the court's ruling would affect lots of employers and lots of employees, amici would pay it special attention. Front groups for corporate America, like the U.S. Chamber of Commerce, would file a brief favorable to employers; similarly, front groups for trial lawyers, like the National Employment Lawyers Association, would file a brief favorable to employees.

Almost every case in America is either too uninteresting or too limited in scope to attract the attention of people wanting to join the fray as amici. When amici are in a case, they are usually in U.S. Supreme Court cases, because its rulings set the law for the entire country, not just a particular region.

17. Summary Judgment

But amici are not always at the U.S. Supreme Court—sometimes (but rarely) they're at the lower levels of federal courts—and they made an appearance in the Cedarville case.

Dan Mach had pulled together an impressive amici list: the American Booksellers Foundation for Free Expression; Americans United for Separation of Church and State; Association of American Publishers; Association of Booksellers for Children; Judy Blume; Center for First Amendment Rights; Children's Book Council; Feminists for Free Expression; Freedom to Read Foundation; National Coalition Against Censorship; Peacefire; PEN American Center; People for the American Way; Student Law Press Center; and Washington Area Lawyers for the Arts.

I was most excited by the appearance of children's author Judy Blume. Anyone who ever read anything as a child is familiar with Judy Blume. Some of her more famous books are *Blubber*, *Summer Sisters*, and *Are You There God? It's Me, Margaret*.

Judy Blume is no stranger to censorship. Her books are regularly targeted. According to the American Library Association, she is one of the most challenged authors in the United States.

Judy Blume fully expected the rash of Harry Potter challenges. As she explained to the *New York Times*, "I knew this was coming.... If children are excited about a book, it must be suspect.... In my books, it's reality that's seen as corrupting. With Harry Potter the perceived danger is fantasy."

Blume's books have been challenged for decades, and time has taught her lessons about dealing with censorship: it must be confronted. "The real danger is not in the books, but in laughing off those who would ban them. The protests against Harry Potter follow a tradition that has been growing since the early 1980s and often leaves school principals trembling with fear that is then passed down to teachers and librarians."

Blume's analysis is spot-on. At least some of the Harry Potter challenges were successful for no other reason than the moral cowardice of institutions facing a vocal minority.

Dan Mach's amici brief listed the amici, gave a brief description of each, and then presented its own legal argument. In addition to attacking the board members' motivations, the amici brief made clear the distinction between a school board's control of curriculum and its control over the library. I had touched on that in my motion, but not as thoroughly as the amici had. The amici also focused on the library committee and its procedure. The amici argued that the library committee's vote in favor of the books should have ended the matter, and the school board had no authority to override it. I had chosen not to make that argument in my motion, but I appreciated Dan backing me up by including it in the amici brief.

* * *

I included the first four Harry Potter books as exhibits to my summary judgment motion, placing "exhibit" stickers on the front of each. They are now part of the official court record and are being stored in a federal archival facility in Dallas, Texas.

Dan Mach and I coordinated our filings—he filed the amici brief the same day as my summary judgment motion. The local paper ran a story; it, like me, was excited to have Ms. Blume make an appearance in our fair town, albeit in a legal brief and via lawyers.

* * *

The school district responded with its own motion—it asked Judge Hendren to throw out the case due to a lack of standing. The motion did not surprise me; I'd been expecting that argument.

"The Plaintiffs are not injured," argued David Hogue. "In her deposition, Miss Counts testified that she owns the first three of the four books of the series. Miss Counts is thus not injured ... she has unfettered access to the 'information.'" David also pointed out that Dakota already had a permission slip from her parents, and thus her claim was moot. How could she complain about the "burden" of accessing the books when she already had overcome the burden? David bolstered his argument with the legal definition of standing. To have standing, Miss Counts would have to have "personally suffered some actual or threatened injury as the result of the challenged conduct." There were many federal cases that had used that definition of standing, but David, wisely, cited to a federal case from Judge Hendren's own court.

David also leveled a shot at Bill Counts. "His only injury is that he felt ignored," and David then cited a Supreme Court case that had held that merely feeling ignored was not enough to convey "standing."

* * *

17. Summary Judgment

"It's awfully short," said Dan Mach after getting a copy of the school district's motion. Dan started laughing. "I can't believe how short it is."

I can understand why Dan—who is an excellent lawyer—was surprised. It was because of his peer group at that time. There is this notion among East Coast lawyers that a brief's length is proportional to its merit. Big firms regard page limits as page goals. Little or no effort is made among the big corporate firms to skinny their briefs.

But the more I practice law, the more I've come to believe in short briefs. I wish I was better at practicing what I'm preaching here, as I've written quite a few long briefs in my time. Nevertheless, short briefs are the goal, and whatever I was going to criticize David Hogue for, it wasn't going to be for being succinct.

✳ ✳ ✳

Both sides had briefed the case; to mix a metaphor and pun, the ball was in Judge Hendren's court now. He would either grant my motion, grant David's motion, or deny both and make us go to a trial. We waited.

18. Carrot and Stick

"Censorship, like charity, should begin at home, but unlike charity, it should end there."—Clare Boothe Luce

I anxiously waited for Judge Hendren to rule on the pending motions. Would he grant my motion and rule against the school district? Would he grant the school district's motion and rule against me? Or would he deny all the motions and make everybody go to trial?

A month after the motions were submitted to the judge, I got my answer.

* * *

"Mr. Meadors, you have a fax coming in. It's long." The receptionist had buzzed me.

At that time, our faxes still came across in paper—we'd not yet upgraded to the computerized faxes—and court decisions usually came via fax. I went to the front and started pulling each page as it came out of the machine. I read the decision at the same speed our antiquated machine could print it.

Judge Hendren began, as he usually did, by keeping the lawyers in suspense. His ruling, entitled "Memorandum Opinion," didn't tell me the result right away.

He started out his opinion by addressing the standing issue, "given that it touches on the jurisdiction of the Court to resolve the substantive issues in this case." Standing, as you may recall, is the legal term for "must have a dog in the fight." This case could only be filed by a student who was actually affected by the policy. Dakota Counts and her parents were the only ones who had stepped up to the plate.

It made sense for Judge Hendren to address the standing issue first.

18. Carrot and Stick

With no standing, there's no case, and nothing else the court said would matter.

Judge Hendren agreed with the school district's arguments and found that Bill Counts had no standing. But he reached a different conclusion with Dakota, who had to have parental permission to get the books. "The Court," wrote Judge Hendren, "is persuaded that Dakota Counts has alleged sufficient injury to give her standing." That injury, "albeit relatively small," was, said the judge, enough.

Judge Hendren made an interesting observation about the fact that Dakota had parental permission to access the books, yet could still have standing to complain about that requirement: "other forms of First Amendment burden pled in the Complaint—that browsers will not find the book on the shelves and those unaware of its existence would not know to ask for permission to check it out—while not applicable to Dakota, demonstrate the importance of allowing standing for even a minimal invasion of First Amendment rights. Those children whose parents do not want them to check out the Harry Potter books could hardly be expected to protect their own First Amendment rights, since they would almost certainly be minors who could not sue in their own right and it is unlikely that their parents would go to court to establish their child's legal right to do that which they did not want the child to be able to do in the first place."

The judge, in discussing standing, also agreed that just because Dakota could access the books at home did not mean that she lacked standing—"access in one forum is not a constitutional substitute for access in another."

Having established Dakota's standing, Judge Hendren then talked about the merits of the case. The opinion went into the facts in more detail and spent several pages reciting them. He then cited *Sund v. City of Wichita Falls*. A good sign, I thought.

Judge Hendren found the *Sund* case persuasive and agreed that the restriction was unconstitutional. "Having concluded that a burden on Dakota's right of access exists, the Court must consider whether the restrictions are justified by some exigency of the educational environment in the Cedarville School District." Judge Hendren considered the deposition testimony of the three school board members, particularly what they said about why they voted to restrict Harry Potter. He found their motivations to be religiously based, and therefore unconstitutional.

Harry Potter and the Cedarville Censors

And then I saw Judge Hendren's footnote that confirmed that I was right to have deposed all three of those school board members at the same time: "The school district attempts to distance itself from this testimony by describing it as 'their individual testimony of their individual viewpoints, rather than the purpose of the Board as a whole in passing the restriction.' This effort must fail, inasmuch as these three Board members comprised the entire voting majority which imposed the policy."

Judge Hendren also rejected the school's "disruption" argument: "There is no evidence that any of the Board members were aware of any actual disobedience or disrespect that had flowed from a reading of the Harry Potter books. Their concerns are, therefore, speculative. Such speculative apprehensions of possible disturbance are not sufficient to justify the extreme sanction of restricting the free exercise of First Amendment rights in a public school library."

The opinion closed with stirring language about how important it was for children to learn about the Bill of Rights—and that the center for that learning, our schools—ought not violate those rights.

Judge Hendren ordered the school district to put the Harry Potter books back on the shelves, and he gave me fourteen days to file my request for attorneys fees.

It was a complete victory, and I savored it for a few minutes before I called Bill Counts with the good news.

* * *

My elation was short-lived. The school district was making noises about appealing. Nothing official, but small towns being small towns, the thoughts of the board members get communicated to their friends, who tell their friends, and so forth. The triple hearsay reported to me was a promised appeal.

And I believed it. I fully believed that the district would put the case on appeal.

Now, I felt comfortable that this case was a winner on appeal. Even with my concerns about the Eighth Circuit's hostility towards civil rights cases, I knew I could hold this case up on appeal—I felt very strongly about that.

But the problem was my clients.

18. Carrot and Stick

When the Countses first bought their house, they thought—and had been told—that it was in the Van Buren school district. But there had been some confusion as to where the exact dividing line was. The Countses later learned that their house is very close to the line, but is still, just barely, within the Cedarville school district.

The Countses were unhappy with that situation. Van Buren's schools had nearly six times as many students as Cedarville's did; Van Buren offered far more extracurricular activities and advanced classes than Cedarville.

This difference did not amount to much for elementary school students like Dakota. But it wouldn't be long before Dakota would be in junior high and high school—when students first start going into advanced classes and having extracurricular activities—and Mary and Bill Counts were simply not the kind of parents to tolerate their children having too few educational opportunities.

Unlike most Cedarville residents, the Countses had not grown up there and did not feel tied to the community. And the whole Harry Potter banning incident didn't help the Countses' view of Cedarville either.

Arkansas law allowed parents to move their children from one district to another under certain conditions, and the Countses researched this. A few weeks before Judge Hendren issued his decision, the Countses had arranged for Dakota to change schools from Cedarville to Van Buren. They submitted their application, and, as required by state law, the application was voted on and approved at a Cedarville School Board meeting. Come August, Dakota would start attending nearby Van Buren schools, not the Cedarville schools.

If Dakota's transfer had happened while the case was still pending before Judge Hendren, that would have been a problem due to "standing." Dakota not attending Cedarville schools would have meant that Dakota was unaffected by Cedarville school policy.

Judge Hendren's decision was issued in July, and Dakota did not officially transfer until August, so we were safe—if there were no appeal. But if there were an appeal, there was a problem. Appeals take a very long time, often a full year.

With Cedarville's school board grousing about a possible appeal of Judge Hendren's decision, it had come full circle. I was back to the standing problem. The case would go up to the Eighth Circuit; Dakota would be at a different school; and I would have a client with no standing. No standing meant no case and a victory for Cedarville.

On the other hand, I thought, surely the courts wouldn't shoot a case out from underneath me based on a standing issue—especially after I'd won it at the district court level. But I wasn't sure, and so I hit the books.

The go-to resource on these kinds of procedural questions was a set of brown and gold law books written by Wright & Miller. Miller used to teach at Harvard Law School. My ex-wife's law school roommate had him for her civil procedure class. She said Professor Miller was good but the students made the class insufferable. In Miller's class, all students seemed to be "gunners," meaning that they preened for Miller's attention. A mediocre gunner listens carefully in law school class, waits for opportunities to say something that appears to be smart or insightful, and then blurts out the allegedly smart comment. A really good gunner prepares those comments in advance of the class and also throws in a pondering question or two.

Wright & Miller had a section on standing, and there I confirmed my worst fears. Sure enough, if a case is won at the district court level, is put on appeal, and then there is suddenly no standing, the whole case evaporates, even the favorable district court decision.

This meant that if there were an appeal, once the Countses changed schools, the whole case was lost.

I considered my options.

Option One: don't tell anybody. But there were two problems with that. First, under the legal ethics rules, I had a duty of honesty to the court. Continuing with a case in which I knew my client had no standing would break those rules. The other problem was that the other side would find out, surely. At some point, somebody over there would realize that the little girl suing them did not even go to that school. Or, at least, they would eventually tell their lawyer that, and he would recognize the significance. In fact, I marveled that I had not heard anything about this from David Hogue. Apparently, nobody on the Cedarville School Board had told their lawyer about the Countses transferring; if they had, I'm sure David would have advised them to go forward with an appeal.

Option Two: if and when the whole standing thing came up, I could argue that it did not apply to this case. There is, like most rules in the law, an exception to the standing rule. In fact, it came into play in the famous

18. Carrot and Stick

abortion case *Roe v. Wade*. The lead plaintiff in that case, Roe, as she was called, was pregnant and wanted an abortion. The Sate of Texas would not allow it. So she sued. Eventually, Roe got all the way to U.S. Supreme Court, but by the time she got there, her pregnancy was long over. The State of Texas argued that Roe's case was moot (no standing)—the anti-abortion laws did not affect her at that time as she was not pregnant.

Normally, that would be a winning argument. But the Supreme Court found an exception—cases that are "capable of repetition, yet evading review." Pregnancy, said the Supreme Court, was exactly that kind of situation, and Roe's case could stand.

I wondered. Could I make the same analogy to the Cedarville case? Maybe Dakota was out of the school, but there were other children there who would want to access the book.

It was a thought. Again I turned to Wright & Miller and read the different cases that they cited. As I read, I became pessimistic. Very few situations got the exception to the standing rule. Once Dakota transferred schools, I wasn't going to win a fight on "standing."

All this weighed heavily on me. We'd gotten the decision. We'd gotten a CNN write-up and other national press. My fee petition was pending and would be granted—the only variable there was the amount. I thought about what it would feel like to have the case mooted while it languished on appeal for the nine months appeals typically take.

I had no good options. I briefly considered a third option—trying to contact J.K. Rowling herself. Maybe she would substitute in as a party. She would have standing since her books were being censored. But that solution seemed so unlikely, I didn't even try. I doubted I would be able to penetrate the wall of agents and lawyers around her. And even if I was able, the ethics rules against cold-calling potential clients were an additional barrier. So I abandoned the J.K. Rowling idea.

My consternation must have shown, because at lunch the next day, some lawyer friends of mine asked what was troubling me, which is unusual, because lawyers are a rather self-absorbed bunch, myself included, so to draw comment from other lawyers is rare.

We were at the Cottage Café, a diner in downtown Van Buren. Van Buren's downtown is quaint and still has its turn-of-the-century buildings—zero lot line structures, all two stories tall, no more, no less. Many of them are antique stores that, somehow, scrape by each year with a sale here, a sale there. Others are nifty craft shops with quilts, wooden apples, and other country-cutesy things.

The Cottage Café was something of an anomaly in that mix, as it was neither scraping by nor country-cutesy. It was a classic meat-and-three-sides lunch place.

That's prevalent in Arkansas—the meat-and-three-sides lunch. Pick a meat—meatloaf, fried chicken, chicken fried steak, plain hamburger patty—and then three sides, typically green beans, pinto beans, okra, black-eyed peas, mashed potatoes, et cetera. I love these kinds of places and missed them terribly when living up North or on the East Coast. In fact, I can quantify that love. I gained thirty pounds when I moved back to Arkansas.

My law partners and I arrived at the café at about noon, opened the wooden door with its little bell, and walked directly to a table. Customers self-seat at the café; there's no teenage girl playing hostess like the franchises. Some other Fort Smith lawyers happened to come in behind us, and since we liked them well enough, we waved them to our table to join us for lunch. They began asking me about the case.

I explained the standing issue to them. One declared that he had no idea what to do and could offer no help; the other opined that my situation was fine, no standing issue existed. But when I quizzed him further about his thoughts, it became plain to me that he really did not understand the issue and had not researched it. Dangerous opinions, those.

It's actually a danger that befalls many lawyers who have practiced for a long time. Lawyers come to believe that they have a sense, when faced with an unanswered legal question, of what the law is. In other words, they believe that they know the answer without looking it up.

Now, to be clear, I'm not saying that all legal questions must be looked up. Certainly not. The bar exam tests basic (and not so basic) questions, so the garden variety contracts question or real estate conundrum should be readily answered by any active attorney.

But for thornier and less obvious issues, such as Supreme Court jurisprudence on standing and the possible exceptions to that rule, a lawyer—any lawyer—needs to go look up the answer instead of intuiting it. I had done that; some of my local brethren at the bar had not. They meant well, but their opinions didn't help me.

My partners had enough sense not to offer uninformed opinions; they

18. Carrot and Stick

just listened sympathetically. Tom Robertson had more practical concerns.

"Just how much of your time and my money have you advanced on this case?"

"A hundred hours and $2,000."

"$2,000?"

"Mostly depositions." Then, defensively, "That's not that much. And my expert was free. I didn't have to pay her."

"Well," drawled Tom, "tell me the clients are paying the costs."

"Tom, we talked about this. You know they're not. It's full contingency, costs included. I'm lucky to even have a client."

Tom grabbed a roll and scooped up gravy remnants. "I understand. Just try to get the costs, at least. I'd hate to lose that money, especially on a case that we've already won."

※ ※ ※

I called Dan Mach. Maybe he'd have ideas.

"Cut your fees."

"Excuse me?"

"Cut your fees," Dan said. "It's the only way."

Dan explained. "You're right about the standing issue. If the case goes up on appeal, you will not have standing. That will be discovered—either you'll have to disclose it to the court, or they will tell the court, which just looks worse for you. And the court of appeals will dismiss on standing, no matter how unfair that may seem."

"So how does the fee issue figure in?"

"Cedarville doesn't know yet about the standing?"

"Apparently not. I know that the Countses' paperwork to transfer has been filed with the school, but I don't think the school has connected the dots or told their lawyer."

"Then you have to give the school board an incentive to not appeal. The only carrot you can give them is to cut your fee request."

"Do you think that will work?"

"Yes, I do. We had a similar problem come up in another case we did, and that's how we solved it. Ought to work here."

Dan was right that we needed to get the case resolved—and quickly. The only carrot I had, in dealing with the school district, was reducing my fees. The stick? The district would, if it appealed, have to pay its own lawyer and, if it were to lose the appeal, pay my appeal fees too.

I decided to approach the school district with both the carrot and the stick. Obviously, my desperate situation—that my case would evaporate because of a lack of standing—could not be revealed to the other side.

I had to act quickly. No settlement could happen without the school board's approval, and the monthly school board meeting was coming up. In fact, it was to take place that night, so I immediately composed a letter to be faxed to the board's lawyer.

> Dear David:
> This is a settlement offer, and I would appreciate it very much if you communicated this to your client prior to tonight's meeting.

Under the legal ethic rules, lawyers can only talk to the other side's lawyers—they cannot talk directly to the other side itself, so I had to go through David Hogue.

I continued, in my letter, by producing "the stick": "Enclosed please find my Petition for Attorney's Fees, which was filed with the Court this same day...."

I then went on to discuss the numbers, telling David why I predicted a $20,000 to $23,000 fee award. In truth, that prediction was puffery. Local lawyers knew Judge Hendren was not overly generous to prevailing civil rights attorneys; I seriously doubt that he would have awarded me fees of that amount. But I didn't think that David Hogue, being from out of town, would know that.

My "stick" continued: "I think we can all agree that if this case were to go on appeal, and your clients were to lose, these numbers would increase by at least $10,000, not to mention your own fees. I think that we can also agree that given the current state of the law and the precedent that is binding on the Eighth Circuit, that the odds of the Eighth Circuit reversing this case are virtually non-existent. No federal appeals court is going to allow a ban of Harry Potter books."

Having shown the stick, I began my introduction of the carrot. But first I wanted to pull at some heartstrings and try to take the moral high ground when it came to "the children": "I think it would be a terrible shame for the Cedarville School District's treasury to be spent on lawyers rather than children. For their sake, I am asking that we put an end to this. Your client and my clients had a disagreement; we took it to court; a federal

18. Carrot and Stick

judge heard the dispute; he made a decision. Let's live by that decision and move on. Cedarville has bigger fish to fry.... It needs to manage the taxpayers' money in a way that ultimately benefits children."

No doubt that some of you readers, particularly the cynical ones, are asking yourselves, "If you were so concerned about the taxpayers' money being spent on children rather than lawyers, then why did you demand any fee at all? If you really cared, you would have waived your fee and not asked the school district to pay it."

And I suppose that if school districts were my charity of choice and that if I'd had neither a mortgage nor student loans to pay, then sure, I'd've waived my fee. But poorly-managed school districts are not my first charity of choice and, frankly, I was unwilling to give away $2,000 of my partners' money and one hundred hours of my time.

I closed with the offer: "If your client agrees not to appeal Judge Hendren's decision, then I would be willing to enter into a consent order setting the total fee and cost award at $13,750. Please ask your clients to consider this. This offer is open until 5:00 p.m. on Friday."

In sum, I was saying that the fee award could be as high as $23,000, but if you stop this silliness, you'll only pay $13,750.

Seemed fair enough to me, especially when compared to the alternative.

But would the board accept it? Did it realize that it had the upper hand on the standing issue?

I faxed the letter and waited.

19. The Fruit of the Litigation Tree

"Resist the devil, and he will flee from you."
—*The Bible*, James 4:7

David Hogue received my fax and called Superintendent Smith. Throughout the case, Superintendent Smith had been his primary contact. Although David's first meeting had been with the school board as a whole, that was the only time David had met with the full board at the same time. Under Arkansas' laws, those meetings had to be public. But at that time, those laws could be skirted by contacting board members an a one-on-one basis; David took advantage of this. He primarily discussed the case with Superintendent Smith, who would then discuss it individually with the board members.

David was unaware that the Countses were transferring out of the district. Convinced that the Eighth Circuit would uphold the opinion, David recommended that the board accept my offer. That advice was not well received, but like all good lawyers, in discussing the prospect of settlement, David distinguished between idealistic notions and the realities of litigation.

* * *

The morning after the school board meeting, I went straight from my bed to get the newspaper. Standing in my robe, I opened and flipped through the paper, right there on the driveway.

I breathed with relief. The board had formally approved the offer. I reread the article several times at the kitchen table. When I got to the office, I faxed David Hogue a letter:

19. The Fruit of the Litigation Tree

Dear David:
  It is my understanding that my offer of yesterday has been accepted—namely, your client has agreed to pay me $13,750 in attorney's fees and has also agreed not to appeal Judge Hendren's April 22, 2003, Order. If this letter accurately reflects our agreement, please sign below and fax this back to me.

He agreed, and I got the fax back on the same day. The case was over. The school put the books back on the shelves and also allowed them to be part of the Accelerated Reader program. The school, had it wanted to, could have kept the books off of the Accelerated Reader list—we had not sued on that point since the Accelerated Reader list was a curriculum issue rather than a library issue—but the school didn't pick that fight. My hopes that the Accelerated Reader list would get a free ride from the coattails of the library litigation had been realized.

* * *

About a week later, I got the $13,750 check from the school district. It had a picture of the school mascot, a pirate, in the upper left hand corner. I wondered how many books could have been bought with that money. Then I deposited the check.

* * *

A few months after the verdict, the school board tossed around the idea of book selection versus book restriction. In other words, prevention rather than a cure. Had the Cedarville School District never purchased the Harry Potter books in the first place, David Hogue had advised them, none of this would have happened.

And David was right. The *Pico*, *Sund*, and *Cedarville* cases established that government entities cannot, constitutionally, remove books from their libraries. But those cases say nothing about schools' failure to purchase certain books for their libraries. At best, the law on this topic is unsettled, although truth be told, when it comes to book acquisitions, the censors have the upper hand. Given the wide latitude that courts give school boards, a failure-to-purchase claim would probably result in a school board victory. Clever school lawyers would analogize a purchasing decision to a curriculum decision; courts would likely agree.

Nevertheless, I'm curious to see how that legal question develops. Like most legal pronouncements in American jurisprudence, it will be built slowly, over the years, and case by case.

Harry Potter and the Cedarville Censors

* * *

After Judge Hendren's order came out, the Associated Press picked up the story. The AP sent a photographer to take my picture. The photographer injected some drama into the shot. She had me holding a Harry Potter book with the Cedarville High School in the background. I had driven to the Cedarville schools to meet her for the picture. I'll admit that I was a little nervous showing up at the school for a photo op, especially when, at that time, the case was not yet fully resolved—the threat of appeal had still been looming. Nobody came out of the school, though, and we got the photos taken in about ten minutes.

The *Dallas Morning News* also ran a story. Rather than copy the AP story, the *Dallas Morning News* relied on a freelance writer, Suzi Parker. She did more in-depth interviews and reviewed quite a few of the court documents. Ms. Parker was one of the more interesting journalists I ran across. She'd published a book, *Sex in the South*, a titillating expose of Southern sexual mores, including the wild success (and simultaneous illegality) of "passion parties." A "passion party" is a Tupperware party, except instead of having lock-top plastic boxes, you have vibrators, massage oils, and other items that I cannot mention lest this book become rated R. It's just a matter of time before some library removes Ms. Parker's book, and when it does, maybe she'll call me.

CNN also picked up the story. It made the ticker at the bottom of the screen. On cnn.com, Judge Hendren's order was the lead story in the "Education" section for about six hours one day. My picture in front of Cedarville High School accompanied the article. Those literal six hours were my figurative fifteen minutes of fame.

Apparently—and I did not know this prior to having this case—there is a company in Florida that scans the news looking for non-famous people. For lack of a nicer term, I'll call those non-famous people "nobodies." The company (properly) identified me as a "nobody," and sent me a brochure. "Capture the moment," it said, or some words to that effect. It offered to take the cnn.com article, purchase the rights to reprint it, and then reprint it, in full color, all nice and pretty, on a plaque. Only $155.

Really, is there any better sales tactic than appealing to the customer's ego? It sure worked on me. I ordered one right away, and it is still on my wall. I love it.

The case also made a splash on Google. For many years, typing my

19. The Fruit of the Litigation Tree

name popped up screen after screen of Harry Potter references, mostly repeats of the AP story. One of the hits was to some right-wing Christian site that casts the suit in a negative light, and there were also hits on various Harry Potter blogs.

After the case was over, I sent Judge Hendren a letter asking him to publish his opinion in the official court reporter, so that other lawyers could cite it as precedent—just as I had cited the *Sund v. Wichita Falls* case. I never got a response to the letter, but ultimately the case was published. It can be found at *Counts v. Cedarville School District*, 295 F.Supp.2d 996 (2003).

A couple of years after the *Counts* decision, another Arkansas school board found itself on the verge of removing some pro-gay books from a school library. The Fayetteville public schools had received a complaint from a parent about three books: *It's So Amazing*, *It's Perfectly Normal*, and *The Teenage Guy's Survival Guide*. The complaining parent found them objectionable because they discussed sexuality and sexual development.

In an effort to appease the complaining parent, the school superintendent moved the books to a special parental permission shelf (sound familiar?). The movement of the books riled other parents, who complained about the censorship.

In the meantime, the original complainer, now emboldened, formed a group of like-minded parents, presented a list of more than fifty objectionable books and demanded they be removed from the school library.

An anti-censorship group formed in opposition, and the Arkansas chapter of the ACLU got involved.

The Fayetteville School Board held a town hall and heard from all sides. At a subsequent school board meeting, the board heard from some librarians, but also its attorney, Rudy Moore.

Prior to that meeting, Moore had called me. He'd heard that I'd litigated a case about books and schools, but didn't know the details and wanted a copy of the opinion. The case had not yet been published, so I faxed him a copy of Judge Hendren's opinion.

At the school board meeting, Moore strongly opposed banning any books or even moving certain books to restricted shelves, telling the board that the *Counts* case was not only on point, but was also right down the road. "When you say that you are going to set the books aside in a restricted place, that's going to be a problem legally ... it is my job to keep us out of litigation." A scholar studying Fayetteville's potential book ban concluded, "In the end it would be Moore's testimony that would appear to have the largest impact on the board's decision. the board voted 4–3 to remove the restrictions...."

* * *

How wonderful it was to learn how *Counts* affected the Fayetteville School Board's decision. Who knew that Bill Counts' principled stand would result in saving Fayetteville from national embarrassment and costly litigation?

And what other affects might that decision have had? I envision a teen who is struggling with the fact that he is homosexual. He'll be looking through the stacks, sad and conflicted, and will run across those pro-gay books—books that tell him that he is okay and that there's nothing wrong with him. He'll find some solace he would not have otherwise found. I hope something like that happens; with those books in school libraries, it's possible. I'm glad to be a part of that.

* * *

Besides keeping local school boards in line, *Counts* had—by virtue of being added to the body of case law—influenced other decisions.

In 2006, a federal court in Florida cited *Counts* when it granted the ACLU's motion to undo the Miami schools' restrictions on books that portrayed Cuba in a favorable light.

In 2012, a federal court in Missouri cited principles annunciated in *Counts* to stop a library from using anti-homosexual internet filtering software.

A few years after the case, Estella Roberts and her husband joined the sea of retirees in Florida. I visited her in Daytona, at a gated subdivision with wide-bladed St. Augustine grass, impeccable landscaping, and stucco houses. I found the subdivision with only one wrong turn. As you may expect, there are several gated retirement communities in Daytona; to the out-of-towners, like me, they were hard to differentiate.

Estella and her husband were quite gracious, inviting me to their house despite the fact that Mr. Roberts had recently been hospitalized. He greeted me pleasantly—far more pleasantly than I would have, had I been recuperating—and Estella offered iced tea, which I accepted. We

19. The Fruit of the Litigation Tree

were in a very large den-kitchen-living room. Two fans hung down from the vaulted ceiling and slowly churned the summer air.

"How long has it been, Estella?"

"A long time." She smiled. And she looked the same. Straight, chin-length gray hair framing a rectangular face with sensible, square, and unimposing glasses. Today her glasses did not have the eyeglass chain that she used to wear.

"Sit here," she said, motioning.

I sat. Estella's kitchen table, small, round and brown, had four chairs—two spots available, two spots not. The not had a pile of magazines, prescription bottles, and a large plastic box. From the box, Estella began pulling out documents, books, and folders, and she set them on the table.

"I saved all the Harry Potter stuff. A girlfriend told me to be sure to save it, but she didn't have to. I would have saved it anyway. I saved all the newspaper articles, the letters, everything." Most of the articles were laminated. Emails had been printed out; phone messages written. "Here is a nice message received from a woman I don't even know." Estella showed me a yellow sticky. "You are very brave," it read. "You are doing the right thing."

"What's this?" I pointed to a videotape.

"I think that's the TV news story. I think. It's been awhile."

After a few minutes of puzzling with her VCR and TV, we got it playing. It was the TV news. The May 2002 school board meeting had been captured and preserved. Estella's presentation to the board received several seconds of air time, as did Pastor Hodges' surly look.

"Do you mind if I punch out this tab?" I asked. I had once, back in my DC law firm, accidentally erased part of a tape that was going to be used in evidence, and ever since then I have been paranoid about punching out the recording tabs on VHS tapes.

"Sure."

I punched the tab.

Estella spent two hours with me that day. We went through the clippings and papers and tape. I collected a pile for copying.

※ ※ ※

"In retrospect, would you do it again?" I posed this question to Angie Haney years after the case; I'd invited her to lunch.

"Absolutely," she said.

"Why?"

"Nothing's changed. The books still have the bad influence as far as the sorcery and all that. They still teach children to be disrespectful and disobedient to teachers. And," Angie smiled, "the lawsuit actually helps my cause. Now everybody's heard my message, not just Cedarville."

A year or two after the Harry Potter debacle, Angie ran for clerk of the circuit court. She had assumed that the voters she met would ask about her role in the Cedarville case, but "it never came up," Angie said. "We figured it would come up. But it didn't."

She lost the election by 913 votes. Four or five thousand had been cast. Not wanting to work for the candidate that had just defeated her, Angie took an office manager job in Fort Smith and, later, became an assistant in the prosecutor's office.

"When my boss found out I was leaving work today to meet with a lawyer," she told me, "he was afraid that I was going to have a job interview and quit on him. I told him that he had nothing to worry about."

We laughed.

* * *

Pastor Hodges did not run for reelection at the end of his school board term. I had visited his church one Sunday night—I just poked my head in the door and looked around a bit—and I saw him running a class in the sanctuary. He didn't see me, and I didn't say hi.

A few years after the case, Pastor Hodges moved to a different church—the Assembly of God in Dierks, Arkansas. Dierks is even more remote than Cedarville; the closest town with more than 50,000 people is more than an hour away. Later, he would find his way closer to Cedarville by moving to a church in nearby Eastern Oklahoma.

* * *

A person meeting Pastor Hodges or Angie Haney would conclude that they are nice people—they are the kind of people who would help pull somebody out of a ditch in a snowstorm or would return a missing wallet, intact, to the owner. On that level I will not fault them, and, in some contexts, we could get along and be friendly.

19. The Fruit of the Litigation Tree

But I will fault them on another level, specifically how they would wield (and have wielded) power when given the opportunity.

I read in a news article that Pastor Hodges objected to being described as the "American Taliban." Yet actions taken by those who identify with the evangelical community are not harmless, nor are their notions merely matters of opinion about the nature of the universe. These people cause palpable harm, and they do so on the basis of demonstrably false ideas.

Evangelicals are getting elected and, imbued with government power, transform their ridiculous ideas into official policy. A Pennsylvania school board mandated teaching creationism over evolution, which is really no different, intellectually, than teaching kids that Earth is flat. In Texas, evangelicals have wormed their way into the bureaucracy that approves textbooks and put their strange notions there. Evangelicals try to prevent teaching teenagers about human sexuality and birth control, in spite of the fact that all evidence shows that depriving teens of this information harms them due to increased STDs and unwanted pregnancies. And in Arkansas—and across the world—evangelicals are banning books even though there is zero evidence that the books cause children any harm whatsoever. Indeed, in the case of Harry Potter, all evidence points to the fact that these books are helpful to children.

I recognize the seeming irony of me criticizing evangelicals for their intolerance and then, simultaneously, being intolerant of evangelicals. But having an open mind does not mean having an empty mind. Government policies should be determined by reason and evidence. This, the evangelicals do not use.

And that struggle continues today—reason and evidence under attack in the political arena. I sometimes wonder if it will ever stop, and I remember the American Civil Liberties Union motto: "Eternal vigilance is the price of liberty."

* * *

At the time of this writing, Dakota is an adult, out of college for several years. She went to the University of Arkansas, got a B.S.B.A with a major in finance, and works as an analyst for a large, publicly traded company.

* * *

Harry Potter and the Cedarville Censors

Even after the verdict, the excitement of the Cedarville case stayed. The Arkansas Library Association asked me to speak at its annual meeting, and I did. I also gave a talk at the Fort Smith Public Library. The good attendance at both flattered me, although I know the topic, not the speaker, was the draw. In Arkansas, for years after the case, people asked me about the case. I never tired of it, preferring to talk about *Harry Potter and the Cedarville Censors* instead of the custody battles or contract disputes that occupied most of my legal time.

And, for years afterwards, before his untimely passing, I would go to Karber's office in the morning. I would sit in front of his desk, drink my coffee, and hear his pithy wisdom. My chair was near his bookshelf, which was cluttered with dusty ACLU plaques, pictures, and some law books.

One of the books was called *The Rights of Students*. It was very thin.

Appendix:
Judge Hendren's Opinion
(*Counts v. Cedarville School District*, 295 F.Supp.2d 996 [2003])

Billy Ray COUNTS, Individually, in his Official Capacity as a library committee member, and Mary Nell Counts, both as parents of Dakota Counts Plaintiffs

v.

CEDARVILLE SCHOOL DISTRICT Defendant

No. CIV.02-2155.

United States District Court, W.D. Arkansas, Ft. Smith Division.

April 22, 2003.

Carey Brian Meadors, Pryor, Robertson & Barry, PLLC, Fort Smith, AR, for plaintiffs.

David R. Hogue, Christian Legal Service, Conway, AR, for defendant.

John L. Burnett, Lavey and Burnett, Little Rock, AR, Theresa A. Chmara, Daniel Mach, Martina E. Vandenberg, Jenner & Block, LLC, Washington, D.C., for amicus.

MEMORANDUM OPINION

HENDREN, District Judge.

Now on this 22 day of April 2003, come on for consideration Plaintiffs' Motion For Summary Judgment (document # 9) and defendant's Motion To Dismiss (document # 13), and from said motions, the supporting documentation, and the responses thereto, the Court finds and orders as follows:

1. Plaintiffs, Billy Ray Counts, Individually, in his official capacity as

Appendix: Judge Hendren's Opinion

a Library committee member, and Mary Nell Counts, both as parents of Dakota Counts (hereinafter called "plaintiffs" or by their individual names, as appropriate) brought suit pursuant to 42 U.S.C. § 1983, alleging that their rights under the First and Fourteenth Amendments to the United States Constitution were being abridged by the decision of the defendant, Cedarville School District, to restrict the access of students, including Dakota Counts, to certain books in defendant's library. (The defendant, Cedarville School District, will hereinafter be referred to either as the "defendant" or the "District.") Plaintiffs prayed for an injunction requiring defendant to return the books to general circulation in its library, and now move for summary judgment.

Defendant denies that any constitutional rights have been violated by its actions and argues affirmatively that the matter should be dismissed because the plaintiffs lack standing to bring their claims.

2. As a preliminary matter, the Court notes that a Brief of Amici Curiae was filed in this matter by numerous groups supporting plaintiffs' motion for summary judgment, to which the defendant has lodged an objection that there is no provision for such a filing. While rare, the Court notes that amicus briefs have been received in cases pending before United States District Courts. *See, e.g., Michigan National Bank v. State of Michigan*, 365 U.S. 467, 81 S.Ct. 659, 5 L.Ed.2d 710 (1961) and *I.C.C. v. Allen E. Kroblin, Inc.*, 212 F.2d 555 (8th Cir.1954). However, given the unusual nature of the filing, the Court believes the better course for it to follow is to simply not include the amicus brief in the matters it will consider in this case. It will, therefore, follow that course.

3. The Court will first address defendant's motion to dismiss for lack of standing, given that it touches on the jurisdiction of the Court to resolve the substantive issues in this case.[1] Standing is a necessary component of the jurisdiction of an Article III court, which exists to resolve cases or controversies. *Broadrick v. Oklahoma*, 413 U.S. 601, 93 S.Ct. 2908, 37 L.Ed.2d 830 (1973).

Generally speaking, there are three elements of standing:

- the plaintiff must have suffered an injury in fact, i.e., an invasion of a legally protected interest which is concrete and particularized and actual or imminent rather than conjectural or hypothetical;
- there must be a causal connection between the injury and the conduct complained of; and

Appendix: Judge Hendren's Opinion

- it must be likely, as opposed to merely speculative, that the injury will be redressed by a decision in plaintiff's favor.

Lujan v. Defenders of Wildlife, 504 U.S. 555, 112 S.Ct. 2130, 119 L.Ed.2d 351 (1992).

(a) Claims by Dakota Counts' parents—The Court first addresses the claims of Billy Ray counts and Mary Nell Counts as parents of Dakota counts. As will be seen from the facts recited in ¶ 5, infra, this case involves restrictions on access to certain books in the school libraries of the Cedarville School District. The restrictions require a student to have parental permission to check out the books. Defendant contends that no injury can be shown (i.e., that the case has become moot) because plaintiff Dakota Counts, a Cedarville student, owns several of the books, and her parents have signed a permission slip allowing her to check the books out of the school library. Thus, defendant argues, Dakota has "unfettered access" to the books.

Plaintiffs counter that Dakota has suffered an injury because there is a burden on her right to access the books—the requirement of parental consent—and that access in one forum is not a constitutional substitute for access in another.

The Court is persuaded that Dakota Counts has alleged sufficient injury to give her standing to pursue her claims in this case. The right to read a book is an aspect of the right to receive information and ideas, an "inherent corollary of the rights of free speech and press that are explicitly guaranteed by the Constitution." *Board of Education v. Pico*, 457 U.S. 853, 102 S.Ct. 2799, 73 L.Ed.2d 435 (1982). The Supreme Court in *Pico* recognized that a school library is an "environment especially appropriate for the recognition of the First Amendment rights of students."

The loss of First Amendment rights, even minimally, is injurious. *Marcus v. Iowa Public Television*, 97 F.3d 1137 (8th Cir.1996). Illustratively, in a case finding political patronage unconstitutional, the Supreme Court has said that "the inducement afforded by placing conditions on a benefit need not be particularly great in order to find that rights have been violated. Rights are infringed both where the government fines a person a penny for being a Republican and where it withholds the grant of a penny for the same reason." *Elrod v. Burns*, 427 U.S. 347, note 13, 96 S.Ct. 2673, 49 L.Ed.2d 547 (1976).

In the case at bar, it is suggested in plaintiffs' Complaint that Dakota's

Appendix: Judge Hendren's Opinion

rights are burdened because the books in question are "stigmatized," with resulting "stigmatization" of those who choose to read them ("[c]hildren carrying the book with them in the school will be known to be carrying a 'bad' book.") In addition, should Dakota want to review a passage in one of the books while at school, she cannot simply walk into the library and do so. She must locate the librarian, perhaps waiting her turn to consult the librarian, then ask to check the book out and wait while the librarian verifies that she has parental permission to do so, before she can even open the covers of the book.

The Court finds that these burdens, albeit relatively small, constitute a sufficient allegation of an actual concrete and particularized invasion of a legally protected interest to establish Dakota's standing to bring this suit.[2] *Cf. Watchtower Bible v. Village of Stratton*, 536 U.S. 150, 122 S.Ct. 2080, 153 L.Ed.2d 205 (2002) (requiring a permit—even one granted without cost or waiting period—as a prior condition on the exercise of the right to speak imposes a burden on speech); and *Lamont v. Postmaster General of the United States*, 381 U.S. 301, 85 S.Ct. 1493, 14 L.Ed.2d 398 (1965) (requiring addressee of mail to request its delivery in writing abridges First Amendment rights).

The fact that Dakota has access to the books at home does not undermine this decision. The Supreme Court has held that "one is not to have the exercise of his liberty of expression in appropriate places abridged on the plea that it may be exercised in some other place." *Reno v. American Civil Liberties Union*, 521 U.S. 844, 117 S.Ct. 2329, 138 L.Ed.2d 874 (1997) (*citing Schneider v. State*, 308 U.S. 147, 60 S.Ct. 146, 84 L.Ed. 155 (1939)).

Defendant also argues that Dakota's claim was not ripe when filed, because she was not in school on July 3, 2002, the filing date, to request the books. No legal authority or supporting facts are cited for this proposition, and the Court will not further examine it except to note that this is not a case where administrative exhaustion or development of the record is called for, and the constitutional issue is presently fit for decision. *Cf. Texas v. United States*, 523 U.S. 296, 118 S.Ct. 1257, 140 L.Ed.2d 406 (1998).

The motion to dismiss will, therefore, be denied as to the claims of Billy Ray Counts and Mary Nell Counts as parents of Dakota Counts.

(b) Billy Ray Counts' Individual Claim—Billy Ray Counts claims—on his own behalf—that the defendant's board's decision "abrogates the library committee's and its members' ability to appropriately determine

Appendix: Judge Hendren's Opinion

suitable material for including in the library without having an improperly motivated School Board override said determinations." This claim is neither fully fleshed out in the Complaint nor persuasively argued in the briefs. Thus, the Court is shown no basis upon which Billy Ray Counts would have standing in his own right to advance a constitutional claim on the facts presented. The motion to dismiss will, therefore, be granted as to the claim of Billy Ray Counts, Individually.

4. Having concluded that plaintiffs have standing to bring a claim of constitutional violation on behalf of Dakota Counts, the Court now turns to the issue of whether summary judgment in their favor is appropriate.

Summary judgment should be granted when the record, viewed in the light most favorable to the nonmoving party, and giving that party the benefit of all reasonable inferences, shows that there is no genuine issue of material fact and the movant is entitled to judgment as a matter of law. *Walsh v. United States*, 31 F.3d 696 (8th Cir.1994). Summary judgment is not appropriate unless all the evidence points toward one conclusion, and is susceptible of no reasonable inferences sustaining the position of the nonmoving party. *Hardin v. Hussmann Corp.*, 45 F.3d 262 (8th Cir. 1995). The burden is on the moving party to demonstrate the non-existence of a genuine factual dispute; however, once the moving party has met that burden, the nonmoving party cannot rest on its pleadings, but must come forward with facts showing the existence of a genuine dispute. *City of Mt. Pleasant, Iowa v. Associated Electric Co-op.*, 838 F.2d 268 (8th Cir. 1988).

5. Pursuant to Local Rule 56.1, plaintiffs filed a statement of facts which they contend are not in dispute. Defendant contested only one—it claims that the "secular intent of the School Board in passing the policy which is the subject of this action is in dispute." From the plaintiffs' uncontested submission—and from other facts appearing in the briefs and evidentiary documents which cannot be considered seriously disputed—the following significant undisputed facts are made to appear:

- In November 2001, Angie Haney (the mother of a child enrolled in the Cedarville School District) and her pastor, Mark Hodges (who is on the Cedarville School Board) became concerned that a series of books known as the Harry Potter books were in general circulation in the school libraries at Cedarville.

- Hodges and Cedarville School Superintendent Dave Smith contacted Estella Roberts, Cedarville High School librarian, about the matter.

Appendix: Judge Hendren's Opinion

Roberts told Hodges and Smith that under school policy, they would need to complete a form—called a Reconsideration Request Form—to bring about any change in the status of the Harry Potter books.

- Hodges gave the blank Reconsideration Request Form to Haney, who completed it and returned it to the defendant. On the form, Haney asked that one of the Harry Potter books, Harry Potter And The Sorcerer's Stone, be withdrawn from all students.

- After receiving the Reconsideration Request Form, and pursuant to its stated policies, the defendant formed a library committee to consider the matter. The library committee consisted of five representatives from the high school, five from the middle school, and five from the elementary school. The five people from each school were the principal, the librarian, a teacher, a student, and the parent of a student from that school.

- The library committee reviewed Harry Potter And The Sorcerer's Stone, and voted unanimously in favor of keeping the book in circulation without any restrictions.

- After receiving the recommendation of the library committee, Roberts made a presentation about the matter to the Cedarville School Board. Defendant's board then voted 3–2 to restrict access not only to Harry Potter And The Sorcerer's Stone, but also to the other three books in the Harry Potter series. Members of defendant's board voting to restrict access were Mark Hodges, Jerry Shelly, and Gary Koonce (hereinafter called "Hodges," "Shelly" and "Koonce").

- The Board members voting in favor of restricted access did not do so because of concerns about profanity, sexuality, obscenity, or perversion in the books, nor out of any concern that reading the books had actually led to disruption in the schools. Only one of the three had even read Harry Potter And The Sorcerer's Stone, and none of them had read the other three books in the series.

- As a result of the vote of defendant's board, Cedarville High School Principal Glennis Cook issued a memo stating that all Harry Potter books were to be removed from defendant's library shelves and placed "where they are highly visible, yet not accessible to the students unless they are checking them out." To check out the books, a student must have "a signed permission statement from their parent/legal guardian." Hodges, Shelly and Koonce intended this directive to be a restriction on access to the books.

- Plaintiffs Billy Ray Counts and Mary Nell Counts sued on behalf of their minor child Dakota Counts, a Cedarville student, alleging that the restrictions placed on the Harry Potter books violate her First Amendment rights to freedom of speech and to receive information. Billy Ray Counts also alleged an individual claim in his official capacity as a member of the Cedarville School District library committee.

• Dakota has already read three of the Harry Potter books, owns the fourth, and has written permission from her parents to check the books out of the school library.

6. Given these undisputed facts, the following issue is presented. Does a school board's decision—to restrict access to library books only to those with parental permission—infringe upon the First Amendment rights of a student who has such permission? Before the Court can decide this issue on a motion for summary judgment, it must first determine if there is any genuine issue of material fact in dispute concerning whether Dakota's rights are so infringed.

Both this issue and the Court's determination of it must be addressed and decided in light of Supreme Court precedent calling for "the most exacting scrutiny [of] regulations that suppress, disadvantage, or impose differential burdens upon speech because of its content." *Turner Broadcasting System, Inc. v. FCC*, 512 U.S. 622, 114 S.Ct. 2445, 129 L.Ed.2d 497 (1994).

7. In support of their assertion that summary judgment is appropriate, plaintiffs rely on *Sund v. City of Wichita Falls*, 121 F.Supp.2d 530 (N.D. Texas 2000), holding that removing a children's book to the adult section of a public library constituted restriction on access because children searching for the book in the designated children's areas would be unable to locate it and browsers risked never discovering the book at all. These particular burdens, of course, do not affect Dakota in the case at bar since she has access to the books as above noted. However, for the same reasons the Court concluded that she has standing to bring this action, it finds that the stigmatizing effect of having to have parental permission to check out a book constitutes a restriction on access. Further, the fact that Dakota cannot simply go in the library, take the books off the shelf and thumb through them—perhaps to refresh her mind about a favorite passage—without going through the permission and check-out process is a restriction on her access. Thus, unless it is shown that such restrictions are justified, they amount to impermissible infringements of First Amendment rights.

Appendix: Judge Hendren's Opinion

8. Having concluded that a burden on Dakota's right of access exists, the Court must consider whether the restrictions are justified by some exigency of the educational environment in the Cedarville School District.

Hodges, Shelly and Koonce testified by deposition that their vote to restrict access to the Harry Potter books was based on (a) their concern that the books might promote disobedience and disrespect for authority, and (b) the fact that the books deal with "witchcraft" and "the occult." The Court will examine these positions seriatim.

(a) The first asserted justification for the restriction appears to be the shared concern among Hodges, Shelly and Koonce that the Harry Potter books might promote disobedience and disrespect for authority. The constitutional soundness of such a restriction depends on whether there is any evidence to support application of a very narrow exception to the First Amendment rights of primary and secondary public school students. While such students do not shed their constitutional rights at the schoolhouse gate, in First Amendment cases the Supreme Court has recognized a very limited restriction where "necessary to avoid material and substantial interference with school-work or discipline." *Tinker v. Des Moines Independent Community School District*, 393 U.S. 503, 89 S.Ct. 733, 21 L.Ed.2d 731 (1969).

The Court in *Tinker* was careful to emphasize how limited this restriction is, and to stress the importance of freedom of speech in the education of America's youth:

In our system, state-operated schools may not be enclaves of totalitarianism. School officials do not possess absolute authority over their students. Students in school as well as out of school are `persons' under our Constitution. They are possessed of fundamental rights which the State must respect, just as they themselves must respect their obligations to the State. In our system, students may not be regarded as closed-circuit recipients of only that which the State chooses to communicate. They may not be confined to the expression of those sentiments that are officially approved. In the absence of a specific showing of constitutionally valid reasons to regulate their speech, students are entitled to freedom of expression of their views.

Tinker also quoted with approval from *Keyishian v. Board of Regents*, 385 U.S. 589, 87 S.Ct. 675, 17 L.Ed.2d 629 (1967), as follows:

Appendix: Judge Hendren's Opinion

The vigilant protection of constitutional freedoms is nowhere more vital than in the community of American schools. The classroom is peculiarly the "marketplace of ideas." The Nation's future depends upon leaders trained through wide exposure to that robust exchange of ideas which discovers truth "out of a multitude of tongues, (rather) than through any kind of authoritative selection." (Internal citations omitted.)

Thus, while it is recognized that Boards of Education "have important, delicate, and highly discretionary functions," it is also recognized that there are "none that they may not perform within the limits of the Bill of Rights. That they are educating the young for citizenship is reason for scrupulous protection of Constitutional freedoms of the individual, if we are not to strangle the free mind at its source and teach youth to discount important principles of our government as mere platitudes." Tinker, id. (internal citations and quotation marks omitted).

Turning to the evidence which might support defendant's contention that the restrictions in question are "necessary to avoid material and substantial interference with schoolwork or discipline," the Court finds the following relevant testimony[3] in the depositions of Hodges, Shelly and Koonce:

- Hodges (the only one of the three who had actually read an entire Harry Potter book) testified that the books are "going to create problems in the school," and "could create ... anarchy." However he did not know of any behavioral problems that had been created by the series, and he admitted that his vote to restrict access was "a preventative measure at that school to prevent any signs that will come up like Columbine and Jonesboro."
- Shelly (who had not read any of the books) testified that books teaching that sometimes rules need to be disobeyed should not be allowed in the school library.
- Koonce (who had not read any of the books in full but "just kind of read here and there" in the first book of the series) testified that he believed it "could" lead kids into juvenile delinquency, but that he was motivated not by what the students were doing, only by what they "might do later."

There is no evidence that any of the three Board members was aware of any actual disobedience or disrespect that had flowed from a reading of the Harry Potter books. Their concerns are, therefore, speculative. Such speculative apprehensions of possible disturbance are not sufficient to justify the extreme sanction of restricting the free exercise of First Amendment rights in a public school library. As the Supreme Court pointed out in Tinker, "in our system, undifferentiated fear or apprehension of disturbance is not enough to overcome the right to freedom of expression.... Certainly where there is no finding and no showing that engaging in the forbidden conduct would 'materially and substantially interfere with the requirements of appropriate discipline in the operation of the school,' the prohibition cannot be sustained." Accordingly, the Court finds no merit in the first asserted justification for the restriction.

(b) The second asserted justification for the restriction is the shared concerns of Hodges, Shelly and Koonce that the Harry Potter books deal with "witchcraft" and "the occult." The Court notes that all three men appear to strongly disapprove of "witchcraft" and "the occult."

This second asserted basis for restricting access to the books is, in the Court's view, no more persuasive than was the first. In the words of Tinker, quoted above, "students may not be regarded as closed-circuit recipients of only that which the State chooses to communicate. They may not be confined to the expression of those sentiments that are officially approved."

Along with the freedom of expression considerations which apply when witchcraft and the occult are viewed simply as ideas to which students have a right to choose to be exposed, another First Amendment consideration comes into play. The proof before the Court shows that Hodges, Shelly and Koonce admittedly want to restrict access to the books because of their shared belief that the books promote a particular religion, e.g.:

- Hodges testified that witchcraft is a religion and that he objected to a book which would expose Cedarville students to the "witchcraft religion."

- Shelly testified that he objected to the books because they "teach witchcraft"—but that if the books "promoted Christianity" he would not object to them.

- Koonce testified that the books "teach about witchcraft," and that witchcraft is a religion.

Regardless of the personal distaste with which these individuals regard "witchcraft," it is not properly within their power and authority as members of defendant's school board to prevent the students at Cedarville from reading about it. As the Supreme Court said in *Pico, supra*,

Appendix: Judge Hendren's Opinion

[o]ur Constitution does not permit the official suppression of ideas. Thus whether petitioners' removal of books from their school libraries denied respondents their First Amendment rights depends upon the motivation behind petitioners' actions. If petitioners intended by their removal decision to deny respondents access to ideas with which petitioners disagreed, and if this intent was the decisive factor in petitioners' decision, the petitioners have exercised their discretion in violation of the Constitution.... In brief, we hold that local school boards may not remove books from school library shelves simply because they dislike the ideas contained in those books and seek by their removal to "prescribe what shall be orthodox in politics, nationalism, religion, or other matters of opinion" [Internal citations omitted].

The Court, therefore, finds no merit in the second asserted justification for the restrictions in question.

9. There is no evidence shown to the Court which might reasonably have led defendant's Board members "to forecast substantial disruption of or material interference with school activities" if students were to be allowed unfettered access to the Harry Potter books (as would be required to bring them within the narrow Tinker restriction), nor can the defendant permissibly restrict access on the basis of the ideas expressed therein—whether religious or secular. These are the reasons given by the three individuals who, by their votes as a majority of defendant's five-member board, made defendant's decision to restrict access.

Accordingly, based upon the testimony of the individuals who cast the deciding votes in favor of the policy herein challenged, the Court finds there is no genuine dispute as to the material relevant facts and that, when the evidence is viewed in the light most favorable to the defendant, the conclusion is inevitable that defendant removed the books from its library shelves for reasons not authorized by the Constitution.

There being no genuine issue of material fact in dispute as to these matters, the Court finds that Dakota Counts' First Amendment rights are being infringed by defendant's decision to restrict access to the Harry Potter books to those students whose parents sign a permission slip allowing them to check out the books. Summary judgment in her favor will therefore be granted.

IT IS THEREFORE ORDERED that defendant's Motion To Dismiss is granted in part and denied in part.

The motion is granted insofar as it seeks dismissal of the claim of Billy Ray Counts, Individually.

The motion is denied insofar as it seeks dismissal of the claims of Billy

Appendix: Judge Hendren's Opinion

Ray Counts and Mary Nell Counts as parents and next friends of Dakota Counts.

IT IS FURTHER ORDERED that Plaintiffs' Motion For Summary Judgment is granted.

IT IS FURTHER ORDERED that plaintiff will be entitled to a reasonable attorney's fee and costs upon application therefor within fourteen (14) days of the date of this Order. Defendant shall have eleven (11) days from service of any such application to lodge its objections thereto.

IT IS FURTHER ORDERED that the Court's decisions in this matter will be given effect by Order entered of even date herewith.

IT IS SO ORDERED.

Notes

1. While plaintiffs contend that defendants' reliance on evidentiary matters converts its motion to dismiss into a motion for summary judgment, that rule only applies to F.R.C.P. 12(b)(6) motions, not motions challenging subject matter jurisdiction, which fall under Rule 12(b)(1). The court therefore has not treated the issues raised by the motion to dismiss under the familiar standards applicable to motions for summary judgment, as requested by plaintiffs, but rather under those applicable to motions to determine subject matter jurisdiction, wherein the court has the power to decide disputed factual issues. See, e.g., *Osborn v. U.S.*, 918 F.2d 724 (8th Cir. 1990).

2. The court notes that other forms of First Amendment burden pled in the complaint—that browsers will not find the book on the shelves and those unaware of its existence would not know to ask for permission to check it out—while not applicable to Dakota, demonstrate the importance of allowing standing for even a minimal invasion of First Amendment rights. Those children whose parents do not want them to check out the Harry Potter books could hardly be expected to protect their own First Amendment rights, since they would almost certainly be minors who could not sue in their own right and it is unlikely that their parents would go to court to establish their child's legal right to do that which they did not want the child to be able to do in the first place. If a minimal burden will not suffice, the district's action would be impregnable to First Amendment attack.

3. Defendant attempts to distance itself from this testimony by describing it as "their individual testimony of their individual viewpoints, rather than the purpose of the board as a whole in passing the restriction." This effort must fail, inasmuch as these three board members comprised the entire voting majority which imposed the policy in question—the other two board members voted to leave the books on the shelves without restriction. Thus the individual viewpoints of these three board members must necessarily be "the purpose of the board as a whole in passing the restriction." Moreover, the "secular purpose" argument advanced in connection with the "purpose of the board as a whole" theory is an aspect of establishment clause jurisprudence, and is not particularly applicable to free speech issues, where a secular purpose to restrict access to an idea may be just as impermissible as a religious one. *Westside Community Board of Education v. Mergens*, 496 U.S. 226, 110 S.Ct. 2356, 110 L.Ed.2d 191 (1990).

Chapter Notes

I wrote this book with the prior express written permission of my clients, the Countses, who were represented by separate counsel when we negotiated, at arm's length, their waiver of privilege and the purchase of the right for me to tell their story.

My sources of information are my own memory, interviews, depositions, letters, billing statements, notes, judicial opinions and orders, court filings, hearing transcripts, newspaper articles, scholarly legal works, and other documents arising from the cases discussed.

Deposition quotes are verbatim or are very close to verbatim. To the extent that any deposition quote has been edited, the edit was done to clean up grammar or tighten the dialogue or standardize capitalization. No meaningful change was made to any deposition quote. Quotes outside depositions are my (or a participant's) best recollection of the conversation.

Sources are discussed in more detail below and are listed in the Bibliography.

Chapter 1

Data regarding Crawford County and the Cedarville School District was obtained from their respective websites as well as U.S. census data.

The scenes with Angie Haney are based on her deposition testimony and exhibits as well as my interviews with her several years later.

Descriptions of Pastor Hodges' background are based on his deposition testimony. The Assembly of God information is from that denomination's website.

In describing the Cedarville School District, both physically and operationally, I relied upon my own observations, interviews with Estella Roberts, and a discussion with a retired teacher from the district who wished to remain anonymous.

Chapter 2

Background on the American Library Association and censorship is from the ALA itself (via its website and the reference books it publishes) as well as my own legal research and

Chapter Notes

prior training in First Amendment law. The history of Harry Potter bans was obtained from various newspaper articles covering those events.

Chapter 3

Sources for the discussions of the *Gobitis* and *Barnette* cases are from both district court and appellate court opinions. I also consulted the following: Irons, Peter, *The Courage of Their Convictions: Sixteen Americans Who Fought Their Way to the Supreme Court* (Free Press, 1988); Manwaring, David R., *Render Unto Caesar: The Flag Salute Controversy* (University of Chicago Press, 1962); and McMahon, Kevin J., *Reconsidering Roosevelt on Race: How the Presidency Paved the Road to Brown* (University of Chicago Press, 2010).

Chapter 4

Information about Estella Roberts is based on my interviews with her during the case. I also interviewed her several years later, after she retired and moved to Florida. The appellate portion of Estella's court case against the Van Buren School District is located at *Roberts v. Van Buren School District*, 731 F.2d 523 (8th Cir. 1984), and *Roberts v. Van Buren School District*, 773 F.2d 949 (8th Cir. 1985).

Angie Haney told me her views on prayer during one of our interviews. Ms. Haney's quotes during the school board meeting are based on my interviews with her, the school board minutes, and her written complaint form. There were also newspaper articles in the *Press Argus-Courier* regarding the school board meetings.

Chapter 5

Sources for the discussion of the *Tinker* case are from the Supreme Court opinion, and Irons, Peter, *The Courage of Their Convictions: Sixteen Americans Who Fought Their Way to the Supreme Court* (Free Press, 1988).

Chapter 6

The descriptions of the two school board meetings are drawn from the board minutes, interviews with Estella Roberts, televised news coverage, and from articles written by and conversations with *Press Argus-Courier* reporter Melinda Bigelow. Ms. Bigelow's articles quoted the dialogue leading up to the vote on the ban, and I reproduced those quotes here.

The memorandum from Glennis Cook was part of the documentary evidence in the court case; Estella Roberts supplied it to me.

Chapter 7

The backstory on *Pico* is from the author's phone interviews with Russ Rieger and Andrea Pepper Friedman; multiple news articles from *Newsday* (Long Island, NY); the district, circuit, and Supreme Court opinions in the case; and the audio of the *Pico* oral arguments before the Supreme Court.

Chapter 8

Estella told me how the Countses came to be my clients, and Bill Counts confirmed this. My impressions of the Countses are based on representing them during the court case plus two interviews with them several years after the case concluded.

Chapter Notes

Chapter 9

My information about Judge Jimm Hendren is based on newspaper articles, his official biography, reported cases, anecdotal evidence from fellow attorneys, and my own personal observations from the various appearances I have made in his court.

The information about "Jeff Thomas" and his case is derived from three sources: my discussions with Greg Karber; the case file; and an interview with Rebecca Bock. The case file had the depositions and a transcript of the hearing. The sources from the case file are public records, and I was careful to not disclose any information that would have been protected under the attorney-client privilege. In an abundance of caution, I changed the names of those involved in this case except for Rebeca Bock and Mitch Llewellyn.

Chapter 10

The information in this chapter is based primarily on an interview with David Hogue several years after the lawsuit. As a practical matter, there is hardly any attorney-client privilege for Arkansas governmental entities; Arkansas's Freedom of Information laws are so broad that a government attorney's private notes about ongoing litigation is considered a public record. David Hogue's recollections are corroborated by Angie Haney; she was present at one of the meetings between the board and David Hogue.

Chapter 11

The *Sund* story is from the opinion in the case; the transcript of its two-day hearing, an interview with the city librarian, Linda Hughes; and an excerpt from the Rev. Robert Jeffress' book, *Outrageous Truth ... Seven Absolutes You Can Still Believe*.

Chapter 12

My quotes from Angie Haney are taken from her deposition transcript. The documents referenced are exhibits to that deposition.

Chapter 13

The quotes in this chapter are taken from the deposition transcripts. Quotes from the depositions are verbatim with a few minor exceptions, and in those exceptions I simply tightened the language, corrected the grammar, and standardized capitalization.

Chapter 14

The Countses' deposition transcripts provided the bases for the quotes in this chapter.

Chapter 15

The information in this chapter is based on discussions with Louise Turner during and after the court case, as well as her deposition transcript.

Chapter Notes

Information about Leah Arendt, the cat lady, is based on the Fort Smith Public Library's file on Ms. Arendt. The file contained newspaper articles and probate filings related to the Arendt litigation.

Chapter 16

My observations of the Eighth Circuit Court of Appeals are based on personal knowledge. The *Bystrom* discussion comes from the Eighth Circuit's decision, the trial court's record, and email interviews with *Tour de Farce* members Jeremy Saperstein and John Collins.

Chapter 17

My information about Judy Blume came from her website and from various newspaper articles.

Chapter 18

Information about the Countses is based on conversations with me during the court case and interviews several years after the litigation.

Chapter 19

Information for this chapter is from interviews with David Hogue, Angie Haney, Estella Roberts, and Dakota Counts. My primary information about cases after the *Counts* decision is from Cortney Smith's essay in *First Amendment Studies in Arkansas* and the cases of *American Civ. Lib. Union v. Miami-Dade Sch. Bd.*, 439 F.Supp.2d 1242 (S.D. Fla. 2006) and *Parents, Families, & Friends of Lesbians & Gays, Inc. v. Camdenton R–III Sch. Dist.*, 853 F.Supp.2d 888 (W.D. Mo. 2012).

Bibliography

Books and Essays

John Carney and Todd DeMitchell, "Harry Potter v. Muggles: Literary Criticism and Legal Challenge," INTERNATIONAL JOURNAL OF EDUCATIONAL REFORM 14: 2–16 (2005).
T. Barton Carter, Marc A. Franklin, Jay B. Wright, THE FIRST AMENDMENT AND THE FOURTH ESTATE: THE LAW OF MASS MEDIA (7th ed. 1997).
Herbert N. Foerstel, BANNED IN THE U.S.A. at 180–188 (2nd ed. 2002).
Peter Irons, THE COURAGE OF THEIR CONVICTIONS: SIXTEEN AMERICANS WHO FOUGHT THEIR WAY TO THE SUPREME COURT (1988).
Robert Jeffress, OUTRAGEOUS TRUTH ... SEVEN ABSOLUTES YOU CAN STILL BELIEVE (2008).
Mary Margaret Keaton, "Harry Potter: A Tool for Sowing Seeds of the Gospel," Vol. 34 No. 6 CATECHIST at 35 (March 2001).
Joan Vos MacDonald, J.K. ROWLING: BANNED, CHALLENGED, AND CENSORED (2008).
David R. Manwaring, RENDER UNTO CAESAR: THE FLAG SALUTE CONTROVERSY (1962).
Kevin J. McMahon, RECONSIDERING ROOSEVELT ON RACE: HOW THE PRESIDENCY PAVED THE ROAD TO BROWN (2010).
Cortney Smith, "Book Censorship in the Fayetteville Public Schools: 'The Chocolate Wars' and 'The Battle of the Books,'" FIRST AMENDMENT STUDIES IN ARKANSAS 75–96 (ed. Stephen A. Smith) (2016).

Court Documents (That Are Not Reported Opinions)

Appellants' Brief, BYSTROM V. FRIDLEY HIGH SCHOOL, 86-5140-MN (8th Cir. 1986) (on file with author).
Appellants' Reply Brief, BYSTROM V. FRIDLEY HIGH SCHOOL, 86-5140-MN (8th Cir. 1986) (on file with author).
Appellees' Brief, BYSTROM V. FRIDLEY HIGH SCHOOL, 86-5140-MN (8th Cir. 1986) (on file with author).
Appellees' Petition for Rehearing En Banc, BYSTROM V. FRIDLEY HIGH SCHOOL, 86-5140-MN (8th Cir. 1986) (on file with author).
Complaint, Answer, and Motions from COUNTS V. CEDARVILLE SCHOOL DISTRICT, CV-02-2155 (W.D. Ark. 2003) (on file with author).
Complaint, Motions, Affidavits, Discovery Documents, and Orders from BYSTROM, ET AL. V. FRIDLEY HIGH SCHOOL, INDEPENDENT SCHOOL DISTRICT NO. 14, ET AL., CV 3-85-911 (D.Minn. 1985) (on file with author).
Depositions and exhibits from THE TALISMAN V. FORT SMITH SCHOOL DISTRICT, CV-94-2005 (W.D. Ark. 1994) (on file with author).
Depositions from COUNTS V. CEDARVILLE SCHOOL DISTRICT, CV-02-2155 (W.D. Ark. 2003)

Bibliography

(Bill Counts, Dakota Counts, Louise Turner, Estella Roberts, Audie Murphy, Mark Hodges, Jerry Shelly, and Gary Koonce) (on file with author).
Hearing transcript (Doc. #29, 29-1, & 29-2), SUND V. CITY OF WICHITA FALLS, 7:99-CV-155 (N.D. Tex. 1999).
Memorandum Opinion, THE TALISMAN V. FORT SMITH SCHOOL DISTRICT, CV-94-2005 (W.D. Ark. 1994) (on file with author).

Interviews

Interviews with Mary, Bill, and Dakota Counts (various times) (plaintiffs in Cedarville case).
Interview with Rebecca Bock Franchione (Oct. 2007) (witness in TALISMAN case).
Interview with Andrea Pepper Friedman (Dec. 2017) (Othalie Pepper's daughter).
Interviews with Angie Haney (Oct. 2007 and 2018) (filed original complaint in Cedarville).
Interviews with David Hogue (2007 and 2018) (lawyer for Cedarville schools).
Interview with Linda Hughes (Mar. 2018) (SUND librarian).
Interview with Russ Rieger (Nov. 29, 2017) (PICO plaintiff).
Interviews with Estella Roberts (various times) (Cedarville librarian).
Interviews with Jeremy Saperstein and John Collins (2007) (TOUR DE FARCE members).

Miscellaneous

"Leah Arendt" file at the Fort Smith (Arkansas) Public Library (accessed 2008).
Arkansas Library Association, INTELLECTUAL FREEDOM COMMITTEE MANUAL (1993) (on file with author).
Incident/Offense Report filed with Crawford County (AR) Sheriff's Office (Estella Roberts reporting verbal harassment after the May 20, 2002, school board meeting) (on file with author).
Meeting Minutes for the Cedarville School Board (May 20, 2002) (on file with author).
Meeting Minutes for the Cedarville School Board (Jun. 17, 2002) (on file with author).
Press release from Association of American Publishers, Inc., "'Muggles for Harry Potter' to Fight Censorship" (Mar. 7, 2000) (on file with author).
Estella Roberts's VHS tape labeled "Harry Potter—Stella—School Board 5/20/02" (on file with author).

News Articles

John T. Anderson, "'Potter' Pickle Pricey: Cedarville School Pays for Book Fight," SOUTHWEST TIMES RECORD at 1A (Fort Smith, AR) (Apr. 25, 2003).
"Battle of the Books in Island Trees," NEWSDAY (Long Island, NY) at 33 (Jan. 11, 1977).
Melinda W. Bigelow, "Books Sequestered," PRESS ARGUS-COURIER (Van Buren, AR) (date uncertain, but in Jun. 2002).
Melinda W. Bigelow, "Federal Lawsuit Filed," PRESS ARGUS-COURIER (Van Buren, AR) (Jul. 10, 2002).
Melinda W. Bigelow, "Potter Back on Shelves: Fight Cost District $13,750," PRESS ARGUS-COURIER (Van Buren, AR) (Apr. 26, 2003).
Melinda W. Bigelow, "Saga of Harry Potter to Continue Monday," PRESS ARGUS-COURIER (Van Buren, AR) at 1A (Jun. 15, 2002).
Melinda W. Bigelow, "School Board Shelves Removing Book," PRESS ARGUS-COURIER (Van Buren, AR) at 1A (May 22, 2002).

Bibliography

Judy Blume, "Is Harry Potter Evil?" NEW YORK TIMES at Op-Ed (Oct. 22, 1999).
"Books Belong on Shelves, Not in Court," SOUTHWEST TIMES RECORD (Fort Smith, AR) at 6A (Mar. 14, 2003).
Margaret Brogley, "My 2 Cents," PRESS ARGUS-COURIER (Van Buren, AR) at 4 (Aug. 3, 2002).
Nancy Edwards, "Judge to Handle Mystery Will," SOUTHWEST TIMES RECORD (Fort Smith, AR) (Feb. 21, 1991).
"Ex-Student in Book Suit Named to Library Board," NEWSDAY (Long Island, NY) at 18 (Nov. 16, 1978).
Tim Farley, "Judge OKs $3 Million Willed to Library," THE DAILY OKLAHOMAN (date unclear; article on file with author).
"Free Harry Potter," ARKANSAS DEMOCRAT-GAZETTE at 4B (Jul. 15, 2002).
Terry Groover, "Librarians to Pick Books," PRESS ARGUS-COURIER (Van Buren, AR) at 2A (Aug. 21, 2002).
Terry Groover, "Parents Sue Over Books," "Students Transferring," SOUTHWEST TIMES RECORD (Fort Smith, AR) at 1A (Jul. 4, 2002).
Nat Hentoff, "Learning Without the First Amendment," NEWSDAY (Long Island, NY) at 57 (Jun. 8, 1977).
Lajuanda Hodges, "Concerns about Potter books," PRESS ARGUS-COURIER (Van Buren, AR) at 4 (Jun. 8, 2002).
"Huckabee: Potter's OK," SOUTHWEST TIMES RECORD (Fort Smith, AR) (Nov. 22, 2001).
"Incumbents Re-Elected to Island Trees Board," NEWSDAY (Long Island, NY) at 28 (May 26, 1977).
Michelle Ingrassia, "Board Chief Denies Abolishing Paper," NEWSDAY (Long Island, NY) at 17 (Oct. 1, 1976).
Michelle Ingrassia, "Board Removal of Books Makes Critics of Students," NEWSDAY (Long Island, NY) at 6 (Mar. 20, 1976).
Michelle Ingrassia, "Suit Filed to Stop School's Book Ban," NEWSDAY (Long Island, NY) at 19 (Jan. 5, 1977).
Michelle Ingrassia, "Book Critic Tied to W. Va. Dispute," NEWSDAY (Long Island, NY) at 7 (Mar. 27, 1976).
Michelle Ingrassia, "Judge Delays Ruling on School Book Ban," NEWSDAY (Long Island, NY) at 19 (Feb. 3, 1978).
Brian Jendryka and Carey Brian Meadors, "John Doe Tells All," Vol. 8 No. 7 THE MICHIGAN REVIEW at 1 (Mar. 1990).
Robert E. Kessler, "School Board Purging 11 Books," NEWSDAY (Long Island, NY) at 3 (Mar. 19, 1976).
Robert E. Kessler, "Island Trees Kills Student Newspaper," NEWSDAY (Long Island, NY) at 3 (Sept. 30, 1976).
Robert E. Kessler, "Island Trees Lifts Its Ban on Paper," NEWSDAY (Long Island, NY) at 19 (Oct. 28, 1976).
Dan Knoll, "Devil Works in Subtle Ways," SOUTHWEST TIMES RECORD (Fort Smith, AR) at 7A (Aug. 15, 2002).
Jack Moseley, "Children Have Right to Read Harry," SOUTHWEST TIMES RECORD (Fort Smith, AR) (Mar. 15, 2003).
Meredith Oakley, "Civics lesson, Cedarville-style," ARKANSAS DEMOCRAT-GAZETTE at 5B (May 9, 2003).
"Parents Suing School Get OK to Move Kids," ARKANSAS DEMOCRAT-GAZETTE at 2B (Mar. 15, 2003).
Suzi Parker, "Legal Battle Brews Over Potter Books," DALLAS MORNING NEWS at 29A (Mar. 8, 2003).
Rose Ann Pearce, "School Board Puts Books Back on Shelves," SOUTHWEST TIMES RECORD at 8A (Fort Smith, AR) (Sep. 16, 2005) (re: prevention of the Fayetteville, AR, book ban).

Bibliography

Angela Robinson, "Book Banning Brings Threat of a Lawsuit," NEWSDAY (Long Island, NY) at 3 (Mar. 29, 1976).
Angela Robinson, "Island Trees Upholds Ban on 9 Books," NEWSDAY (Long Island, NY) at 9 (Jul. 29, 1976).
Angela Robinson, "School Chief Decries Book Seizure," NEWSDAY (Long Island, NY) at 9 (Mar. 31, 1976).
Fern Shen, "Who Should Decide What Books You Read?" WASHINGTON POST at C14 (Sep. 24, 2002).
"Students Transferring," SOUTHWEST TIMES RECORD (Fort Smith, AR) at 2A (Mar. 13, 2003).
"Vote Till You Get It Right," ARKANSAS DEMOCRAT-GAZETTE at 4B (May 9, 2003).
"Will Causes Commotion," SOUTHWEST TIMES RECORD (Fort Smith, AR) (Nov. 13, 1990).
"A Win for Book Access," ARKANSAS DEMOCRAT-GAZETTE at 4J (Sep. 18, 2005) (re: prevention of the Fayetteville, AR, book ban).

Reported Opinions

AMERICAN CIV. LIB. UNION V. MIAMI-DADE SCH. BD., 439 F.Supp.2d 1242 (S.D. Fla. 2006).
BARNETTE V. WEST VIRGINIA STATE BOARD OF ED., 47 F.Supp. 251 (S.D. W. Va. 1942).
BYSTROM V. FRIDLEY HIGH SCHOOL, 822 F.2d 747 (8th Cir. 1987).
COUNTS V. CEDARVILLE SCHOOL DISTRICT, 295 F.Supp.2d 996 (2003).
GOBITIS V. MINERSVILLE SCHOOL DIST., 24 F.Supp. 271 (W.D. Pa. 1938).
MINERSVILLE SCHOOL DIST. V. GOBITIS, 108 F.2d 683 (3rd Cir. 1940).
MINERSVILLE SCHOOL DIST V. GOBITIS, 310 U.S. 586 (1940).
PARENTS, FAMILIES, & FRIENDS OF LESBIANS & GAYS, INC. V. CAMDENTON R–III SCH. DIST., 853 F.Supp.2d 888 (W.D. Mo. 2012).
PICO V. BOARD OF EDUCATION ISLAND TREES UNION FREE SCHOOL DISTRICT NO. 26, 474 F.Supp. 387 (E.D. N.Y., 1979).
PICO V. BOARD OF EDUCATION ISLAND TREES UNION FREE SCHOOL DISTRICT NO. 26, 638 F.2d 404 (2nd Cir. 1980).
PICO V. BOARD OF EDUCATION ISLAND TREES UNION FREE SCHOOL DISTRICT NO. 26, 457 U.S. 853 (1982).
ROBERTS V. VAN BUREN SCHOOL DISTRICT, 731 F.2d 523 (8th Cir. 1984).
ROBERTS V. VAN BUREN SCHOOL DISTRICT, 773 F.2d 949 (8th Cir. 1985).
SUND V. CITY OF WICHITA FALLS, 121 F.Supp.2d 530 (N.D.Texas 2000).
TINKER V. DES MOINES SCHOOL DISTRICT, 393 U.S. 503 (1969).
WEST VIRGINIA STATE BOARD OF EDUCATION V. BARNETTE, 319 U.S. 624 (1943).

Websites

"Arkansas Parents Sue Over Restricted Access to Harry Potter," www.ala.org/alonline/news/2002/020715.html#cedarville (visited Jul. 15, 2002).
The Assemblies of God (USA) official website (visited in 2007; current site is ag.org).
"Attorney Reveals Details of Harry Potter Case," www.arkansasnbc.com/global/story.asp?s=1374894&ClientType=Printable (visited Aug. 3, 2003).
www.cedarvilleschools.org (retrieving student population data) (visited in 2007).
www.census.gov (retrieving population data for Crawford County, AR) (visited in 2007).
Diane Weaver Dunne, "Look Out Harry Potter!—Book Banning Heats Up," www.educationworld.com/a_admin/admin/admin157.shtml (visited Oct. 1, 2007).
Janell Edwards, "Love Every Moment," store.cdbaby.com/cd/edwardsjanell (background on Judge Hendren's family) (visited Jul. 29, 2018).

Bibliography

"Harry Potter Beats His Foes—Again," https://www.cbsnews.com/news/harry-potter-beats-his-foes-again/ (visited Jul. 29, 2018).

"Harry Potter Tops List of Most Challenged Book of 21st Century," www.ala.org/ala/press releases2006/september2006/HarryPottermostchallenge.htm (visited Oct. 1, 2007).

Tom Hess, "Putting Harry in His Place," www.family.org/cforum/citizenmag/features/a0023430.html (accessed in 2002 via Google cache).

"Jimm Larry Hendren," www.fjc.gov/history/judges/hendren-jimm-larry (visited Jul. 29, 2018).

www.judybloom.com (visited 2007).

Oral arguments in PICO V. ISLAND TREES, www.oyez.org/cases/1981/80-2043 (visited May 5, 2018).

Suzi Parker, "Legal Battle Brews Over Potter Books," www.dallasnews.com/sharedcontent/dallas/tsw/stories/030803dntexarpotter.1d999.html (visited Mar. 8, 2003).

"Potter Books Banned in Arab Schools," news.bbc.co.uk/cbbcnews/hi/world/newsid_1816000/1816793.stm (visited Jul. 4, 2002).

"Russ Rieger, Teen Plaintiff in Pico v. Island Trees, Talks About His Role in the Landmark Supreme Court Case," ncac.org/blog/russ-rieger-a-teen-plaintiff-in-pico-v-island-trees-talks-about-his-role-in-the-landmark-supreme-court-case (visited Oct. 28, 2017).

Karen Roggenkamp, "Harry Potter Series-Selected Challenges," faculty.tamu-commerce.edu/kroggenkamp/PotterChallengeList.doc (visited Oct. 10, 2007).

Stephanie Shea, "Texas Trouble for Harry Potter," www.bookweb.org/home/news/btw/3932.html (visited Jul. 4, 2002).

Index

Accelerated Reader list 7, 33–34, 54–55, 103, 175
age appropriate 136, 139–144
Ahrens, Richard 44
Allensworth, Thomas 93–94
Alliance Defense Fund 82
Altman, William 93–94
American Civil Liberties Union 28, 38, 44–49, 65, 69–70, 93, 178, 181
American Library Association 13–14, 24, 44, 89, 94, 160
American Rule *see* fees
amici 160–162
answer 87–88
Arendt, Leah 135
Arkansas Freedom of Information laws 31–32
Arkansas Library Association 11, 98, 182
Assemblies of God 7–8
Associated Press 176

Barnette case see *West Virginia State Board of Education v. Barnette*
bates-labelling 99–100
Best Short Stories by Negro Writers 46
The Bible 15, 17
Bill of Rights 55–56
Black Boy 46–47
Blackmun, Harry 51
Blume, Judy 161–162
Board of Education, Island Trees Union Free School District No. 26 v. Pico 43, 48–53, 145, 148, 157, 160, 175
Bock, Rebecca 66–72
book challenges (in general) 14, 178
book challenges (Harry Potter series) *see* Harry Potter series (other challenges)
Booklist 136
Burger, Warren 51
Bystrom, Cory 150–155
Bystrom v. Fridley High School 148, 155–158

case law 3, 175
Cedarville School Board 25–27, 31–34, 82, 165–166
Cedarville School District 9–10, 24–25, 36, 81, 96–97, 165, 175
censorship (restriction rather than banning) 34, 90, 94–95, 132, 158, 162, 165
Childress, Alice 41
chilling effect 16
Christian Legal Service *see* Hogue, David
circuit split 18, 29, 47–48
Citizen 104
CNN 176
Coca-Cola 117
The Code (at UM-Ann Arbor) 36–39
Collins, John 150–155
complaint (legal document) 54–56, 60, 71–74, 77–80, 87–88, 155, 159
Comstock laws 13
Cook, Glennis 34
Cottage Café 169–170
counterclaim 88
Counts, Bill 25, 57–60, 119–123, 162, 165–167
Counts, Dakota 3, 25, 57–60, 119–132, 162, 164–167, 181
Counts, Mary 57–58, 167
Counts v. Cedarville School District (reported case) 1, 3, 164–167, 175, 177
The Courage of Their Convictions 29
court reporters 102–103
Court Review 159

Daddy's Roommate 91–94
Dallas Morning News 176
decisive factor test 101, 105, 112–114, 166
depositions (in general) 100–102, 106
disruption 29–30, 70–76, 101, 106, 113, 152, 155–159, 166
Down These Mean Streets 46, 48
Drakes (coffee shop) 38–39

205

Index

Eighth Circuit 76, 148–149, 156–158
English Rule *see* fees
ethics, legal 56–57, 96, 120, 168–169
expert witness 72–73, 133–138, 141–143

Fayetteville School Board (Arkansas) 177–178
federal courts (as opposed to state courts) 146
fees 56, 59–60, 6, 70, 85, 89, 166, 171–175
filing 77
First Amendment 13, 17–20, 29–30, 40, 55–56, 60, 90, 95, 154–156, 165–166
The Fixer 41–42, 46
flag salute laws 17–20
Foley, Steve 154–155
Fort Smith Public Library (Arkansas) 134
Fort Smith School District (Arkansas) 70–72
Frankfurter, Felix 19–20
Franklin, Betty 57, 97–98, 121–122
Fridley High School *see Bystrom v. Fridley High School*
funneling 109, 113

general denial 87
Go Ask Alice 46
Gobitis case *see Minersville School District v. Gobitis*
Gold, Jacqueline 47
Gould, Kristen 79
Griffin, Debbie 97

Haney, Angie 5–9, 11–12, 25–27, 81–83, 101–108, 110–111, 179–180
Hansel & Gretel (fairy tale) 139–140
Harry Potter series (awards) 14
Harry Potter series (historical accuracy) 14
Harry Potter series (other challenges) 15–16
Heather Has Two Mommies 91–94, 158
heckler's veto 29, 93
Hendren, Jimm 64–65, 72–77, 95, 160–166, 172, 176–177
A Hero Ain't Nothing but a Sandwich 41, 46
Hill, Janie 94
Hodges, Mark 6–12, 24, 26, 31, 33, 80, 103–118, 159, 179–181, 187–188
Hogue, David 81–83, 88, 102, 107, 111, 118–132, 138–144, 162–163, 168, 174–175
Horany, John 93–94
Hughes, Linda 91–94

Ingvalson, Brian 151, 154
Irons, Peter 29
Island Trees School Board 40–47

Jeffress, Robert 92–94
Jehovah's Witnesses 17–20, 29
John Birch Society 40–41

Karber, Greg 56–57, 61–78, 84–85, 182
Koonce, Gary 32–33, 105, 117–118

The Last Temptation of Christ 36
Laughing Boy 46–47
Levittown, New York 40
libel 101, 154–159
Library Committee (of Cedarville schools) 24–25, 31, 119–120
litigator's myopia 85–86
Llewellyn, Mitch 74–75, 78, 80, 83

Mach, Daniel 89–90, 160–163, 171
magistrates, federal 62
Malamud, Bernard 41–42
mandatory disclosures 99–100
The Michigan Daily 38
The Michigan Review 38–39
Minersville School District v. Gobitis 17–18
Minnesota Civil Liberties Union 153–154
A Modest Proposal 41
Moore, Rudy 177
Morris, Desmond 46
motion to dismiss 87–88
Murphy, Audie 33

The Naked Ape 46
Newsday (Long Island, NY) 44–45, 47
Northside Grizzly 66–76
Northside High School (Fort Smith, Arkansas) 66–76

obscenity 13, 44, 46, 101, 111–112, 154–159
O'Connor, Sandra Day 51
Outrageous Truth ... Seven Absolutes You Can Still Believe 92

Parker, Suzi 176
Partain, Sharon 33
Pepper, Othalie 42–43
Perry Mason 97–98
persuasive authority 95, 165
Pico, Steven 47–48
Pico v. Board of Education, Island Trees see *Board of Education, Island Trees Union Free School District No. 26 v. Pico*
Playboy 142–144
plurality (concept) 51, 148
Powell, Lewis 51
Presidents Council, District 25 v. Community School Board #25 48–49

206

Index

Press Argus Courier (Van Buren, Arkansas) 79–80
Publishers Weekly 91

Rehnquist, William 51
Rieger, Russ 42–43, 47–48
The Rights of Students 182
Roberts, Estella 10–12, 21–27, 31–34, 57, 97–98, 104, 178–179
Roberts v. Van Buren School District 23–24
Robertson, Tom 83–85, 171
Rowling, J.K. 14, 55, 109, 169

Saperstein, Jeremy 150–155
School Library Journal 136
Sedition Act 13
service of process 78, 80
settlement conference 146–147
Shelly, Jerry 33, 105, 107, 114–115
Shumard, Mike 33
Slaughterhouse Five 41, 46
Smith, Dave 10–11, 25, 27, 34, 79–80, 82, 97, 174
Sochinski, Paul 47
Soul on Ice 46
Southside High School (Fort Smith, Arkansas) 37
Southwest Times Record (Fort Smith, Arkansas) 78–79
standing 53–54, 59, 120, 123, 126–127, 132, 160, 162, 164–165, 167–173
Stanton, Richard 151, 153–154
Stark, Matthew 153–155
Stites-Jones, Beverly 146–147

summary judgment 147–148, 158–163
Sund v. Wichita Falls 89–95, 148, 158–159, 165, 175, 177
Swift, Jonathan 41

The Talisman 65–74
Teacher Fair Dismissal Act 23
Tinker, Mary Beth 28–30
Tinker v. Des Moines School District, 28–30, 158
Tour de Farce 150–156
Turner, Louise 133–144

Uniontown, Arkansas 6
Uniontown Assembly of God 5–7
United States Supreme Court 18–20, 29–30, 40, 50–52, 148, 169
University of Michigan, Ann Arbor 36–39

Van Buren School District (Arkansas) 21–24
Vonnegut, Kurt, Jr. 41
vulgarity 49, 101, 111, 156–159

West Virginia State Board of Education v. Barnette 20, 29
White, Byron 51
Wichita Falls (Texas) 91–94
witchcraft 6–7, 12, 14–15, 27, 66, 103–104, 108–110, 113–117
Wright & Miller 167–169
Wynne, Wesley 38–39

Yarris, Glenn 47

www.ingramcontent.com/pod-product-compliance
Lightning Source LLC
Chambersburg PA
CBHW021856230426
43671CB00006B/414